Ethical eye

Animal welfare

French version:

Le bien-être animal

ISBN-10: 92-871-6015-5
ISBN-13: 978-92-871-6015-7

Cover design: Graphic Design Workshop, Council of Europe
Photo: Getty Images
Text proofreading and layout by the Documents and Publications Production Department, Council of Europe

Edited by Council of Europe Publishing
F-67075 Strasbourg Cedex
http://book.coe.int

ISBN-10: 92-871-6016-3
ISBN-13: 978-92-871-6016-4
© Council of Europe, November 2006
Printed in Belgium

Contents

Contributors

Donald M. Broom

Donald M. Broom has been Professor of Animal Welfare at Cambridge University since 1986 and has published over 300 papers on welfare, behaviour problems and ethics of animal usage, and seven books including *Stress and animal welfare* (Broom and Johnson, 1993, Kluwer), *Farm animal behaviour and welfare,* 3rd edn (Fraser and Broom, 1997, CABI) and *The evolution of morality and religion* (2003, CUP). He has served on UK, Council of Europe and OIE committees and has been Chairman or Vice-Chairman of EU Scientific Committees on Animal Welfare since 1990.

Elisabeth de Fontenay

Honorary Professor of Philosophy at Paris 1 University (Panthéon-Sorbonne), Elisabeth de Fontenay is the author, *inter alia,* of *Les figures juives de Marx* (Galilée, 1973), *Diderot ou le matérialisme enchanté* (Grasset, 2001), *Le silence des bêtes* (Fayard, 1999) and *Une tout autre histoire: Questions à Jean-François Lyotard* (Fayard, 2006).

Birte Broberg

Having graduated (DVM) from the Royal Danish Veterinary and Agricultural College, Copenhagen, in 1974, Birte Broberg is Senior Veterinary Officer at the Danish Veterinary and Food Administration. She has taken part in EU and Council of Europe negotiations on animals kept for farming purposes and the protection of animals during transport. From 1999 to 2006, she has been Chairperson of the Standing Committee of the European Convention for the Protection of Animals kept for Farming Purposes. Birte Broberg has given presentations on the protection of animals at training courses in EU candidate countries.

Jacques Merminod

After studying veterinary medicine in Bern, Switzerland, and completing a doctorate (1975-1985), Jacques Merminod has been working as a scientific officer at the Federal Veterinary Office in Bern, in the field of animal protection legislation (since 1986) and deputising for the head of the legal department (since 1998). He is chair of the working group on the Council of Europe Convention for the Protection of Animals during International Transport.

Roman Kolar

Roman Kolar is a biologist and has been working for the Animal Welfare Academy, the scientific affiliation to the German Animal Welfare Federation (Deutscher Tierschutzbund), since 1994. He is Deputy Director of this Academy and scientific advisor to Eurogroup for Animal Welfare, the umbrella organisation of the major animal welfare associations in the EU. He is a member of various national and international committees and bodies that deal with animal experimentation issues. In numerous publications and conference presentations, he has strived to raise awareness of animal protection in science and research.

Charles Laroche

Charles Laroche joined Unilever in 1974. Since then, he has held various positions in Finance and Marketing within the Unilever Group. In 2000, he was appointed Vice-President Corporate Relations and Public Affairs for Unilever Home & Personal Care Europe. Charles Laroche is currently President of the AISE (International Association for Soaps, Detergents and Maintenance Products). He is also a Board member of several other European trade associations such as Colipa, ASSURRE and Cefic. With Unilever and several other leading companies, he has been heavily involved in the development and implementation of EPAA (European Partnership for Alternative Approaches to Animal Testing).

Mickey Gjerris

Mickey Gjerris is Assistant Professor at the Centre for Bioethics and Risk Assessment at The Royal Veterinary and Agricultural University, Copenhagen. He has a Master's Degree in Theology and a PhD in Bioethics from the University of Copenhagen.

Anna Olsson

Anna Olsson is trained as an animal scientist and ethologist. She is a researcher in animal welfare and bioethics at the Institute for Molecular and Cell Biology in Porto, Portugal.

Peter Sandøe

Peter Sandøe is Professor of Bioethics at The Royal Veterinary and Agricultural University in Copenhagen. He is Director of the Centre for Bioethics and Risk Assessment, an interdisciplinary and inter-institutional research centre founded in January 2000. Since 1992, he has served as Chairman of the Danish Ethical Council for Animals, an advisory board set up by the Danish Minister of Justice.

Andreas Steiger

Professor Andreas Steiger received his Diploma as veterinarian from the Faculty of Veterinary Medicine, Bern in 1969. He has conducted numerous research projects on ethology and pathology and also research in the pharmaceutical industry. From 1979 to 1997, he was Head of the Animal Welfare Division of the Swiss Federal Veterinary Office in Bern. Professor Steiger was Chairman of the Standing Committee of the European Convention for the Protection of Farm Animals from 1987 to 1993 and was Chairman of the Committee of Experts on the European Convention for the Protection of Pet Animals in 1995. He is now Head of Division of Animal Housing and Welfare of the Vetsuisse Faculty, University of Bern.

Daniel Chevassut

Physician at the Centre Hospitalier Régional Universitaire Nord de Marseille, Daniel Chevassut is also founder and organiser of a pain clinic at Hôpital Nord de Marseille. He is a representative of and speaker for the Union Bouddhiste de France on the "Health care ethics, human rights and morality" course at the Université Pierre et Marie Curie – Paris VI.

Brother Maurizio Pietro Faggioni

Friar Minor, Brother Faggioni graduated in Medicine and Surgery, specialising in endocrinology; he has a Doctorate in Moral Theology and is Full Professor of Bioethics at the Alphonsian Academy, Rome and a consultant for the Congregation of the Doctrine for the Faith. He is also a member of the Pontifical Academy for Life. He has published numerous articles on the subject of bioethics.

Raoutsi Hadj Eddine Sari Ali

Raoutsi Hadj Eddine Sari Ali is a member of the European Federation of Scientific Networks (FER) and a lecturer at the school of medicine in Paris. He also broadcasts weekly on Radio France Maghreb on religious education in a secular environment (*"L'esprit des religions"*).

Albert Guigui

Albert Guigui is the Chief Rabbi of Brussels and of the Central Israeli Consistory of Brussels. He is co-author of numerous articles and books and has contributed a chapter on Judaism and bioethics in an encyclopaedia on bioethics.

Alexandre M. Stavropoulos

Emeritus professor of Theology and Psychology at the Faculty of Theology, University of Athens, Alexandre Stavropoulos is still teaching in the postgraduate research programme: "Pastoral theology and education". He is an active member of numerous associations and scientific committees in Greece and elsewhere.

Karsten Lehmkühler

After studying Protestant theology in Basle, Erlangen and Strasbourg, Karsten Lehmkühler obtained a Doctorate in Theology in 1995 with a thesis entitled *Kultus und Theologie. Dogmatik und Exegese in der religionsgeschichtlichen Schule* (published in 1996 by Vandehoeck & Ruprecht, Göttingen). In 2002 he was accredited to supervise research (thesis: *Inhabitatio. Die Einwohnung Gottes im Menschen,* published in Göttingen in 2004). A lecturer in systematic theology from 1998 to 2004 and Professor of Ethics in the Protestant Theology Faculty of Marc Bloch University in Strasbourg since 2004, Karsten Lehmkühler was ordained Minister of the Baden United Church in autumn 2005.

Elisabeth Hardouin-Fugier

A university professor (Lyons) and historian of the arts and mentalities, Elisabeth Hardouin-Fugier has never, in her many books, separated images from cultural facts. Among the subjects broached, animals enjoy pride of place: *Le peintre et l'animal en France au XIXe siècle* (2001), *La Corrida* (1995, translated into Japanese), *Zoo: a history of zoological gardens in the West* (2003) (with E. Baratay, also translated into German from the French), *Histoire de la corrida en Europe* (2005). Elisabeth Hardouin-Fugier is also interested in the animal from the legal aspect, particularly German legal thinking.

Ingvar Ekesbo

After military service, Ingvar Ekesbo studied at the Royal Veterinary College and obtained a PhD in 1966. Ingvar Ekesbo became a Professor in Animal Hygiene in 1970 and was Head of Department from 1977 to 1993. Ingvar Ekesbo has been a member of national and international committees on animal health, welfare, and husbandry and was Chairman of the

Council of Europe Standing Committee of the European Convention for the Protection of Animals kept for for Farming Purposes from 1979 to 1998. He has published about 200 scientific articles and a great number of popular science articles.

Aleš Brecelj

Aleš Brecelj (DVM, MSc) graduated from the Veterinary Faculty in Ljubljana, Slovenia in 1989. He started his career in a small animal practice and since 1998 has been working for the Veterinary Administration of the Republic of Slovenia, currently as Head of the Animal Health and Animal Welfare Sector.

Nathalie Melik

Leading a team of seven people, Nathalie Melik, a veterinary inspector, has been head of the animal protection bureau in Paris for over twelve years. The bureau is responsible for drafting and negotiating all legislation and regulations concerning animal welfare at EU, international and national level. Nathalie Melik's responsibilities have led her to take part in numerous training courses and information campaigns in the field of ethics and animal protection in general.

Martin R. Gamero

Former representative of Spain for the Council of Europe's work on animal welfare, Martin R. Gamero was the Spanish veterinary surgeons' delegate to the Federation of Veterinarians of Europe (FVE). He was also President of the Veterinary Surgeons' Association of Andalusia.

Egbert Ausems

Egberts Ausems is a lawyer from the University of Amsterdam. He joined the Council of Europe in 1968 and was in charge of the drafting and implementation of the 1979 Convention on the Conservation of European Wildlife and Natural Habitats (Bern Convention, ETS No. 104) and several conventions on animal welfare. He is the former Head of the Animal Welfare Section of the Directorate of Legal Affairs of the Council of Europe.

Colin Tudge

Colin Tudge is a biologist by education and inclination but also has a lifelong interest in various areas of philosophy, religion, and politics, and a special passion for food and agriculture. He has always earned his living by writing and formerly worked full-time for *The New Scientist* and BBC Radio 3. But mainly he writes books including, most recently, *So shall we reap,* on the future of agriculture; and *The secret life of trees.* He has recently become a director of Britain's Food Ethics Council.

Introduction – Concepts of animal protection and welfare including obligations and rights

by Donald M. Broom

A brief history of attitudes to animals

The idea that animals used by people should not be treated like inanimate possessions but should be protected from actions that might cause suffering is very old and widespread in human society. Irrespective of any law, many people have condemned those perceived as being cruel to animals. On the other hand, cruelty was part of some forms of human entertainment. In Europe, laws intended to prevent cruelty to dogs and horses were passed as long as 200 years ago and were gradually extended to other kinds of animals. Most early laws referred to companion animals and working animals but not to farm animals. Some laws protected animals against the forms of animal experimentation which were considered likely to cause them substantial pain. Laws were also passed which proscribed some forms of entertainment involving animals as being cruel but others were still permitted. Laws aimed at preventing poor welfare in animals have become more wide-ranging, both in terms of species and the different animal uses, and have been passed in more and more countries.

The treatment of animals is an area in which codes of conduct and descriptions of good practice exist. Even amongst groups of people whose objective was to kill animals, there have long existed unwritten codes of conduct concerning what actions were or were not permissible. For example, as discussed by Serpell (1996, 1989), people using guns and dogs to hunt mammals or birds would expend energy and resources trying to ensure that firstly, animals were shot in a way likely to kill quickly and secondly, that shot animals were found and killed rather than being left to die slowly. More recently, codes of practice relating to animals kept for food production and other purposes have been produced by various organisations (see below).

The way in which animals are treated is much affected by the way in which the human user or carer thinks about those animals. If the animal is thought of as an object to be used which is little different from something inanimate, actions which cause poor welfare in the animals are much more likely than if the animals are considered to be similar in many ways to humans. Hence knowledge of animal functioning tends to engender respect where the animal is sentient, that is to say that it has significant capacity for awareness of itself and its relationships with its environment (see below). In recent years, knowledge of animal functioning, particularly their behaviour and physiology, has increased rapidly and has been the subject of much media attention.

This is a major reason why public concern about animal welfare has increased in many countries during the last thirty years and especially in the last ten years. Evidence of this is summarised in Table 1.

Table 1 – Evidence of increased concern about animal welfare
1. Letters from the public, media coverage.
2. References in parliamentary discussions and government statements.
3. Requests for scientific evidence concerning animal welfare.
4. Activity of scientific and other advisory committees.
5. Funding of scientific research on animal welfare.
6. Increased teaching and conferences.
7. More legislation.

(from Broom, 1999)

Members of the public exert influence by letters to government, other public bodies and commercial organisations and by statements which appear in the media. Members of the European Parliament report that they receive more letters about animal welfare than on any other topic. Politicians respond by raising the issues, including them in manifestos, seeking scientific information, encouraging further research and teaching, and by passing laws.

People who own or work on farms, or other commercial organisations using animals, are influenced by a variety of factors when they are deciding on animal housing and management policies and when they are executing these policies. They will be endeavouring to make a profit so the monetary costs which they incur and the potential financial returns which they are likely to get for their product will be factors of major importance to them. A cost to those involved in animal industry, which may not be fully appreciated by many of them, results from consumers who do not like some aspect of production and refuse to buy the product (Broom, 1994).

The attitudes of animal users depend upon early training, traditional practices, acquisition of knowledge from others subsequent to any training, personal experience and general beliefs and philosophy. Training did not, until recently, include much information about animal welfare except where it impinged on profitability. Even diseases were often mentioned in agriculture training only in relation to effects on growth, offspring production or product quantity and quality. Today's training courses are more likely to include information about the welfare of the animals (Broom, 2005) and most agricultural trade journals nowadays cover animal welfare issues. Traditional practices are often deemed by farmers or others keeping or using animals, to be right for the sole reason that "this is the way that we have always done it". Although some of these methods are the best ones to produce good welfare, others are not and traditional methods and practices should not persist just because they are traditions.

Farmers and other animal users have to live with their families, friends and neighbours. If these people are critical of the effects on the welfare of animals of the methods used, the farmer may change these methods. In some cases, the animals are very obvious to all who pass by the farm. If a sheep or cattle farmer has many animals which are noticeably lame, it is likely that someone will comment on this to the farmer. Similarly, horse establishments or zoos whose animals are lame may be criticised. People in charge of animals do not like to be thought of as incompetent or uncaring, so they may respond to such comments by giving the animals veterinary treatment or changing the management system so as to avoid lameness. If the animals are inside a building or otherwise hidden from public view, the number of people who might comment on poor welfare will be smaller and there is a greater chance that the farmer or other person responsible can persuade him or herself that there are no significant welfare problems.

Meetings with others in the same business and trade magazines will tend to help animal users to arrive at common views about their various problems. A farmer, laboratory animal technician, or zookeeper who has to reconcile him or herself to poor welfare in some animals will find it easier to do so with the support of others. Such influences can slow down change towards better welfare for the animals, especially if economic factors mitigate against such change.

The views of the general public are largely made known to farmers and others involved in animal usage via the media. There is frequent coverage of animal welfare issues in newspapers, on radio and television and this, by bringing scientific knowledge about animal complexity to the attention of people, affects their attitudes. Farmers and some other animal users may see themselves portrayed as uncaring. Some such portrayals are unfair but others are correct and the farmer cannot hide from them by putting animals in buildings and associating only with other farmers. When public demonstrations about animal welfare issues occur, the people who use the animals need to take note of them. The demonstrations by great numbers of largely orderly and apparently normal people against the shipping of calves under conditions which were illegal within the United Kingdom had a big influence on farmers and politicians alike. It is not the most vociferous people, some of whom may be rather extreme in their views, who have the greatest influence on animal users or politicians but the moderate people who represent a groundswell of public opinion. In many recent surveys in Europe, animal welfare has been shown to be an important issue for the general public. For example, about three quarters of people questioned in France regarded animal welfare as a problem affecting their decision to purchase veal or eggs (Ouedraogo, 1998) and of 420 school-girls questioned in Dublin, 34% stated that they avoided eating meat, principally for animal welfare (53%) rather than nutrition (29%) reasons (Ryan, 1997).

Welfare and related concepts

Animal protection is a human action but animal welfare is a varying quality of any living animal. The scientific study of animal welfare has developed rapidly during the last fifteen years. The concepts have been refined and a range of methods of assessment have been developed. Substantial challenges to animal functioning include those resulting from: pathogens, tissue damage, attack or threat of attack by a conspecific or predator, other social competition, complexity of information processing in a situation where an individual receives excessive stimulation, lack of key stimuli such as a teat for a young mammal or social contact cues, lack of overall stimulation, and inability to control interactions with the environment. Hence potentially damaging challenges may come from the environment outside the body, for example, many pathogens or causes of tissue damage, or from within it, for example, anxiety, boredom or frustration which come from the environment of a control system. Systems that respond to or prepare for challenges are coping systems and coping means having control of mental and bodily stability (Broom and Johnson, 1993). Coping attempts may be unsuccessful, in that such control is not achieved, but as soon as there is control, the individual is coping. Systems for attempting to cope with challenge may respond to short-term or long-term problems, or sometimes to both. The responses to challenge may involve activity in parts of the brain and various endocrine, immunological or other physiological responses as well as behaviour. However, the more that we learn about these responses, the clearer it becomes that these various types of response are interdependent. For example, not only do brain changes regulate bodily coping responses but adrenal changes have several consequences for brain function, lymphocytes have opioid receptors and a potential for altering brain activity, heart-rate changes can be used to regulate mental state and hence further responses.

Some coping systems include *feelings* as a part of their functioning, for example, pain, fear and the various kinds of pleasure, all of which are adaptive (Broom, 1998). Bad feelings which continue for more than a short period are referred to as *suffering.* Other high or low level brain processes and aspects of body functioning are also a part of attempts to cope with challenge. In order to understand coping systems in humans and other species it is necessary to study a wide range of mechanisms including complex brain functioning as well as simpler systems. Investigations of how easy or difficult it is for the individual to cope with the environment and of how great is the impact of positive or negative aspects of the environment on the individual, are investigations of welfare. According to Broom (1986, 1996, 1998) the *welfare* of an individual is its state as regards its attempts to cope with its environment and this includes feelings and health. Welfare is a characteristic of an individual at a certain time and the state of the individual can be assessed so welfare will vary on a range from very good to very poor. Welfare concerns how well the individual fares, or goes through life. Some authors place sole emphasis on feelings when defining welfare (Duncan and Petherick, 1991). Equivalent words in other languages include *bien-être, bienestar, bem estar, benessere, Wohlergehen, welzijn, velfærd,* and *dobrostan. Health,* like welfare, can be qualified as good or poor and varies over a range. It refers to body systems, including those in the brain, which combat pathogens, tissue damage, or physiological disorder. All of this is encompassed within the broader term welfare so, according to this approach, health is a part of welfare. This view is gaining in acceptance amongst scientists and veterinary practitioners but there are still some who do not accept it.

The assessment of welfare (Broom and Johnson, 1993) should be carried out in an objective way, taking no account of any ethical questions about the systems, practices or conditions for individuals which are being compared. Once the scientific evidence about welfare has been obtained, ethical decisions can be taken. Much of the evidence used in welfare assessment indicates the extent of poor welfare in individuals but it is also important to recognise and assess good welfare, that is, happiness, contentment, control of interactions with the environment and the possibility to exploit abilities. Good welfare in general, and a positive status in each of the various coping systems, should have effects which are part of a positive reinforcement system, just as poor welfare is associated with various negative reinforcers. We need to identify and quantify indicators of good welfare as well as those of poor welfare.

Most people who speak of *stress* refer to a situation in which an individual is subjected to a potentially or actually damaging effect of its environment. However, the usage of the term is sometimes confusing as it is used to mean three different things: an environmental change which affects an organism, the process of affecting the organism, or the consequences of effects on the organism. Some people react with limited stress to one kind of physiological response mechanism, hypothalamic-pituitary-adrenal cortex (HPA) activity, or to mental rather than physiological responses. However, it was demonstrated by Mason (1971) and many other studies that several different responses to challenges can occur: HPA activity is temporarily increased during courtship, mating, active prey catching and active social interaction, none of which would be considered to be stressful by the majority of the general public or of scientists. To equate stress with HPA axis activity renders the word redundant and is considered unscientific and unnecessary by most scientists working in the area. If every impact of the environment on an organism is called stress, then the term has no value. Another meaning which has been ascribed to stress makes it largely synonymous with stimulation. Many stimuli which affect individuals in beneficial ways would never be called stressors by most people. Stress is an environmental effect on an individual which overtaxes its control systems and results in adverse consequences, eventually reduced fitness (Broom and Johnson, 1993). The ultimate measure of fitness is the number of offspring reaching future generations and there are many different ways in which challenges overtax control systems and have such effects.

The environment of an animal is appropriate if it allows the animal to satisfy its needs. Animals have a range of functional systems controlling body temperature, nutritional state, social interactions, etc. (Broom, 1981). Together, these functional systems allow the individual to control its interactions with its environment and hence to keep each aspect of its state within a tolerable range. The allocation of time and resources to different physiological or behavioural activities, either within a functional system or between systems, is controlled by motivational mechanisms. When an animal is actually or potentially homeostatically maladjusted, or when it must carry out an action because of some environmental situation, we say that it has a need. A need can therefore be defined as a requirement, which is part of the basic biology of an animal, to obtain a particular resource or respond to a particular environmental or bodily stimulus. There are needs for particular resources and needs to carry out actions whose function is to obtain an objective (Toates and Jensen, 1991; Broom, 1996). Needs can be identified by studies of motivation and by assessing the welfare of individuals whose needs are not satisfied (Hughes and Duncan, 1988a, b; Dawkins, 1990; Broom and Johnson, 1993). Unsatisfied needs are often, but not always, associated with bad feelings whilst satisfied needs may be associated with good feelings. When needs are not satisfied, welfare will be poorer than when they are satisfied.

Some needs are for particular resources, such as water or heat, but control systems have evolved in animals in such a way that the means of obtaining a particular objective have become important to the individual animal. The animal may need to perform a certain behaviour and may be seriously affected if unable to carry out the activity, even in the presence of the ultimate objective of the activity. For example, rats and ostriches will work, in the sense of carrying out actions which result in food presentation, even in the presence of food. In the same way, pigs need to root in soil or some similar substratum (Hutson, 1989), hens need to dust bathe (Vestergaard, 1980) and both of these species need to build a nest before giving birth or laying eggs (Brantas, 1980; Arey, 1992). In all of these different examples, the need itself is in the brain and is not physiological or behavioural but may be satisfied only when some physiological imbalance is prevented or rectified, or when some particular behaviour is shown.

The effects of legislation on welfare

Legislation has effects on how people house and manage animals. It is generally initiated by pressure from voters on elected politicians. In a scientific area the politicians need to know the latest state of scientific knowledge on the subject. As a consequence, the European Union has set up scientific committees on a range of subjects. The former committees considering animal welfare were the Scientific Veterinary Committee, Animal Welfare Section and the Scientific Committee on Animal Health and Animal Welfare. The present committee is the European Food Safety Authority Scientific Panel on Animal Health and Welfare.

Legislation within European countries and EU directives and regulations have usually been preceded by recommendations from Council of Europe committees such as the Standing Committee of the European Convention for the Protection of Animals kept for Farming Purposes. This last Committee has produced recommendations on: poultry kept for egg production, pigs, cattle, animals used for fur production, sheep, goats, chickens kept for meat production, ducks, etc. There are other conventions on the protection of pet animals, animals for slaughter, animals used for experimentation and animals during transport. The information in the conventions and recommendations has formed the basis for legislation and codes of practice in many countries.

On a worldwide scale the Organisation Internationale des Epizooties (OIE) or World Organisation for Animal Health is now producing sets of recommendations which are likely to be treated as laws by most nations in the world, just as OIE recommendations on animal disease are respected.

The actual effect of legislation on the welfare of animals depends upon the responses of those owning and managing the animals. This response, in turn, depends upon the nature of any enforcement. Some systems for farm animal production will not continue if they are made illegal because they depend upon large manufacturers who are easily forced to change to a legal system. Other aspects of legislation can be enforced only by checks on farms, transport vehicles, markets, slaughter-houses, etc., and the extent of law-breaking will be significantly affected by the frequency and quality of the checks. For many transgressions, unannounced inspections are necessary if transgressors are to be discovered. There are regional and national differences in the seriousness with which legislation is viewed by those involved in the animal production business.

Retailer-produced codes of practice

Farmers often sell animals or their production of milk, eggs, etc. to single purchasers who represent large retail chains or wholesale distribution companies. The increase in direct selling to supermarket chains has led to considerable power being placed in the hands of these companies. It is possible for these purchasers to lay down conditions for animal production and to enforce these by inspection. The standards set by the super-market chains are determined by what people will buy and by their reputation with the public.

The public image of large companies which retail food, including supermarket chains and fast-food companies, is of great importance to them. Bad publicity because of a risk to public health, a risk to the environment or the occurrence of poor welfare at any stage of the production process can be very damaging. Hence it is in the interest of such food companies to avoid any scandal which might threaten their good image. When these companies receive many letters from consumers complaining about a product which they sell, they have to take notice of the points which are being made.

As a consequence of consumer pressure, food retail companies are adopting standards which they impose on their suppliers. In some cases, these standards are quite simple, for example,

Albert Hein in the Netherlands and elsewhere limited their sales of eggs to scharreleie which meant that the hens were reared in conditions where they could scratch in litter. Marks and Spencer in the UK and elsewhere stopped selling eggs from battery cages. In other cases, elaborate standards have been described in detail and sent to suppliers. One of the first systematic attempts to provide comprehensive information about the conditions under which animals were kept in the course of food production was the "Freedom Foods" scheme run by the RSPCA in the UK. Under this scheme, the standards for housing and management have been set by a widely respected animal protection society and farms are inspected by Freedom Foods staff. Retailers who subscribe to the scheme are allowed to use the Freedom Foods logo which is accepted as honest by the purchasing public. Acceptance by the public of products which are produced in such a way that the welfare of the animals is good, depends upon trust in the organisation which is carrying out the labelling and inspection. Some large supermarket chains and other food retailers are trusted because it is thought that they could not afford to be found out if they were not labelling and policing adequately.

The enforcement of standards by food retailers has led to substantial changes in the welfare of animals on farms because every producer has to conform to the standards in order to sell their products. The rapid development of such schemes in several countries has, in general, been based on scientific evidence about animal welfare.

Obligations to animals: do they have rights?

Moral actions are directed more towards those identified as "us" than towards those considered to be "them" (Broom, 2003, 2006 in press). Categories included as "us" may be:

a. individuals readily recognised as close relatives,

b. all of those who know who I am,

c. those who might have access to the same information that I have, or

d. sentient beings who share characteristics with me.

Increased communication efficiency is revolutionising our degree of concern for other humans and extending our area of moral concern to other species. Companion animals will be in category (a) for some people. Serpell and Paul (1994) found that many pet owners stated that they regarded their pets as part of their family. Most pet owners would include their pet in category (b) and all who consider animals to be sentient, or who know that most mammals have over 90% of the same genes as humans, would include some or many other species of animals in categories (c) or (d). In many societies today, education levels are high and there is easy access to good quality information about people in other countries and about animals whose abilities are complex. Hence the likelihood that people will cause, or tolerate poor welfare in foreign people or animals is declining. It is of particular interest that changed attitudes to animals appear to be linked more closely to education levels than to affluence. In countries which are relatively poor but well educated, interest in animal welfare may be such that people are willing to incur some degree of financial loss rather than benefit from poor welfare in animals.

If we use a living animal in a way which is beneficial to us, we have some obligations to that animal. One obligation is to avoid causing poor welfare in the animal except where the action leads to net benefit to that animal, or to other animals, including humans, or to the environment. A utilitarian approach is not sufficient to determine all obligations, however, and a deontological approach is also needed because there are some degrees of poor welfare which can never be justified by benefit to others.

It is my view (Broom, 2003, p. 130) that all human behaviour and laws should be based on the obligation of each person to act in an acceptable way towards each other person and each animal which is used. It is better for strategies for living to be based on our obligations rather than to involve the concept of rights. This is because many so-called rights can result in harm to others. There are occasions when people state that they have a right to say what they like, or drive as fast as they want, or carry a gun, or select the sex or genetic make-up of their children. In each of these cases the action could hurt others which would be accepted by very few people. Whilst arguments based on a concept of rights may sometimes be clearly wrong, arguments based on the obligation of one individual towards others do not suffer from such problems. Hence my conclusion that the concept of rights is not the best to use and that each person should always focus on how they ought to behave. As far as animal rights are concerned, no legal rights are stated but there are many statements, codes of conduct, or unwritten rules which explain the obligations towards animals of those people who use the animals.

The argument presented above criticising the use of the term rights also applies to references to the freedom which an individual asserts or which it is said should be given. Efforts to list the freedoms which should be allowed to the animals which we keep have been of use as a general guide to management but with the development of information about the needs of animals, it is now possible to be more precise in laws or guidelines for animal care and all of these should refer to needs rather than to freedoms.

The most widely accepted obligation to animals which we use concerns avoidance of poor welfare so learning about animal welfare and its scientific basis is very important for all those who have frequent contact with animals.

Bibliography

Arey, D.S., "Straw and food as reinforcers for prepartal sows" in *Applied Animal Behaviour Science* 33, 1992, pp. 217-226.

Brantas, G.C., "The pre-laying behaviour of laying hens in cages with and without laying nests", in *The laying hen and its environment*, R. Moss (ed.), *Current Topics in Veterinary Medicine and Animal Science* 42, 1980, pp. 129-132.

Broom, D.M., *Biology of behaviour*, Cambridge University Press, Cambridge, 1981.

Broom, D.M., "Indicators of poor welfare", in *British Veterinary Journal*, 142, 1986, pp. 524-526.

Broom, D.M., "The valuation of animal welfare in human society", in R.M. Bennett (ed.), *Valuing farm animal welfare*, University of Reading, Reading, 1994, pp. 1-7.

Broom D.M., "The effects of production efficiency on animal welfare", in E. A. Huisman, J.W. M. Osse, D. van der Heide, S. Tamminga, B.L. Tolkamp, W.G.P. Schouten, C.E. Hollingsworth and G.L. van Winkel (eds.), *Biological basis of sustainable animal production, Proc. 4th Zodiac Symp.*, EAAP Publ. 67, Wageningen Pers, Wageningen, 1994, pp. 201-210.

Broom, D.M., "Animal welfare defined in terms of attempts to cope with the environment", in *Acta Agriculturae Scandinavica, Section A – Animal Science Supplement*, 27, 1996, pp. 22-28.

Broom, D.M., "Welfare, stress and the evolution of feelings" in *Advances in the study of behavior*, 27, 1998, pp. 371-403.

Broom, D.M., "Welfare and how it is affected by regulation", in M. Kunisch and H. Ekkel (eds.), *Regulation of animal production in Europe*, K.T.B.L. Darmstadt, 1999, pp. 51-57.

Broom, D.M., "Coping, stress and welfare", in D.M. Broom (ed.), *Coping with challenge: welfare in animals including humans*, Dahlem University Press, Berlin, 2001, pp. 1-9.

Broom, D.M., *The evolution of morality and religion*, Cambridge University Press, Cambridge, 2003.

Broom, D.M., "Animal welfare education: development and prospects", in *J. Vet. Med. Educ.,* 32, 2005, pp. 438-441.

Broom, D.M. and Johnson, K.G., *Stress and animal welfare,* Kluwer, Dordrecht, 1993.

Dawkins, M.S., "From an animal's point of view: motivation, fitness and animal welfare", in *Behavioral and brain sciences,* 13, 1990, pp. 1-61.

Duncan, I.J.H. and Petherick, J.C., "The implications of cognitive processes for animal welfare" in *Journal of Animal Science* 69, 1991, pp. 5017-5022.

Hughes, B.O. and Duncan, I.J.H., "Behavioural needs: can they be explained in terms of motivational models?" in *Applied Animal Behaviour Science,* 19, 1988a, pp. 352-355.

Hughes, B.O. and Duncan, I.J.H., "The notion of ethological 'need', models of motivation and animal welfare", in *Animal behaviour,* 36, 1988b, pp. 1696-1707.

Hutson, G.D., "Operant tests of access to earth as a reinforcement for weaner piglets", in *Animal production* 48, 1989, pp. 561-569.

Mason, J.W., "A re-evaluation of the concept of 'non-specificity' in stress theory", in *J. Psychiat. Res.,* 8, 1971, pp. 323-333.

Ouedraogo, A.P., "Ethical consumers? Social representations of stock farming in France", in I. Veissier and A. Boissy (eds.), *Proceedings of the 32nd Congress of the International Society for Applied Ethology,* INRA, Clermont-Ferrand, 1998, p. 204.

Ryan, Y.M., "Meat avoidance and body weight concerns: nutritional implications for teenage girls", in *Proceedings of the nutrition society,* 56, 1997, pp. 519-524.

Selye, H., *The physiology and pathology of exposure to stress,* Acta, Montreal, 1950.

Selye, H., *The Stress of Life,* 2nd edn, McGraw-Hill., New York, 1976.

Serpell, J.A., *In the company of animals: a study of human-animal relationships,* Cambridge University Press, Cambridge, 1996.

Serpell, J.A., "Attitudes to animals", in D. Paterson and M. Palmer (eds.), *The status of animals: ethics education and welfare,* CAB International, Wallingford, 1989, pp. 162-166.

Serpell, J. and Paul, E., "Pets and the development of positive attitudes to animals" in A. Manning and J. Serpell (eds.), *Animals and human society,* Routledge, London, 1994, pp. 127-144.

Toates, F. and Jensen, P., "Ethological and psychological models of motivation: Towards a synthesis", in J.A. Meyer and S. Wilson (eds.), *From animals to animats,* MIT Press, Cambridge, 1991, pp. 194-205.

Vestergaard, K., "The regulation of dust bathing and other behaviour patterns in the laying hen: a Lorenzian approach", in *The laying hen and its environment,* R. Moss (ed.), Current Topics in Veterinary Medicine and Animal Science 8, Martinus Nijhoff, The Hague, 1980, pp. 101-113.

Do animals have rights?

by Elisabeth de Fontenay

The question of animal rights recently raised its head again in spectacular fashion following a call to extend human rights to chimpanzees launched by a group of philosophers and primatologists, backing an initiative by Peter Singer[1] and Paola Cavalieri.[2] The extravagance of a demand of this kind can naturally only prove counterproductive, firstly because it seems to disregard the undeniable difference between animals and humans. Although the discovery of the 99% of genes common to human beings and chimpanzees brings the two species considerably closer together, this difference is self-evident and a matter of common sense, since all humans are capable of establishing and observing rules, something which is impossible without articulated language.

It is necessary to take stock of the history of human rights before broaching the issue of animal rights. The American rights of 1773 are not the same as the French ones of 1789, 1791 or 1793, nor those of 1848, which considerably revised the earlier rights, to the point that they almost contradict those of 1789. As to the Universal Declaration of 1948, it represents both a summing-up and a new step forward and is the instrument which humanitarian movements cite as their authority.

Nor does the concept of natural law afford grounds for attributing rights to living beings other than humans. The ancient philosophers concerned with the law of nature – the Epicureans, the Stoics, in particular Cicero – refused to recognise animal rights which imposed a duty on humans.[3] This was because they believed that, although humans were part of the system of natural law common to all living beings, they were in addition subject to a natural law of man as man, proper to them as rational, autonomous agents capable of entering into contracts. Modern philosophers of natural law have not departed from that principle. It is accordingly virtually impossible, within traditional thinking, to venture even to suggest that human rights may also apply to the great apes. If this is

1.
Singer, P., *Animal liberation*, The New York Review of Books, New York, 1990.

2.
Cavalieri, P., *Le débat*, No.108, January-February 2000, and No. 109, March-April 2000.

3.
De Fontenay, E., *Le silence des bêtes. La philosophie à l'épreuve de l'animalité*, Fayard, Paris, 1998, Chapter IV.

how the *jus naturalis* tradition and the concept of human rights are linked, animal rights have nothing to gain.

It is moreover a known fact that the assertion of human rights has constantly been surrounded by considerable ambiguity. What exactly does the term mean? Liberty rights, such as those claimed by the revolutionaries of 1789? Or can one add – without fear of contradiction – the entitlement rights which were embodied in the Declaration of 1848 and which can be defined as individuals' power to require society to guarantee them assistance, health care or a job, for example? The stance adopted in this legal, political and social debate determines the relevance of considerations on the fair treatment possibly owed to animals. For without a thorough grasp of the philosophical, historical and legal tenor of discussions on human rights, claims that animals have rights are necessarily distorted. It is only by taking account of the complementarity of the two kinds of rights, freedoms and entitlements, a complementarity which social movements struggled to have recognised, that the substance of the claims on behalf of animals can be clarified.

Solely for writers of the continental European philosophical tradition which takes animals into consideration ontologically – those who follow the phenomological approach of Husserl[4] and Merleau-Ponty[5] – animals are not just natural beings since they can be presumed to have their own "subjectivities" correlative to "worlds" which may coincide with human ones. This theory entails going beyond the still very anthropocentric obsession with the great apes, in order to attribute to mammals, and more broadly vertebrates, something like a culture,[6] to conceive their relations with human beings possibly in terms of empathy, *Einfühlung*, that is to say a potential capacity for comprehension, which would enable us to have some access to their worlds.

Such an analysis, which ties in with the most astonishing advances of ethology, has nothing in common with the theories of deep ecology, nor more generally those of environmentalism. Its attempt to recognise animal subjectivity or consciousness can be regarded as being in tune with what is

4.
See the phenomological magazine *Alter*, No. 3, "L'Animal", 1995, pp. 88, 91, 97.

5.
Merleau-Ponty, M., "La nature", course notes, Collège de France, Editions du Seuil, Paris, 1995.

6.
Richir, M., *Phénoménologie et institution symbolique*, Jérôme Millon, Grenoble, 1988. See also Merleau-Ponty, op. cit.

termed "pathocentrism", the assumption that the ability to feel or suffer is common to all life, as to be found in the work of Schopenhauer. The pathocentrist approach consists in showing, giving more or less short shrift to metaphysical or juridical humanism, that the moral community is made up not just of "moral agents", capable of mutual responsibilities and of informed consent, but also of "moral patients", which include certain categories of human beings and animals. One could say that the phenomological attempt to understand animal realities and the utilitarian Anglo-Saxon call for an extension of the moral community might work in animals' favour, so as to afford them greater protection and ally humans with them, despite the mutual antagonisms and antipathies.

It must be noted that this is an area where criminal law is ahead of civil law. Criminal law is tending towards "the concept of an animal as both a commodity and a sentient being, recognised by law as having the right to live in accordance with its genetically programmed dispositions, a clause incorporated in the Treaty of Amsterdam, which uses the term "animal welfare", whereas the Civil Code is struggling to give a precise legal definition of an animal."[7] In civil law, animals are neither objects nor persons.

Marguénaud's approach

Nonetheless, it would seem that two contemporary thinkers offer an acceptable basis for arguing that animals have legal rights. The issue will be broached first from the standpoint of positive law and the distinction between being a bearer of rights and obligations in law and having legal personality, and second from that of legal philosophy and the difference between liberty rights and entitlement rights.

Firstly, adopting the standpoint of modern French law, a French legal specialist, Jean-Pierre Marguénaud, has shown, through a conclusive analysis,[8] that giving animals legal personality has nothing to do with a form of anthropomorphisation and accordingly does not undermine human dignity. He considers that making animals bearers of rights merely results in adoption of a legal technique suited, at a given moment in

7.
Suzanne Antoine in *Bulletin d'informations de la Ligue française des droits de l'animal*, No. 45, October 2004.

8.
Marguénaud, J.-P. (Director of the Observatory of Institutional and Legal Reform – Observatoire des mutations institutionnelles et juridiques - OMJ, Limoges), *Bulletin juridique international pour la protection des animaux* (BJAPA) and *Recueil Dalloz*, 1998, No. 20, "La personnalité juridique des animaux".

time, to the protection, deemed necessary, of certain animals' interests. The convenience of opting for animals' "symbolic promotion" and for this legal technique in no way leads to a trivialisation of human rights, since the concept of "legal personality", not to be confused with that of "rights bearer", does not entail any erasure of the borderline between humans and animals.

In addition, Jean-Pierre Marguénaud shows that under current French law animals are no longer things but indeed juristic persons, contrary to what Luc Ferry suggested, on the sole basis of the Grammont law of 2 July 1850, in his *Le nouvel ordre écologique.*[9] The one and only article of the Grammont law simply made it reprehensible to ill-treat a domestic animal in public without due reason, thereby punishing the mere offence against public decency not the abuse of animals' sensitivity. It was the former justice minister Edmond Michelet who provided the impetus for repeal of the Grammont law and its replacement by a decree of 7 September 1959, which was conducive to far stricter protection, since it contained a provision which, while continuing to punish ill treatment, did away with the restrictive condition of the offence's public nature. This means that the animal is protected for its own sake and is accorded a right. Into the bargain, it can be noted that further progress has since been made towards protection of animals in their own interest. The authorities have successively introduced penalties for cruelty to domestic animals, whether or not perpetrated in public, deliberate abandonment and serious ill treatment. It has become an established requirement that an ill-treated animal should be handed over to an animal protection organisation. Animals are now protected for their own sake, including from their owners. Jean-Pierre Marguénaud is accordingly able to conclude that an animal:

> "[...] is no longer a piece of property ... As there is a logical inconsistency between the right of ownership and its restriction in the interests of the thing owned ... it is difficult to continue to assert that animals are subject to the law on property. The new Criminal Code imposes a fine for deliberately killing an animal. *Abusus*, which is a prerogative of the owner, is accordingly subject to restrictions in the animal's interest. An animal is no longer a thing or a chattel, since the new Criminal

9.
Ferry, L., *Le Nouvel ordre écologique*, Grasset, Paris, 1970.

Code creates a separate category of offence for acts of cruelty against animals, which do not qualify as offences against the person, property, the state, the nation, public order or humanity."

It can moreover be assumed that this novel category of offence, "a halfway house between offences against property and against the person", will not last long and that the "technical" solution of the legal personification of animals will in the end prevail, since any "group with a possibility of collective expression for the defence of lawful interests" is already vested with legal personality. The two requirements – separate interests and the existence of a body likely to pursue them – are fulfilled. Like legal entities, animals are accordingly juristic persons without being bearers of rights and obligations, and it is this legal truth which had to be demonstrated in order to put an end to the nonsensical debate, and in order for people, or at least animal-lovers, to also understand that it will never be possible to eradicate a minimum of anthropocentrism. This selfish focus on ourselves, this speciesism to use the right term, which must indeed be amended, is an outcome of our finiteness rather than a sign of our power. But it also gives us a responsibility towards all the beings that sleep while we keep watch.

Feinberg's analysis

Secondly, the reasoning followed by Joel Feinberg, an American law philosopher,[10] seems nonetheless to offer the most fruitful approach to the question. Not only does he explain and unravel the ambiguities inherent in the concept of rights, clarifying the essential distinctions drawn by legal specialists, but he also satisfies the utilitarian, Darwinian requirement that we enlarge the circle of beings to which we accord moral consideration. I shall base my description of his ideas on the remarkable account of them given by Jean-Yves Goffi in *Le philosophe et ses animaux* and the collection of essays *Si les lions pouvaient parler*.

It can be said that, as a general rule, we always hold a right to something against someone, that is, I have a right vis-à-vis someone, who then ends up with a corresponding obligation.

10.
See Goffi, J.-Y., *Le philosophe et ses animaux*, Editions Jacqueline Chambon, Nîmes, 1994, pp. 93-107 and pp. 161-163. See also his contribution to the collection of essays *Si les lions pouvaient parler*, Cyrulnik, B. (ed.), Gallimard, Paris, 1998, pp. 892-897.

The most common example is the creditor's right vis-à-vis a debtor. Far from being mere subjects of human duties, animals possess such rights, to the extent that laws punish certain ways of treating them and contain not just prohibitions, but also obligations. For example, animals have the right to be sheltered from cruelty. However, as we saw earlier, that does not mean that they are bearers of rights in law. Since they have no consciousness of the offence, of the authority, or of the symbolic nature of the punishment, they cannot take legal action or exercise legal prerogatives.[11] According to Feinberg, the fact nonetheless remains that the law can protect them, and in this respect he is at odds with the tradition of juridical humanism, whereby a being which has no legal capacity to act, possess or contract qualifies as a thing.

This philosopher of law moreover compares animals' situation, or at least that of certain animals, with the status of the insane, people with mental disabilities, the senile elderly and infants, who are present in law merely as represented beings. He nonetheless points out that humans are incompetent only by chance and are moreover represented solely when their interests must be defended, whereas animals are by nature incapable of asserting their interests, which would suggest that they do not possess rights per se. For Feinberg there are two different ways of being represented, by a lawyer who strictly follows instructions or by a guardian who exercises some discretion in defending the ward's interests. This is where his theories conflict with those of juridical humanism, with their emphasis on contracts rendering the basis of law the capacity to make a rationally informed choice. According to Feinberg, there are other ways of enjoying rights – one need but think of children, who merely have a potential but are entitled to an education, which will allow them to develop as autonomous beings, bearers of rights and obligations in law. From this standpoint, Feinberg asserts that certain conditions of poverty, scarcity or indignity may reveal rights which do not need to be claimed or even recognised by their holders in order to exist. This is a key assertion, which is universally valid, and embodies the very essence of entitlement rights. Accordingly, one need but apply the traditional distinction between liberty

11.
This leads Feinberg to conclude that they are not persons, in the legal sense, a conclusion which Marguénaud disputes as we have seen.

rights, of which political rights are a paradigm, and entitlement rights, of which social rights are the most perfect example, to understand that animals have rights despite the fact that they are not bearers of rights in law.

But what does "having rights" mean if it is not being in a situation to have one's interests promoted or defended. That cannot apply to things, although they may be valuable, rare and even unique, such as works of art or historical monuments.

Responsibility for protecting and preserving them, however, does not fall to a guardian or trustee but to a curator. To possess what are termed interests, one must have what Feinberg calls a "conative life", made up of drives, unconscious instincts and conscious desires and goals which can be fulfilled or hampered. The Latin term *conatus* has long been used in physics and philosophy. Hobbes and Descartes, for example, used it to describe the principle of inertia: an object maintains its current state of inertia or motion unless another object counters its *conatus*. With his proposition on *conatus*, "Each thing, as far as it can by its own power, strives to persevere in its being",[12] Spinoza focuses on the very being of what perseveres. However, to gain a better understanding of the concept of "conative life" proposed by Feinberg, reference must above all be made to the *oikeiosis*, or indeed the *homologia*, of the Stoics, although – one of the inconsistencies resulting from their anthropocentric orientation – they paradoxically refused to recognise any rights for animals, which they regarded as entirely destined for human use. *Oikeiosis* is the affinity, the natural, spontaneous disposition of all living beings for self-protection, to preserve themselves by appropriating what they need and avoiding what is dangerous. There is a tendency, founded on a form of self-awareness, to extend this trait to other beings, beginning with those that are near and progressing to those that are increasingly distant. Writings by Diogenes Laertius[13] and Cicero[14] refer to what Seneca describes as each animal's love for itself. This self-love leads to a desire for survival and it is this innate, albeit dim and vague, instinct that allows an awareness of something other than the animal itself.[15]

Feinberg accordingly in turn believes that attachment to one's own welfare is a trait specific to animals, which makes them

12.
Spinoza, *Ethics*, III, VI, VII, VIII.

13.
Diogenes Laertius, *Lives and opinions of eminent philosophers*, VII, 85.

14.
Cicero, *The extremes of good and evil*, II, XLVII, 122; III, V, XVI.

15.
Seneca, *Epistles*, 121, 5-24.

fear death. This conative life is structured by tendencies, desires and goals, which at the same time entail having conscious beliefs about the desired object, since one cannot say that a plant lacking water, which has no consciousness of its thirst, has a conative life. However, it has to be acknowledged that this system of living beings is subject to a restriction: not all animals qualify as having conative life, not all are individual bearers of interests and accordingly not all have rights. It is not unreasonable, at least in principle, to establish a hierarchy, whereby certain animals have rights and others do not. "It is not as if one were saying that the square roots of even numbers are concupiscent and the square roots of odd numbers are chaste!"[16] This witticism is a very useful rejoinder to those who claim rights for fleas, in order better to deny the rights of dogs.

What therefore are these animal interests protected by law, which naturally also belong to humans? As will now be clear, they concern well-being, life, health, physical integrity, lack of suffering and so on. Humans for their part are capable of having what can be termed "further" interests, which consist in the individual's goals and ultimate aspirations. This is why animals' interests, including the right to life, are less important than human rights. Jean-Yves Goffi seeks to challenge this restriction. If animals have nothing more than life, is it not therefore all the more precious? Is the insignificance of animals' interests not a reason for greater protection? The answer is no doubt yes, but will this justified observation be turned to account in order to lapse back into the unworkable extreme of maintaining that an animal life is of equivalent, if not greater, worth than a human one.

Two problems can nonetheless be seen to be hard to overcome. Feinberg writes: "without awareness, expectation, belief, desire, aim, and purpose, a being can have no interests; without interests, it cannot be benefited; without the capacity to be a beneficiary, it can have no rights."[17] As we have seen, that rules out plants, on the one hand, and, on the other hand, the lower animals, animal species and "human beings in a vegetative state", all jumbled together. As regards the protection of species, since animal rights do not come into the picture, it would seem that a more appropriate approach to the great pre-

16.
Goffi, J.-Y., in *Si les lions pouvaient parler*, op. cit.

17.
Cited by Goffi, J.-Y. in *Le philosophe et ses animaux*, op. cit., p. 105.

sent-day problem of safeguarding threatened animal species is to be found in the context of protection of works of art and heritage objects. Feinberg regards species as mere groups of individuals, which, as such, cannot have a conative life. However, he gets around the resulting legal vacuum by saying that as caretakers and not owners of the planet, apart from any question of animal rights, we protect threatened species on account of multiple human interests and on the strength of our duties to future generations.

As for Feinberg's argument concerning the lack of rights of "human vegetables", this is a really worrying proposition, since the profound thinking on the conditions of poverty that engender rights, without their beneficiaries necessarily having any awareness thereof, does not concern this category of patients. However, Feinberg in a way revises his disqualification of them by stating that there are all kinds of reasons for treating these human beings as if they had rights. This use of "as if", that effective, subtle analogical operator, naturally entails having recourse to another line of logic and raises new problems which cannot be addressed in the context of this paper. The fact remains that Feinberg's legal reasoning is strongly anchored in philosophical tradition and appears to be both the most benevolent and the least inconsequent of those I have had occasion to acquaint myself with.

The position adopted by Georges Chapouthier,[18] entailing a gradualist legal approach, would seem appropriate if it did not consist in giving scientists the excessive power to decide which species should be aided by animal rights and how they should be defended, in other words empowering the possessors of positive knowledge to assess species' right to rights on a differential basis. This approach poses problems in that it tends to use science to legitimise rights. True, it is a good thing that recent work in the fields of biology and psychology should teach us about our similarities with rats and that we should not trust entirely in the hierarchy of beings that has existed in the western world for time immemorial. However, by campaigning for the introduction of a gradualist legal approach, do we not irresponsibly surrender our power to make laws?

18.
Author of *Au bon vouloir de l'homme, l'animal*, Denoël, Paris, 1990.

In the sphere of animal rights it is important to be eclectic and possibly even opportunist. The debate is worthwhile and one which the scientific, legal and moral specialists should not lose interest in pursuing. This is also a field where France has a lot of ground to make up, which should be possible thanks to the more advanced European legislation.

Ethical issues

Farming and rearing

by Birte Broberg

The domestication of farm animal species

A large number of animal species – mainly mammals, birds and fish – are kept as farm animals. The domestication of many of today's farm animal species is believed to have started in different parts of the world some 8000 to 10000 years ago. The first animal species to be kept by man were probably sheep, goats, pigs, cattle, poultry and horses. Domestication of rabbits started much later, probably not until Roman times, and only recently farming of other species such as fur animals, deer and ostriches began.

The purpose of keeping these animals was then and is still to produce meat, milk, eggs, honey, wool, skin, and fur, or to use them for other farming purposes, such as draught animals.

Today's farm animals live in a very different environment from that of their wild ancestors. The process of domestication and later selection especially for faster growth, higher milk yield, etc. has resulted in animals that may look markedly different from their ancestors. They differ in colour and size, their reproduction abilities are changed so that they can reproduce all year round, they grow much faster, they have larger muscles, they have better feed conversion, etc. However, even though a number of mainly production-related traits have changed, and research has found modifications in behaviour, such as the animal's attitude towards humans and reduced sensitivity to changes in their environment (Price, 1999), it seems that modern farm animals still have most, if not all of the behavioural patterns of their wild ancestors. An example of this is the behaviour of domestic pigs when released into nature. These pigs, even after having been kept for generations under modern farming conditions, showed behavioural patterns similar to wild boar, for example, they tended to form the same type of groups, pregnant sows about to give birth left the group to seek a suitable farrowing site, and they built a nest (Jensen, 2002).

Different farming methods and farming of different animal species

Farm animals are kept in a variety of different farming systems, ranging from smallholdings to large intensive "factory-like" farms to extensive outdoor systems.

The extensive outdoor systems where the animals are left to seek food, typically grass over vast areas, such as marshes or mountainous areas, are normally regarded as animal-friendly systems, which give animals large freedom of movement and the possibility to express their normal range of behaviour. However, even these systems may have drawbacks from an animal welfare point of view. The animals may be inspected at long or irregular intervals, which means that disease and injury may be discovered late; they may in certain areas be the target of predators, such as wolves and bears; they may be kept outside in adverse weather conditions without a shelter and a proper dry lying area, or they may – if not removed in time – be caught on land in danger of being flooded, etc.

It is the intensive farming systems and the living conditions given to animals in these systems that are the main target for animal welfare concerns. These systems are characterised by having a large number of animals in a relatively small area, often in a barren environment; the animals are cared for by a relatively small number of people, as many functions such as feeding, watering, mucking out and even milking and collection of eggs have been mechanised. This means that less attention is being paid to the individual animal, this being more predominant in some production systems, for example, broilers, than in others, for example, milking cows. Another aspect of intensive animal production is breeding programmes aimed at animals that produce more, for example, milk or eggs, or grow faster. A factor of major importance in the development of intensive systems has been the incentive to reduce production costs in order to compete on a market with an increasing demand and competition for cheaper food.

Although a small minority do not eat meat or other animal products because of animal welfare reasons, it is generally accepted, that the keeping of animals for production of food for human consumption is an acceptable farming activity, provided the animals are kept under satisfactory conditions. Whether this is an acceptable farming activity is hardly ever debated and if discussed, it is the conditions given to the animals in a given system that are debated, not the farming activity itself. Consequently it is legitimate to keep farm animals for production of meat, milk, eggs and honey. Products such as skin, wool and down could be regarded as side products of food production, so these productions would also be generally accepted.

When it comes to fur animals the situation is different. Public debate has shown that attitudes towards farming of fur animals cover a wide field. At one end there are those who find that fur is a non-essential luxury product, and therefore it is not acceptable to use animals in such a production. Even though not justifiable in relation to farm animals this point of view might also be influenced by cruel trapping methods used for catching wild fur-bearing animals, the killing of baby seals, and lately, imports from Asia of skins from dogs and cats killed under totally unacceptable conditions. Other parts of the field are occupied by those who find that the farming of fur animals should be regarded in line with farming of all other farm animals, although some find that the welfare standards for fur animals should be higher, because fur is after all a luxury product. This latter point of view gained support from a report that compared the welfare situation of farmed mink to that of other farmed animals (Spruijt, 1999). It could be concluded that indicators of poor welfare in certain systems for sows and laying hens were more numerous and more severe than those in mink. However, the Scientific Committee on Animal Health and Animal Welfare (2001) in its Report on the Welfare of Animals Kept for Fur Production seems more sceptical in its conclusions and recommendations. There is still room for improvement.

Animal welfare concerns

The trend towards intensive production systems started in the 1950s, and at that time – and also later – the main focus was to keep the animals free of disease and provide them with a nutritious feed so that they could survive and be efficient producers. It could be postulated that good animal welfare was regarded as being equal to healthiness, the provision of a nutritious feed, and production ability, and indeed progress was made in these areas. It cannot be questioned that good health, a nutritious feed and good management and stockmanship are important elements of animal welfare, but research has confirmed that there are other contributory factors if the welfare of farm animals is to be considered as good.

The first evidence of a reaction against intensive farming systems came in 1964 when Ruth Harrison's book *Animal Machines* was published. The book mainly focused on chickens kept for meat production (broilers), hens kept in battery cages, and calves kept for the production of white veal. It gives food for thought that a recent survey (European Commission, 2005), after measuring the perceptions of consumers regarding the welfare of certain species, concluded that the level of welfare of laying hens and broilers must to be improved as a priority.

The reaction to the book was sharp criticism concerning intensive farming systems and their effect on animals kept in them. This gave rise to a number of initiatives, for example, in the UK the Brambell Committee was established with the task of looking into intensive farming methods. The committee emphasised the importance of education of farmers, it stated that welfare is a wide term that covers both physical and mental well-being of the animal, and it suggested that farm animals should at least have freedom to stand up, lie down, turn around, groom, and stretch their legs. These recommendations were named the five freedoms, and could be regarded as a first attempt to define the elements which should be taken into account when determining (good) animal welfare. It gives food for thought that even though formulated in 1965 some of them have not yet been achieved, for example, hens in battery cages, sows in stalls, tethered cattle. They did, however, only focus on an animal's freedom to move and on the space given to the animals, and did not touch upon other important elements such as health (disease and injury), enrichment of the environment (the quality of the space given to an animal), nutrition, social contact, etc.

Over the years research aimed at different aspects of animal welfare expanded, and a range of methods for assessing animal welfare was developed, a summary of these is included, for example, in reports from the Scientific Committee on Animal Health and Animal Welfare. As knowledge grew it became evident that the original five freedoms needed revision. The Farm Animal Welfare Council in the UK took up this task, and has formulated the following five freedoms:

- Freedom from thirst, hunger and malnutrition – *by ready access to fresh water and a diet to maintain full health and vigour*
- Freedom from discomfort – *by providing an appropriate environment including shelter and a comfortable resting area*
- Freedom from pain, injury and disease – *by prevention or rapid diagnosis and treatment*
- Freedom to express normal behaviour – *by providing sufficient space, proper facilities and company of the animal's own kind*
- Freedom from fear and distress – *by ensuring conditions and treatment which avoid mental suffering.*

The five freedoms should be regarded as a set of guiding principles for all those engaged in one way or another in the welfare of farm animals, such as farmers, agricultural advisors, veterinarians, consumers, welfare organisations, politicians, legislators, etc.

When trying to judge a given husbandry system against the five freedoms it becomes evident that the different systems have their strengths and weaknesses. However, few if any of the existing intensive systems meet the comprehensiveness of the five freedoms, and the difficulty lies in taking proper account of the often conflicting interests: the need of the farmer to make a profit in a global market situation against the needs of the animals.

Farm animals are under the influence of a variety of factors, and whether their welfare can be judged as good or bad will depend on a complex range of components. Animals are affected by their whole environment, such as management and stockmanship, physical limits, enrichment factors, air quality, temperature, social interaction with other animals, and breeding programmes aimed at selection for production traits such as faster growth, higher production of milk, eggs, etc. This breeding strategy has been successful from a production point of view, but its negative effect is an increase in production-related diseases. These problems may become even more evident if animals are given a substance that would promote their production abilities. An example of this is the use of BST in dairy cattle. Its use was banned in the EU following recommendations from the Scientific Committee on Animal Health and Animal Welfare (1999).

The environment is appropriate if it allows the animal to satisfy its needs. A need can, according to Broom (2001), be defined as a requirement which is part of the basic biology of an animal to obtain a particular resource or respond to a particular environmental or bodily stimulus. Hence animals need to obtain specific resources, for example, water and feed but they also need to carry out certain actions, for example, pigs need to root and hens need to dust bathe. When the needs of an animal are not satisfied the welfare of that animal will be poorer than when its needs are satisfied. Malnutrition, injury and disease are obvious signs of poor welfare, and other indicators include abnormal behaviour such as stereotypies (for example, tongue rolling in calves and bar biting in sows), tail biting in pigs, feather pecking in hens, etc.

The two elements of intensive farming systems that have given rise to most criticism are probably reduced space and barren environments given to animals. Barren environments deprive animals from carrying out at least some of their natural behavioural patterns. Reduced space will limit the animal's possibility of movement and activity, and it may interfere with normal social interactions, including the possibility to withdraw from other animals. All animals including humans need the possibility to keep a minimum distance from others, when they so wish. This distance is known as individual or social room. If this minimum distance is overstepped the animal will try either to attack or escape. This distance may vary depending on whether the animals are of gregarious or solitary nature. The effect of reduced space and a barren environment may elicit abnormal behaviour, some of which may be detrimental to the animals and therefore unwanted. Examples of this are tail biting in pigs and feather pecking in hens, the solution is tail docking and beak trimming. In future solutions should be sought by which the environment and management fulfil the animals' needs rather than trying to "adapt" the animal to the environment by procedures such as mutilations.

Consumer awareness and attitudes

The intensification of farm animal production that started in the 1950s has resulted in relatively lower market prices on food, thus consumers in northern Europe today only spend about 10% of their income on food while in the 1950s, it was typical to spend between one quarter and one third (Sandøe et al., 2003). It is evident that to a great extent the animals have paid the price of this development. This has led animal welfare organisations to campaign against the conditions of animals in intensive farming systems, and consumer concern about animal welfare to increase in a number of countries during the last thirty years, but especially during the last ten years (Broom, 1999).

Consumer concern, campaigns from animal welfare organisations, and the attention given to animal welfare issues by the press, both in newspapers, on radio and television, have had an effect. Supermarket chains have imposed requirements concerning production systems on their suppliers, a number of labelling systems have emerged, farmers' organisations have introduced information campaigns to increase awareness amongst their members, national advisory committees on animal welfare and on ethics have been established, and legislation that sets standards, limits or even bans the most restrictive husbandry systems has been passed in a number of countries.

Consumers and their willingness to pay the cost or to influence the market mechanisms with their buying behaviour are an important basis for further improvements. A recent survey

(European Commission, 2005) carried out in the 25 EU member states on the attitude of consumers to the welfare of farmed animals may give an indication of future possibilities in this field. The survey indicated that visits to farms seem to increase awareness and concern for animal welfare, and that knowledge obtained through farm visits seems to affect purchasing behaviour, so that people who have visited a farm are most likely to think about animal welfare when buying animal products. However, the number of people who have visited a farm at least once varies considerably from country to country, from more than 90% in Scandinavian countries to only 29% in one southern EU member state. There is also a marked difference from country to country when people are asked if they are thinking of animal welfare when purchasing meat – in two-thirds of the countries the majority state that they never or only very rarely think of it. In spite of that almost three in four people in the survey think that they can influence the welfare of farmed animals by their purchasing behaviour, and more than half (57%) state that they are willing to pay more for eggs from animal-friendly systems.

Examples of concerns in relation to the keeping of different farm animal species

As mentioned, it is mainly the effect that intensive farming systems impose on animals that has given rise to concern. Some concern stems from impressions obtained from different media, which may not show the whole truth, and from the way humans themselves would perceive a given situation. However, it is important to note that concerns must be based on how the animal perceives its situation. Scientific knowledge concerning the welfare of the different farm animal species has increased over the last decades thus giving information on various problems related to the different farming systems, although it must be realised that there are still areas where further research is needed. Some species have been studied more intensively and for a longer period than others. For example, the focus on fish welfare is relatively new.

A few examples are given below. There are numerous other issues that could be given attention, such as the welfare of farmed fish, the impact of limited space on slaughter pigs, high mortality rates observed in certain categories, the production of foie gras in ducks and geese, whether or not mink should have access to swimming water, lameness in housed dairy cows, fattening rabbits in barren cage systems, light intensity and lighting regime especially for poultry, disease and injury that – generally speaking – may need more attention, such as foot rot in sheep and decubital ulcers in the shoulder region of sows.

Chickens kept for meat production (broilers)

The time required for a broiler to reach 1 500 g live weight has been reduced from 120 days in 1925 to 30 days in 2005 (Bessei, 2005). Many welfare concerns are linked to this fast growth, and the Scientific Committee on Animal Health and Animal Welfare (2000) concluded that the major welfare problems in broilers were those which could be regarded as side effects of the intense selection mainly for growth and feed conversion. The problems include leg disorders, ascites and sudden death syndrome, and the committee concluded that leg disorders were a major cause of poor welfare in broilers. This is supported by studies referred to by Bessei (2005) which showed that walking was significantly improved in lame birds after treatment with analgesic and anti-inflammatory drugs, and that lame birds selected more drugged feed than intact birds when given the choice. Hunger in breeding birds (parents of the broilers) is also a problem that needs to be addressed.

Laying hens

Laying hens are kept in either conventional cage systems, in furnished (also called enriched) cage systems or in alternative (non-cage) systems, such as aviaries, percheries, deep litter systems or free-range systems. These systems give the hens different possibilities to perform normal behaviour such as dust bathing, scratching, perching, and nesting. Concern over the welfare of laying hens has for many years been aimed at hens kept in conventional cage systems, and in 1996 the Scientific Veterinary Committee in its Report on the Welfare of Laying Hens concluded that conventional cage systems provided a barren environment for the birds and that the cage because of its small size and its barrenness had inherent severe disadvantages for the welfare of hens. The report acknowledged the benefits and deficiencies of the system. Deficiencies mentioned were that nesting behaviour, perching, scratching, dust bathing, and most movements were prevented or modified, that stereotyped behaviour occurred, that there was increased fear, and that the hens had weak bones caused by lack of movement. This was an important basis for the decision within the EU (Directive 1999/74/EC) to ban the conventional cage systems, the ban had effect on new establishments from 2003, and it will phase out existing systems by 2012. The EU directive also lays down provisions for alternative systems, and it introduced a new type of cage system, enriched cages, in which hens are offered a nest, a perch and an area with litter for foraging and dust bathing.

Enriched or furnished cage systems are fairly new, but undoubtedly scientific knowledge and established experience will lead to further improvements in design, and to better knowledge of the welfare aspects of this system. In its Opinion on Welfare Aspects of Various Systems of Keeping Laying Hens, the Scientific Panel on Animal Health and Welfare (2005) indicates that studies have shown that hens in furnished cage systems have significantly stronger bones compared with hens in conventional cage systems, and also that the increased space in furnished cage systems appears to be beneficial for welfare, allowing a wider behavioural repertoire with no adverse effects on feather pecking, cannibalism, or aggression, even though the behavioural repertoire is still restricted compared with birds in non-cage systems.

Consumer reaction to the furnished cage systems still remains to be seen. It is a question of whether consumers will acknowledge the possible improvements from an animal welfare point of view or whether they will judge any cage system for laying hens as unacceptable.

Slaughter pigs

Slaughter pigs are typically kept on partly or fully slatted floors at a rather high stocking density. Scientific studies summarised in the Report of the Scientific Veterinary Committee on the Welfare of Intensively Kept Pigs (1997) (the SVC report) have shown that exploratory behaviour, which includes rooting, smelling, chewing is important for the welfare of pigs. In the report it is recommended that materials for investigation and manipulation should be provided whenever possible for pigs. Deformable material, such as wood with bark on it or thick rope, is especially attractive to pigs. Straw would also be attractive to pigs, but they will lose interest in artificial objects, such as chains or footballs, when their novelty decreases, hence these objects should not be regarded as suitable objects for investigation and manipulation. As a consequence of the recommendation in the SVC report a provision to provide pigs with such material has been inserted in the Council of Europe recommendation concerning pigs as well as in EU legislation (Directive 91/630/EEC as amended).

Farrowing and lactating sows

Farrowing and lactating sows are typically kept in separate units either loose or in crates. By far the largest numbers of sows are kept in crates. Crates restrict the movements of the sows throughout the farrowing and lactation period, furthermore sows are strongly motivated to build a nest before giving birth. The SVC report summarises by saying that it is beyond doubt that there is an internally triggered need to perform nest building behaviour during the last 20 hours or so before farrowing, and that some of the nest building activities may be possible for the sow to carry out in a farrowing crate, in particular if she is offered straw, but a large part of the behavioural patterns are inhibited by the physical limitations of the crate. In practice the possibilities of giving straw to farrowing sows are very limited either because they are on a fully slatted floor or because straw will block the slurry system. The main advantage of the crates is that they reduce piglet mortality, which is an important welfare parameter. The effect of the crates from this aspect is mainly due to a reduction in the number of piglets that die due to crushing or overlying by the sow. It is necessary to weigh the poorer welfare of the sow in a crate against the better welfare of the piglets, and in the SVC report it is recommended that further development of farrowing systems in which the sow can be kept loose and carry out normal nest building, without compromising piglet survival, should be strongly encouraged.

Bibliography

Bessei, W., "Welfare of meat producing poultry – An overview", in *Animal Science Papers and Reports,* 23, Supplement 1, 2005, pp. 205-216.

Broom, D.M., "Welfare and how it is affected by regulation" in "Regulation of animal production in Europe", International Congress, Wiesbaden, KTBL Darmstadt, 1999, pp. 51-57.

Broom, D.M., "Assessing the welfare of hens and broilers", in *Proc. Aust. Poult. Sci. Sym.,* 13, 2001, pp. 61-70.

European Comission, Special Eurobarometer No. 229, *Attitudes of consumers towards the welfare of farmed animals,* European Commission, Brussels, February-March 2005.

Farm Animal Welfare Council: http://www.fawc.org.uk/free-doms.htm

Jensen, P., *The ethology of domestic animals – An introductory text: behaviour of pigs,* CAB International, Wallingford, UK, 2002.

Price, E.O., "Behavioural development in animals undergoing domestication" in *Applied Animal Behaviour Science* 65, 1999, pp. 245-271.

Sandøe, P., Christiansen, S.B. and Appleby, M.C., "Farm animal welfare: the interaction of ethical questions and animal welfare science" in *Animal Welfare,* 12, 2003, pp. 469-478.

Scientific Committee on Animal Health and Animal Welfare, *Report on animal welfare aspects of the use of bovine soma-totrophin,* European Commission, Brussels, 1999.

Scientific Committee on Animal Health and Animal Welfare, *The welfare of chickens kept for meat production (Broilers),* European Commission, Brussels, 2000.

Scientific Committee on Animal Health and Animal Welfare, *The welfare of animals kept for fur production,* European Commission, Brussels, 2001.

Scientific Panel on Animal Health and Welfare, "The welfare aspects of various systems of keeping laying hens" in *The EFSA Journal,* 197, 2005, pp. 1-23.

Scientific Veterinary Committee, *Report on the welfare of laying hens,* European Commission, Brussels, 1996.

Scientific Veterinary Committee, *The welfare of intensively kept pigs,* European Commission, Brussels, 1997.

Spruijt B.M., *The welfare situation of farmed mink as compared to other farmed animals and the question of domestication,* Animal Welfare Centre, Utrecht University, 1999.

International transport and animal slaughter

by Jacques Merminod

People have transported animals since time immemorial. Admittedly, cavemen followed and tracked animals, forcing them over cliffs or guiding them towards marshland in order to isolate them and kill them for their meat, their fur and their bones, with which they made tools, ornaments or musical instruments, and these animals were therefore not transported in the true sense of the word, but travelled "under their own steam". They were killed in a rather primitive fashion with clubs or wooden spears. They died terrified, exhausted and wounded, and nobody thought anything of it. Humans needed food and clothes to survive in a sometimes harsh environment and animals provided what they needed.

Over time, humankind has managed to domesticate some animal species, such as horses, sheets, goats and cattle. The relationship between people and animals may have become closer as the latter were domesticated but it did not always improve. People kept animals for their milk, meat or skins, among other things. Some species were used as draught animals, for riding, and for both civilian and military activities. The domestication of animals coincided with their use for breeding: animals were carefully selected with a view to improving not only production but also their physical performance and appearance. This relationship remained virtually unchanged for centuries.

Avoiding animal suffering

The first laws on animal protection appeared in the 19th century, first in England, then in Germany. Little by little, each European country enacted legislation of this kind, mainly for the purpose of protecting animals from human cruelty.

Like means of transport, slaughter methods have improved over the last few centuries, with particularly striking improvements in the 20th century. It is considered extremely important to stun animals to spare them pain by making them lose consciousness before they are slaughtered. In the past there were no technical means of rendering animals almost immediately unconscious prior to slaughter; the methods used mainly involved physical force and bordered on brutality. Nowadays, the most common methods of stunning, depending on the type of animal, are gunpowder, which activates a captive bolt, electricity and various types of gas. Each method has advantages and disadvantages and it is difficult to identify the "best" method for each animal species – even the experts often disagree. Nevertheless, it is not overstating the case to say that huge progress has been made in this respect. The problems encountered nowadays are quite different.

As a result of the industrialisation and specialisation of farming and the emergence of much more efficient and less expensive means of transport than in the past, there has been a massive expansion in animal breeding, transport and slaughter. Growing financial constraints have accentuated this trend. In the past animals were transported only within the local or regional area, or sometimes to another part of the country. Nevertheless, there are documents dating back to the Middle Ages which refer to thousands of cattle being driven to Germany for slaughter, mainly from Poland, Hungary or Russia. Other routes were used to take animals over the Alps into Italy. Nowadays, millions of animals, mainly pigs and cattle but also sheep and horses, are transported across and beyond Europe, usually from north to south or from east to west, to be fattened or slaughtered for meat production. In most countries the duration of animal transport has increased significantly owing to the fact that, for economic reasons, slaughterhouses are concentrated in certain parts of Europe. Ever-larger slaughterhouses are capable of dealing with ever-greater numbers of animals within ever-shorter times. Although stunning methods are usually technically reliable, short deadlines mean there are now greater risks that an animal may not be properly stunned and may suffer pain. Globalisation and the opening up of markets mean that these risks are, unfortunately, liable to persist and even worsen.

Attitudes to animal protection depend very much on not only the moral and ethical values of the different societies and cultures but also, let it not be forgotten, on how affluent they are. People whose main concern is to find the means to feed their families and ensure their survival do not have either the time or, in particular, the energy to think about animal protection and the relationship between people and animals. Even in a small continent like Europe, a specific situation may be perceived differently from one country to the next or from one region to the next. Nor do town-dwellers look at things in the same way as people living in rural areas. Generally speaking, however, European consumers have come to realise not only that animals – which are living beings just like themselves – must be protected against ill-treatment but also that it is necessary to provide proper care and living space and to ensure that they are transported and slaughtered under suitable conditions. The first demands for this type of protection were made in the late 20th century – at the instigation of, *inter alia,* animal protection organisations. National governments, the EU and the international community have now taken up the cause and begun to introduce regulations to protect animals during transport or slaughter.

For years now, national and international animal protection organisations have been protesting against the long distances over which animals are transported in Europe to be slaughtered far from where they were bred. They quite rightly point out that animals are not accustomed to being transported and that they may therefore suffer great stress. Admittedly, the longer the journey, the greater the risk of inflicting suffering on the animals concerned. The animals, which find themselves in unfamiliar surroundings and are not accustomed to standing up for so long, get tired of having to stand and struggling to keep their balance all the time in a means of transport that is constantly in motion. Depending on the weather, it can also be hot and humid inside or, on the contrary, very cold. In such situations, animals need extra energy to keep warm or to lower their body temperature when it is too high. Despite this, they are seldom, if ever, fed and watered during transit and consequently lack both energy and water. As a result, they cannot recover their strength and arrive at their destination exhausted.

Council of Europe activities

All of the aforementioned factors have influenced Council of Europe activities. In the early 1960s, the Consultative Assembly of the Council of Europe addressed the issue of the international transport of animals, adopting a recommendation on the subject on 22 September 1961, in which it called for a convention for the regulation of the international transit of animals. Two years later, the Committee of Ministers decided to set up a committee of experts to draft such a convention. The committee, made up mainly of the representatives of the various member states of the Council of Europe, was assisted by several non-governmental organisations concerned in one way or another by the issue. On 13 December 1968 the Committee of Ministers opened the European Convention for the Protection of Animals during International Transport for signature by Council of Europe member states.[1] Between 1969 and 2004, 24 Council of Europe member states ratified and signed this treaty, which came into force on 20 February 1971.

A few years later, in 1973, the Consultative Assembly of the Council of Europe adopted a recommendation on slaughter methods for meat animals. It proposed that the Committee of Ministers call on member states to conclude a European convention on the humanisation and harmonisation of slaughter methods. The Committee of Ministers assigned this work to a committee of experts, and several non-governmental organisations again took part. Finally, on 10 May 1979, the Committee of Ministers opened the European Convention for the Protection of Animals for Slaughter[2] for signature by member states of the Council of Europe. Between 1980 and 2004, 20 member states ratified the convention and four merely signed it. It came into force on 11 June 1982.

The two conventions lay down general conditions ensuring the welfare of animals during transport and slaughter respectively. One lays down rules governing the preparation of animals for loading, the loading itself, the design of the means of transport, the animals' fitness for transport, transport conditions, veterinary checks, the handling of animals, certificates and specific aspects of the various modes of transport (rail, road, water or

1.
European Convention for the Protection of Animals during International Transport (ETS No. 65).

2.
European Convention for the Protection of Animals for Slaughter (ETS No.102).

air). The other convention lays down rules concerning the unloading of animals, their lairaging in slaughterhouses, the way in which they should be treated, and stunning methods. Before the provisions of a convention become legally binding, the Parties must transpose them into their national legislation. They must then have the political resolve to ensure that the situation is monitored and consequently provide the bodies responsible for applying the rules with the human and financial resources required to carry out the necessary checks. Without strict monitoring, laws are often not properly applied. This was one of the conclusions reached in 1996 by the Parties to the 1968 Convention for the Protection of Animals during International Transport.

Indeed, most of the offences ascertained during the international transport of animals are breaches of existing national or international legislation. Initially, trains or boats were used for the large-scale international transport of animals. There were fixed routes and points where animals could be fed and watered, that is, railway stations and sea ports. The authorities in charge of applying animal protection rules and regulations therefore usually knew where the animals were and could, if necessary, inspect them. Nowadays, animals are usually transported by road because road transport is faster, more flexible and requires fewer staff than rail transport. Routes and places where the animals can rest and are fed and watered – assuming that they are – not only vary from one haulage company to the next, but also depend on traffic conditions, anticipated traffic jams, weather conditions, etc. To provide a better overview of international transport, the revised convention requires that an attendant be appointed for each consignment and that it be possible to obtain information concerning the transport from that person at any point during the journey. Moreover, as is the case in the European Union, it requires that a special document be drawn up for long journeys, namely, those lasting more than eight hours. This document sets out the arrangements made for the journey, in particular the point of departure and the places where the animals are to be transferred or unloaded so that they can rest. These requirements should help to improve the situation. Nevertheless, everything will depend on the authorities' willingness to meet these requirements and the resources available to them for monitoring the situation effectively.

In the late 1980s, the parties to the two conventions decided that there ought to be detailed provisions concerning the persons directly or indirectly responsible for the transport or slaughter of animals. They decided to draw up five recommendations concerning transport, in particular the transport of horses, pigs, cattle, sheep, goats and poultry, and one on animal slaughter. These recommendations not only contain the relevant binding provisions set out in the respective conventions but also a raft of rules to be followed to safeguard animal welfare. Some of the non-governmental organisations concerned helped to draft the recommendations.

In 1996, after extensive media campaigns drawing attention to serious irregularities in the transport of animals in Europe, the Council of Europe member states that had signed the European Convention for the Protection of Animals during International Transport met to take stock of the situation. They first took note of the recommendation of the Parliamentary Assembly of the Council of Europe, which the Committee of Ministers had forwarded to member states, and discussed it in depth. In this recommendation, the Assembly had said that it was:

> "particularly worried about many reports on the ill treatment of animals during international transport and on suffering caused to animals due to unnecessary waiting times at border crossings"

and suggested that the Committee of Ministers:

> "ask the parties to the European Convention for the Protection of Animals during International Transport [...] to improve as a matter of urgency the conditions for the international transport of livestock [and] to strengthen the control mechanisms for the implementation of legislation."

Secondly, the countries that had signed the European Convention for the Protection of Animals during International Transport decided to revise the old convention and amend it in the light of the lessons learnt from its implementation over a period of 30 years and the scientific results obtained during that time. The revised convention,[3] which includes the main principles set out in the original text, also contains provisions designed to remedy its shortcomings and facilitate the application of the principles of the convention. It was designed as a framework convention laying down essential principles applying to all vertebrate species. It stipulates that there should be technical protocols concerning minimum space allowances and the maximum duration of journeys, minimum intervals for watering and feeding the animals and minimum periods of rest. These protocols have still to be drawn up by the parties to the convention, as do the new recommendations concerning transport, which are no longer to be drafted according to species but according to the mode of transport (road, sea, air or rail). The new convention came into force on 14 March 2006 after four states had ratified it. At present six states are linked up by this convention.

At the end of the last century, the European Union drew up legislation on this subject at almost the same time as the Council of Europe, or shortly afterwards. It was therefore possible for the two organisations to co-ordinate their efforts and introduce very similar legal instruments. These had a greater impact because they did not concern only EU countries but the whole of Europe.

Some countries are dragging their heels

Council of Europe debates on the new convention have shown, however, that some European countries are reluctant, or even opposed, to introducing new regulations for the protection of animals during international transport. Although it was possible to read between the lines and surmise that the reasons for this reluctance or refusal were economic ones, these reasons have never been explicitly stated. Those opposed to introducing new regulations claimed either that there were not enough scientific data to draw up rules on a specific aspect (for example, stocking density in the various means of transport), or that there were not enough international rules covering the world as a whole. But is it really necessary to have scientific data to decide at what intervals an animal should be fed and

3.
European Convention for the Protection of Animals during International Transport (Revised) (ETS No. 193).

watered? Why do animals have almost permanent access to food and water while they are on the farm but have to wait hours to be fed and watered when they are being transported? Transport conditions vary from one case to the next and it will never be possible to have scientific data that applies to every case. That is no reason, however, for refusing to draw up regulations which ensure that animals are properly treated during transport or slaughter.

The initial enthusiasm has therefore given way to a certain apathy. Even when the European Community had only 15 member countries, they dominated Council of Europe debates. Now that there are 25 member countries, no decisions can be taken without the agreement of all 25. Given the diverging interests of animal-producing countries, countries of transit and countries specialising in animal slaughter, and given the economic constraints to which farming is subject, it is increasingly difficult for them to reach an agreement. Nowadays, these interests differ so much that it is virtually impossible to draw up common rules for the transport of animals which go further than those already agreed on, despite all the efforts made by the various committees at several levels in the different institutions. Economic interests, backed up by neo-liberal policies advocating globalisation, unfortunately take precedence over any form of animal protection worthy of the name. Very few legislative improvements have been made and they are, as a rule, only "cosmetic". This is not to criticise the revised European Convention for the Protection of Animals during International Transport, which the Committee of Ministers finally opened for ratification in November 2003 and which came into force in March 2006. It is undoubtedly an improvement on the original 1968 convention and should help to better the lot of animals being transported across Europe, provided that the different countries demonstrate their goodwill and make the necessary resources available for the application of the rules set out in the convention.

Animals whose backs are injured because the ceilings of the wagons in which they were transported were too low, animals which have died in transit because they have been neither fed nor watered and animals sticking their heads out of vehicles because they cannot get enough air inside: these shocking scenes are fortunately an exception in international animal transport. And it would be unfair to those who are aware of their responsibilities towards animals in transit to claim that all animal transport is cruel. Admittedly, animals always suffer a certain amount of stress when they are transported. But they do not always lead a stress-free life in a field, stable, byre or pigsty either. Nevertheless, these images clearly show that it is too early to rest on our laurels. By improving general transport conditions, it should be possible to provide a suitable environment, better adapted to the needs of the animals concerned. If this is to be achieved, the staff responsible for their transport or slaughter should be properly trained. They should know about the behaviour and needs of the species concerned and have experience in dealing with them. This requirement is one of the improvements in the revised Convention for the Protection of Animals during International Transport.

What is lacking at European level is the political resolve to do something about animal welfare, be it with regard to lairaging, transport or slaughter. Instead of agreeing that something must be done to protect animals and take account of their needs, on moral grounds, the different countries look only to their national interests, which are usually economic. There is therefore little, if any, chance of finding a joint solution which will definitely improve animals' lot, be it within the Council of Europe or the European Union. Given that animal transport and slaughter are often closely linked to farming, the latter's public image has been tarnished and consumers no longer fully accept that it should be subsidised. Unfortunately, most consumers do not realise that they have a major responsibility in this respect. By demanding ever-cheaper produce (in particular milk, meat and eggs), consumers contribute to the industrialisation of agriculture, and farmers can no longer take account of animals' needs as a result of economic constraints and the fact that animals are transported across Europe to slaughterhouses in countries where labour is cheaper. We must wake up at last to the fact that it costs money to protect animals and that, if we do not want to feel guilty about the way animals are treated, we must be prepared to pay the price. A commitment to animal welfare does not mean wholesale opposition to animal transport and slaughter, or to the industry or the prosperity resulting from these activities, but an attempt to pave the way for a more humane attitude to animals.

As in the past, however, as long as consumers do not put pressure on politicians, producers, hauliers and slaughterhouses to improve animal protection in their respective spheres, it will take years to ensure proper conditions for the transport and slaughter of animals. Meanwhile, alas, there will be no significant change in the plight of animals in Europe.

Animal experimentation

by Roman Kolar

Animal experimentation is a unique issue when looking at the relationship between humans and animals. In animal experiments pain, suffering and distress are deliberately inflicted on animals, whereas in other fields this would be regarded an illegal mistreatment. It is also for this that the animal welfare community can accept only one final goal in connection with animal research: its total abolition. In addition to ethical considerations, scientific arguments are put forward. Scientific shortcomings of animal experiments have been demonstrated on various occasions. It is particularly the questionable relevance of findings in animals for the situation in humans that is a matter of concern in this context. But even when acknowledging that animal experiments may provide results that could provide valuable gain of knowledge and contribute to biomedical research or toxicological classifications, from an ethical perspective it seems unacceptable that we, as humans, put sentient beings into states of suffering that we would never accept for ourselves.

Despite all of this, animal experimentation has become a cruel reality in the world of today. In the 15 "old" EU member states alone, during the year 2003 about 10 million vertebrate animals were used for scientific and other experimental purposes according to the latest official statistics. It must be assumed that the real number is considerably higher, as serious shortcomings have been reported regarding these statistics. As the animal experiment has only become of major importance as a scientific method in the last century, nearly any effort to reduce animal suffering in biomedical research has been counteracted by new applications and new technologies for animal use in science. The most recent dramatic example can be found in the area of genetic engineering. The increasing use of and demand for transgenic animals that began in the 1990s was responsible for a rise in the numbers of animals used for scientific purposes (Fig. 1) – a number that had been declining in many countries since the 1980s because of stronger legislation and increasing awareness about the need to reduce animal experiments within the research community.

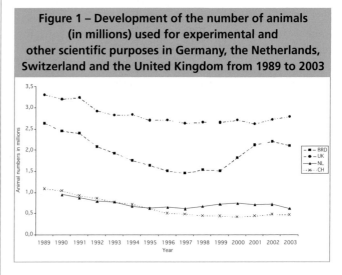

Figure 1 – Development of the number of animals (in millions) used for experimental and other scientific purposes in Germany, the Netherlands, Switzerland and the United Kingdom from 1989 to 2003

In the light of this reality many animal welfare organisations have decided to participate in any effort that could contribute to diminishing the suffering of animals in the laboratories. This should not be misunderstood as giving up the vision of abolishing all animal experiments but rather taken as a first aid measure.

What is an animal experiment?

Definitions

The term *animal experiment* is used beyond biological and semantic specificity. Without a given frame an animal experiment would be understood as any experimental procedure carried out on an organism from the zoological (taxonomic) category *Animalia*. However, in existing legislation mostly reference is made to *vertebrate* animals, thus actually excluding the majority of animal species. The restriction of legislation to vertebrate animals has historical reasons, based on the assumption that only vertebrates would have the capacity to feel pain and to suffer. Whereas there is no scientifically accepted rationale for that assumption, in the last decades overwhelming scientific evidence has been collected to demonstrate that a number of non-vertebrate species possess a well developed nervous system that makes them capable of suffering in a way that we would assume for most vertebrates. This evidence has resulted in increased attention to certain species, as can be demonstrated by the fact that octopus had been included in UK legislation on protection of laboratory animals. More recently, evidence has also been collected for demonstrating the suffering capacity of "lower" species such as snails.

Another restriction to the potentially wider interpretation of the term animal experiment is to be seen in the fact that, particularly in legislation (see below), it is normally only used in connection with experiments on *live* animals. This means that if animals are killed, and experiments are carried out after their death, these are not regarded as animal experiments in the legal sense. It is for this reason that the majority of animal use for educational purposes is not in the scope of legislation or statistical record. Also, the use of animal organs and tissues for scientific purposes is not regulated by legislation. However, only recently in some countries requirements have been changed so that such use at least has to be reported and is taken into account in the statistics.

Areas of animal experimentation

The reality in laboratories in the 21st century reveals a variety of purposes and applications of animal research. The following major fields of use can be distinguished:

- Basic (biomedical) research
- Applied (biomedical) research
- Regulatory testing of drugs, compounds and products
- Regulatory (routine) testing of biological substances and products
- Educational purposes.

These categories can be further sub-divided as is done in the official statistics. Here, the above categories are used to exemplify the procedures the animals have to undergo:

In *basic research* almost anything that can be done to animals is done to investigate biological phenomena and/or their medical or veterinary implications. In many areas, such as physiology, animals are examined rather as "machines" and individual functions of their body are investigated in more or less painful procedures. Often single "parameters" (that is, body functions) are artificially altered (for example, mechanically, biochemically, or by genetic engineering) to observe effects.

In *applied biomedical* research and testing, either healthy animals, or animals that are called "disease models", and in which specific pathological symptoms have been created artificially, are used. Disease models are created mostly either by deliberate feeding of toxic substances or genetical engineering. In surgical research (but not only there), physical injuries are also inflicted on animals, such as breaking their bones, burning their skin, etc.

Before the putting on the market of drugs, compounds and products, according to existing *testing* regulations, animals are (force-)fed or injected with the substances in question, in other cases these are applied to the skin, eye or other organs, or the animals are forced to inhale them. Then the animals, or their offspring, are observed for adverse effects. These effects range from none to the sometimes extremely painful death of an animal.

Biologicals, such as vaccines, have to be tested more than once before they are placed on the market, as is the case for chemicals or drug compounds. As the *safety* and *efficacy of biologicals* has to be demonstrated for each production unit (batch) for regulatory purposes, these tests are carried out routinely, thus resulting in huge numbers of animals used. Moreover, these are extremely severe procedures, in which there are always control groups that, for example, are not given the vaccine in question and have to develop the symptoms of the disease that the vaccine is to prevent.

In *education* animals are mostly killed before they are used, for example, in dissection classes, at least at the undergraduate level. In graduate education, also experiments on live animals are common, for example, in physiology. Such experiments are not only problematic from an animal welfare point of view. Often students have no chance to escape such experiments if they wish to obtain a specific degree, independent of their personal attitude.[1]

Animal species

The animal species used in experiments range from non-sentient protozoa to great apes. The most common laboratory animal species are rats and mice. The number of fish used in experiments is constantly rising as these animals are increasingly used in environmental investigations. Almost all animal species that are kept as pets are also used in research and testing, like hamsters, guinea pigs, cats and dogs. Primates are also used widely in many areas, and are being imported from breeding colonies in third countries where they are often bred under questionable conditions. Also, a lot of research is carried out on so-called farm animals (pigs, cows, horses, poultry).

Some historical remarks

Resistance to animal experimentation probably dates back exactly to the moment in history when man first used animals to experiment upon them. From that moment the various attitudes towards animal research ranged from total acceptance to total rejection. Whereas the fundamental ethical standpoint of abolitionists was (and is) that man has the responsibility not to inflict pain and suffering on his fellow-beings for his own benefit, more than 200 years ago there were already attempts to distinguish between "ethical" and "unethical" animal experiments by defining conditions under which animal experiments would seem legitimate. For example, in 1797 the German philosopher Immanuel Kant stated in his *Metaphysics of Morals* that "painful, physical experiments for the pure purpose of speculation, if the aim can be reached without them, are to be abhorred". One year later, Thomas Young, Fellow of Trinity

1.
Numerous studies have proven that from a pedagogic point of view the motivation and learning effect is equal or even better in courses where the countless available alternative methods are used.

College, Cambridge demanded that animal experiments would have to provide "good and useful knowledge" and should aim at "a great and public benefit". Franz Volkmar Reinhard, a High Court priest in Saxony, only accepted animal experiments for the benefit of mankind (1816).

The idea of discriminating between "ethical" and "unethical" animal experiments is reflected by efforts both in research and in legislation to set parameters to provide for an authorised, that is, "ethically acceptable" use of animals in science. The principles to be applied for such use can best be demonstrated by having a closer look at what are nowadays globally recognised as the "three Rs in animal research".

The three Rs concept

In addition to the guiding principle that animal experiments would presuppose utmost relevance for mankind, early in history the requirement that animal experiments must be replaced by alternative methods was formulated. For instance, the German priest Adam Dann demanded in 1822 that animal experiments should be replaced by examinations of human bodies.

Nowadays *replacement* is known as one of the Rs within the so-called three Rs principle that is particularly referred to when the ethics of animal experimentation is addressed. This principle was "invented" by the English zoologist William M.S. Russell and his fellow countryman, Rex L. Burch, a microbiologist, and published in 1959 in their book *The principles of humane experimental technique*. Russell and Burch defined:

- *refinement* as "decrease in the incidence of severity of inhumane procedures applied to those animals, which have to be used",

- *reduction* as "lowering the number of animals used to obtain information of a given amount and precision", and

- *replacement* as "employing non-sentient material which may replace methods which use conscious living vertebrates".

The term *alternative*, that was originally branded exclusively for replacement methods, is nowadays being increasingly used to describe any of the three Rs. Historically, animal protection-ists used (and often still use) it to indicate the need to abolish animal experiments and find new ways to gain scientific knowledge.

Ethical and welfare principles in legislation on animal research

Legislation to regulate the use of animals for scientific pur-poses ranges back to the Cruelty to Animals Act that was established in the United Kingdom as early as in 1876. In many countries animal welfare legislation was enacted in the 19th or 20th centuries, and sometimes it also covered animal experi-mentation. From early on there was strong resistance against specific legislation on animal experimentation within the scientific community. For instance, the American Association for the Advancement of Science (AAAS), in its resolution on animal experimentation of 1937, denounced initiatives to enact specific legislation on animal experiments as "attempts fostered largely by erroneous statements and accusations and false sen-timent and prejudice".

At the level of the Council of Europe and of the European Union, regulations on animal experimentation were set up only in the 1980s: Directive 86/609/EEC and the Convention for the Protection of Vertebrate Animals used for Experimental and other Scientific Purposes (Council of Europe, ETS No. 123). At that time the public debate on animal experiments had reached a climax, and opposition to animal research received media attention to a yet unknown extent.

From an animal welfare point of view the above mentioned regulations have proved to be of limited efficiency as is demonstrated by the reality of animal experimentation today, which still allows for performing animal experiments for even the most absurd purposes, and for grievances in laboratories and housing facilities that are beyond imagination. On the other hand, at least in theory, these regulations incorporated the most common principles for the protection of laboratory animals:

• experiments must be indispensable for specified purposes

- pain, suffering or distress must be ethically justifiable
- the three Rs must be applied wherever possible
- animal experiments, as well as the breeding and housing of laboratory animals, have to be practically regulated by controlling and authorising systems.

Ethical decisions with regard to animal experiments

Legislation on animal experimentation mostly stipulates that an ethical decision is made on whether an animal experiment is to be authorised, and lays down the basic parameters for that decision. Regulations also include an assignment of this responsibility to authorities and other bodies, particularly so-called ethics committees.

There are various levels at which in fact ethical decisions concerning animal experiments are made. First of all there are the scientists and technicians who are directly involved in the experiment. Mostly they must prove that they have undergone a more or less relevant type of education before they are permitted to perform the experiment. Some institutions also employ an animal welfare officer who is specifically assigned to support in providing this care and treatment. This person may also have a controlling and/or licensing function.

Ethics committees for animal experimentation normally have an advisory function. They consist of individuals who either provide some expertise relevant to the science that an experiment is based on, or knowledge on ethical and/or specific animal protection issues, and sometimes include persons that are to represent (part of the) society such as lay members with various backgrounds.

There are different levels at which ethics committees function. In some countries, like the United States, the committees are directly connected to the institution at which the animal experiments are undertaken (so called IACUCS, Institutional Animal Care and Use Committees), in other places they work at local, regional and/or national level. There are also ethics committees employed by funding bodies, for example, the European Commission has installed ethics panels to decide on the ethical acceptability of research proposals submitted for funding, and these panels, *inter alia,* also look at specific animal experimentation issues.

The final decision to authorise, and therefore officially legitimate on ethical grounds, an animal experiment is mostly taken by a licensing authority which often bases this decision on the advice of an ethics committee.

Ethical evaluation of animal experiments: theory and practice

There is a vast amount of literature on the functioning, and deficits, of ethics committees in the field of animal experimentation. It is evident that the ethical evaluation process cannot protect from unethical use of animals. The reasons for this grievance include, but are not limited to, the following:

- not all animal experiments undergo an ethical evaluation process. For example, regulatory demanded tests, that make up about 30% of all animal experiments, in many places (for example, in Germany) do not have to be justified or evaluated by an ethics committee (see below).

- in ethics committees ethicists or animal welfare representatives are usually in the minority whereas users of animals are in the majority.

- ethics committees' members may lack the expert knowledge on ethics, the three Rs or the scientific problem that is being discussed.

- the evaluation process requires a "weighing" of the "cost" for the animals, that is, their suffering, against the supposed "benefit", namely, the purpose of the experiment. This, however, is an extremely difficult task, and there is a lack of knowledge, common understanding, and advice on how to perform it.

- neither a limit for the cost nor a minimum standard for the benefit exists (see below).

- thus, typically, the issues discussed in ethics committees are often restricted to the three Rs, in particular reduction and refinement. The question whether an experiment is at all ethically justified is mostly neglected.

Case studies: Defining minimum standards for the benefit and a limit for the cost

Defining minimum standards for the benefit

One of the problems when trying to assess whether an animal experiment is justifiable on ethical grounds is that there is not a defined minimum standard for purposes that would be regarded acceptable in this context. In other words, no regulation exists to define that for specific ("unimportant") purposes it would be unethical to let animals suffer or die.

The cosmetics case

However, in one specific case there has been a societal controversy over this issue with concrete consequences on legislation. After year-long campaigning and lobbying of animal welfare organisations, and following debates in the public and in parliaments (particularly the European Parliament), the EU has issued an animal testing ban in the field of cosmetics, and also a marketing ban for cosmetics tested on animals.

Despite the many exemptions and loopholes the new EU regulations on cosmetics still entail, and despite year-long delays until now and in the future, they must be regarded as a milestone. A broad societal consensus has been reached with regard to the research on and production of cosmetics, a field where animal experiments are not justified from an ethical point of view. Despite the fact that decades ago it had to be clear to anyone showing an interest in this issue that the public regarded animal experiments for cosmetics to be unacceptable, this attitude had no consequences at all on their legitimacy, and on the ethical evaluation of such experiments by the authorities in Europe, except those few countries where similar national bans were already in place.

It is somehow understandable that large parts of the European cosmetics industry are opposed to the new EU regulations as they interfere with their present strategy for innovation and strive for economic success. But it is at the same time regrettable that the potential to produce products in a way that is in line with the ethical principles of the societies whose citizens are expected to buy these products is not seen as a chance. This chance consists of getting an economic advantage over companies that produce in an unethical way on a global scale. Many European companies have already gained a lead over others in terms of know-how in alternatives to animal experiments.

At present the EU plans to assign large budgets for the development and validation of alternative methods. The EU cosmetics industry has therefore the chance to export a success story to the rest of the world. And the experience of animal welfare organisations is that even in countries that do not have a history of good animal welfare regulations and conditions, there is resistance to the acceptance of animal testing for cosmetics purposes. Last but not least there is scientific proof of the fact that animal testing for safety purposes is highly problematic because the results are of questionable quality and relevance for humans. Thus, assessing the safety of their products by modern non-animal testing methods, whose reliability and relevance has been proved in challenging validation and acceptance schemes, is beneficial also in terms of consumer protection.

Other areas of concern

From the animal welfare point of view a minimum standard for the justification of animal experiments as has been negotiated in a democratic way for cosmetics, has to be applied in other fields, too. What is the justification for animal testing to put a new paint for cars on the market? Why should household products be treated differently from cosmetics? In many countries, when animal tests for licensing a substance or product are required by the (national) law, no ethical evaluation of these experiments is undertaken. The license for such experiments will be granted automatically by the authorities. However, even if one regards animal tests as necessary for the safety testing of cosmetics products or ingredients – a view that is not shared by the author of this article – when the marketing of these substances requires the suffering of thousands of laboratory animals, it would be indispensable to assess the justification for this suffering.

There is no golden rule yet on how to ethically address this issue in practice, but it seems clear that whenever animal testing is involved, the assessment of its justifiability would require addressing society's need for the substance or product in question, as long as the law requires animal tests for the marketing of that substance or product.

Defining a limit for the cost

Until now, there has been a lack of limiting the "cost" of an animal experiment; according to the existing legislation even the most extreme suffering is still acceptable.

Two examples for setting a predefined limit to the "cost" in animal experiments are to be mentioned here. The one focuses on the sensitivity of certain categories or species of animals that provides for assigning them protection from being used in any scientific procedures, independent of the supposed "benefit" this would generate. The other example entails a limit for pain and suffering independently of the species to be used by foregoing the experiment if it may result in a certain degree of pain and suffering.

The case of great apes

The need to grant great apes specific protection has been acknowledged increasingly in the last decade. The more we learn about our closest relatives in the animal kingdom the more it becomes clear that there are no scientific grounds on which to base the assumption that they would experience the world differently from human children up to a certain age. In many countries experiments on great apes have not been performed for years as if there was a silent agreement on this, but New Zealand was the first country in the world to specifically enact a law that prohibits using great apes in experiments in 1999.

Whereas there is agreement within the animal welfare community that great apes possess a capacity to suffer that forbids using them in scientific procedures, there is also agreement that – even if possibly to a slightly lower degree – other animals possess a similar capacity, for instance the entire category of non-human primates.

The case of the Swiss Academy of Sciences

The Swiss Academy of Sciences provides for the second example of efforts to define a limit for the cost when animal experiments are performed. In its Ethical Principles and Guidelines for Scientific Experiments on animals, the revised version of which was approved in 1995, Paragraph 4.6. states that "Experiments apt to cause the animal severe suffering must be avoided by modifying the hypothesis to be tested in such a way as to allow the choice of alternative experimental procedures, or by forgoing the anticipated gain of knowledge."

Unfortunately, this type of self-restriction within the scientific community, well known from a variety of issues in human ethics, is not common in the field of animal experimentation. For this and other reasons it must be regarded as necessary to have such a type of restriction laid down in legislation.

The way forward

Regarding human ethics there is broad consensus about the fact that certain things may not be done to human patients independently of how mankind could profit from the results. It is time to include animals in our considerations concerning these matters. Modern societies are by no means at the end of the process of giving animals the status and the protection that they would deserve on both ethical and scientific grounds. This also concerns the field of animal experimentation. There are two approaches as to how to achieve progress in this respect. The one is to exclude by law the use of animals in painful procedures, and, if at all, only to allow this for specific exemptions, instead of generally sanctioning animal experiments and only defining a regulatory framework around them as is done nowadays. Where this cannot be achieved by democratic means in the short term, legislation must be improved towards more strict and better defined regulations, and the implementation and enforcement of these regulations has to be significantly improved.

The second approach is a scientific one, and it aims at replacing all animal use in science and research by alternative methods. Where this cannot be achieved by democratic means in the short term, all efforts have to be undertaken to reduce and refine that use to the utmost extent. It is important in this respect that the aim should not be to replace existing animal tests one-by-one. Instead, the design of scientific studies that currently rely on the use of animals, and the questions they are based on, have to be modified so that they can be answered by employing non-animal methods.

From a scientific point of view, in fact, the most humane science has always proved to be the best science, as Russell and Burch phrased it. From the point of view of consumer and environmental protection there is hope for better methods than outdated animal experiments to understand the risks to humans and the environment of new substances or products. And from the point of view of animal welfare it is time to end the unimaginable suffering of millions of animals that are susceptible to pain and suffering, and capable of expressing fear and distress. A society without animal experiments must not be one with hampered scientific progress, but it would be one that had made a major step forward towards a more responsible role of mankind on planet earth.

Product safety-related aspects of animal testing

by Charles Laroche

For decades, animal testing was the most obvious and most effective way of testing the safety of products before they were put on the market. Animal testing and product safety are therefore closely linked together in industrial history. Industry as a whole, but above all the pharmaceutical, chemical, cosmetics, agro-chemical and agri-food industries, used animal testing to ensure that the use of their products presented no danger to the health of future consumers.

There has been much criticism made to the industry for failing to take due account of animal welfare and rights. To put an end to this "excessive" use of animal testing, the European Union and its member states adopted a protocol on the protection and welfare of animals, appended to the EU Treaty, which aims at recognising animals as sentient beings. During the drafting and adoption of this protocol, the different parties undertook to look after the welfare of animals used for tests. As a result, industry as a whole must now apply the available methods in order to "Refine, Reduce and Replace" animal testing, generally known as the three Rs, in accordance with the animal welfare directive.[1]

The 7th amendment to the cosmetics directive[2] lays down specific requirements for the cosmetics industry regarding the use of alternative methods based on animal safety studies. It also introduces a ban on animal testing for cosmetics and on sales of products tested on animals. The deadlines set in this amendment are 2009 and 2013 (total ban), even when no alternative methods have been developed.

According to the 4th report on the statistics on the number of animals used for experimental and other scientific purposes in the European Union member states, the total number of animals used in 2002 was 10.7 million. The recent REACH proposal (registration, evaluation and authorisation of chemicals) drew the attention of decision makers and the public at large

1.
Directive
86/609/EEC.

2.
Directive
76/768/EEC.

79

to the continuing need for animal testing as a means of protecting both human and animal health and the environment. There is, however, considerable pressure from civil society and policy makers to improve the understanding of risks facing human beings and the environment in general and to ensure product safety. In the absence of validated alternative methods, animal testing remains the only effective means of ensuring product safety.

Therefore it appears essential, to study the workability of substitution methods replacing animal testing while guaranteeing product safety for consumers. Major companies are heavily involved in the application of the three Rs and are increasingly investing in research on alternatives to animal testing. However, this must not lead to a decrease in product safety. ECVAM (European Centre for the Validation of Alternative Methods) therefore has a vital role to play in ensuring real continuity in product safety for European consumers, but also in the field of innovation, despite the gradual phasing out of animal testing.

The role of animal testing in product safety

It is essential to ensure that the use of the products placed onto the market is safe for consumers. Most countries have laws upholding this principle and making manufacturers and retailers responsible for consumer safety, which seems legitimate. Innovation in the area of consumer products often involves introducing new formulations, new molecules or new packaging systems. Testing is necessary to determine the safety of using these new materials or these new product formats. In most cases, because alternative methods have not yet been discovered, animal testing is still part of the safety evaluation process.

The safety of a product is determined on the basis of an evaluation of the risks, in the course of which hasards are identified and risks clearly defined. This leads to a decision by the risk management department. This evaluation usually involves a decision as to how the risk can/must be addressed (for example, by means of specific on-pack labelling). When the use of an ingredient is proposed in the manufacture of a product, it is always on the basis of a particular function. This functionality is the starting point for the identification of any adverse effects on consumers. The structure of the molecule is studied and compared with that of other molecules whose safety or lack of safety is already known. However, if the possible effects are unclear, the necessary information is sought through test methods which, in most cases, do not call on animal testing.

Animal testing procedures are usually fairly simple. Several groups of animals, usually consisting of the same number of individuals, are exposed to the product for a given period of time. Each group receives a different dose of the substance being tested, except for a control group which is kept under the same conditions as the exposed groups. The doses to which the animals are exposed usually differ exponentially from one group to another. The behaviour of the animals is then observed, samples may be taken, and functional tests are sometimes carried out. An autopsy is carried out on any animals which die during the test and a range of blood and urine analyses are performed. The next stage is to compare the groups exposed to the substance with the control group. The differences are studied and interpreted. Among the exposed animals, the level up to which no adverse effects are observed is known as NOAEL (No Observed Adverse Effect Level). Establishing this level is usually the first step in the traditional risk evaluation process. The consumer's exposure is accordingly evaluated on the basis of the amount of a given ingredient contained in the product, how it is used and how he or she will be exposed to it (ingestion, skin contact, inhalation).

These techniques permit a fairly accurate assessment of the impact the tested products will have on consumer health and safety. At present, however, risk evaluation based on animal testing remains the most reliable means of ensuring the fullest possible consumer safety when using a product. Nevertheless, since the 1960s, there has been a growing interest in finding alternatives to animal testing as it is still practised throughout the industry.

It should, however, be pointed out that although animal testing is sometimes the only means of making sure that a product is safe, non-animal testing is still generally the rule, and animal testing the exception. Companies are increasingly receptive to issues related to health, safety and the environment. Accordingly, it seems essential to point out that most of the industry sectors only use animal testing if all of the following criteria are met:

- no **alternative method is available** and there is a potential threat to human health;

- there is a **scientific justification** for the test proving that the results generated by it are intended to provide scientific data needed for risk evaluation or to determine the product's effectiveness;

- the test protocol is **approved from an ethical standard** in keeping with society's standards;

- the test clearly **benefits the consumer** and justifies new product development.

Compliance with the three Rs (Refinement, Reduction and Replacement) with regard to animal testing has become a key issue throughout industry. As has already been emphasised, most consumer products now come onto the market without any of their constituent elements having been tested on animals.

The cosmetics directive and its 7th amendment

Animal testing is a subject which frequently gives rise to emotional debates since opinions often differ on its moral justification. Governments, institutions, non-governmental organisations (NGOs), professional associations and businesses take different positions and regulating measures justifying their viewpoints and practices regarding the use of animal testing .

The cosmetics industry is part of a sector which has been heavily criticised in the context of animal testing. For many years, animal welfare organisations were violently critical of the fact that innovation in the cosmetics sector entailed tests on animals, although the proportion of tests carried out for the purposes of this branch of industry was tiny compared to the massive testing carried out by all other industry sectors.

Although a ban on animal testing has been called for and planned for many years, the cosmetics industry has not yet managed, at the edge of the 21st century, to convince all stakeholders involved of its commitment to developing alternative approaches or of the scientific reality of the issue. In this context, under pressure from civil society expressed via animal welfare organisations, the Council and the European Parliament found themselves in a political deadlock when the 7th proposed amendment to the cosmetics directive was submitted to them by the European Commission in 2000. The only policy choice open to them was to adopt this 7th amendment to the cosmetics directive (76/768/EEC) which provides for a ban on sales within the European Union of cosmetics containing ingredients tested on animals from anywhere in the world, starting from 2009 (for most tests) and 2013 (for all tests). In this legislative context, the term "cosmetics" includes products such as soap, shampoo, deodorants, anti-perspirants and toothpaste, which play an important part in daily personal hygiene. One of the consequences of the 7th amendment might be that consumers in the European Union will no longer have access to new cosmetic products, for which innovation involves the use of new ingredients. Animal testing is indeed very often part of the validation process for ensuring safety of new products. The challenge put forward by the Cosmetics Directive is to continue innovating in this category of products while maintaining the same level of consumer safety without using animal testing processes.

The debate surrounding the adoption of this new legislation has made it possible to identify the main issues, namely that, in the context of human safety, a ban on animal testing is only possible to the extent that significant advances are made in the development of alternative approaches. These debates constitute strong founding principles for consensus on an action plan to facilitate the development of alternatives.

European Partnership for Alternative Approaches to Animal Testing (EPAA): the way ahead

After four years of work on the project, on 7 November 2005, the "European Partnership for Alternative Approaches to

Animal Testing" (EPAA) was launched. The idea was put forward for the first time in 2001, during the discussions on the 7th amendment to the cosmetics directive and its ban on animal testing – an approach which did not offer any real solutions in terms of progress on alternatives. The need to form this partnership became clear with the upcoming implementation of the REACH regulation on chemicals, whose requirements in terms of consumer safety would result in an unacceptable amount of tests on animals. This legislative activity, combined with a genuine desire of all decision makers to speed up the process for eliminating animal testing, has paved the way for the setting up of a validated programme for replacing this type of test without endangering the health and safety of consumers or company employees.

In such a context, this project found a natural ally in Dagmar Roth-Behrendt, at the time a Member of the European Parliament and Rapporteur for the 6th and 7th amendments to the cosmetics directive, and currently Vice-President of the European Parliament. Without her unfailing support, this project would not have become what it is now.

Unilever, which had long since become involved in the development of alternative approaches, led the discussions with other companies on the possibility of forming a network to fund and promote research in this area. The underlying idea of this partnership, originally named "foundation", is to enhance the considerable progress already made in this field while capitalising on the opportunities offered by the new legislation. The aim of this partnership between animal protection organisations, the European institutions, regulatory authorities, universities and businesses is to act as an umbrella organisation, facilitating, leading and ensuring the promotion of research into alternative approaches. In short, the aim is to link up existing initiatives such as ECVAM,[3] DG Research, Colipa,[4] the member states, Frame[5] and Ecopa[6] with new research initiatives such as the 6th Framework Programme, the Innovative Medicines Platform, the LRI[7] developed by Cefic,[8] or the Sustainable Chemistry Platform.

Following a meeting with Philippe Busquin, European Commissioner for Research, Thomas Hartung (ECVAM) and Julia

3.
European Centre for the Validation of Alternative Methods.

4.
European Cosmetic Toiletry and Perfumery Association.

5.
Fund for the Replacement of Animals in Medical Experiments.

6.
European Consensus Platform for Alternatives.

7.
Long-range Research Initiative.

8.
European Chemical Industry Council.

Fentem (Unilever), a paper to identify and define the basis and needs of such an organisation was jointly produced. After a series of meetings involving over 20 companies from the pharmaceutical, chemical, agri-food, cosmetics, detergents and other sectors, and following a series of events, some of which were held at the European Parliament, the partnership began to take shape, while some conflicts of interest were emerging. These various factors jeopardised the development and actual setting up of the project. However, with growing pressure from public opinion and the imminent implementation of REACH, urgent action was needed. Günther Verheugen, European Commissioner for Enterprise and Industry, decided to take up the challenge. It was therefore thanks to a general and individual commitment that the partnership was officially launched on 7 November 2005 during the "Europe goes alternative" conference.

The principles underlying this partnership were defined as follows:

- to aim at stimulating the development, validation and implementation of alternative approaches via appropriate resources and financing tools and their regulatory acceptance;

- to identify European and international opportunities to address barriers to progress, foster acceptance and harmonisation of tests by regulators, ensure mutual acceptance and avoid redundancy wherever possible (through OECD, ICH[9] and other mechanisms);

- to build on past achievements from the different partners in applying the three Rs to animal use. This will require effective mapping of existing efforts in order to provide a starting-point;

- to support development and use of other modern approaches to gradually change the way safety assessment is carried out;

- to ensure a mechanism for dialogue and communication with other relevant stakeholders on developments that effectively contribute to animal welfare;

9.
International Conference on Harmonisation (ICH) of technical requirements for registration of pharmaceuticals for human use.

- to be mindful of the need to consider innovation, the protection of intellectual property arising from innovation and the implications for the overall competitiveness of the European industry.

The launching of this partnership is therefore only a beginning: a detailed joint work programme is to be drawn up and implemented to enable us to honour our commitments. In this context, companies are currently working with the European Commission to implement a strong structure, supported by investment from a range of partners, who will support the necessary work identified by the partnership. For their part, scientists are already busy implementing the action plan so as to ensure that the partnership is based on shared priorities and clear deadlines.

The action programme will identify the objectives to be achieved in the short, medium and long term. In the near future, the partners will seek to achieve rapid success in the area of validation. In the medium term, they will endeavour to develop intelligent testing strategies and, in the longer term, to acquire a genuine knowledge in complex research fields. The success of the partnership will be measured in several ways: improved animal welfare, a set of validated agreements on safe testing, contributions to future draft legislation and more straightforward validation, requiring, among other things, fewer resources.

The partnership must become an open and progressive forum in which all partners will have the same opportunities to become involved. We are currently working on a structure comprising an organising group seeing to the running of the partnership and working groups taking charge of specific projects. Our plan is that this organising group should be assisted by a group of partners whose members will have observer status. The purpose of this will be to facilitate the communication process and help ensure consistent activities. In addition, an annual conference is to be held in November to review the progress made.

Co-operation between the partners will therefore be vital to the success of this initiative. We all have a role to play in this project and we hope that, thanks to the ongoing support of the European Commission, the partnership will find the political support that it needs for its future development.

Although in some circumstances product safety still depends on animal testing, it is important to note that this approach is used less and less in processes for validating product safety, no doubt as a consequence of the adoption of the 7th amendment to the cosmetics directive and the imminent implementation of REACH. European companies must apply the three Rs (Refinement, Reduction and Replacement), which represent the first stage in the process leading to a total ban on animal testing in Europe in 2013. Hence it is likely that companies in some sectors of the industry will in the long term be able to ensure consumer safety without having recourse to animal testing. Scientific advances in this field and initiatives such as the "European Partnership for Alternative Approaches to Animal Testing" will make it possible to guarantee the safety of consumers while continuing to offer them new products. All this should eventually also permit an appropriate review of legislative requirements in the animal welfare area.

Animal biotechnology and animal welfare

by Mickey Gjerris, Anna Olsson and Peter Sandøe

During the past 30 years biotechnology has been used to develop a range of useful types of animal. These animals have made huge contributions to basic research and biomedicine and are beginning to enter the agricultural production system. This development raises a number of ethical questions. The central issue, as is so often the case, is about the boundaries of ethical acceptability.

Most people would readily agree that there is a difference between what humans *can* do and what they *ought* to do. Equally, most people would happily acknowledge that it is good to do the morally right thing. However, the harmony usually ends there, because although it is easy to agree that a good thing should be promoted, it is often hard to reach consensus on what that good thing is, how it can be promoted, and where to draw the line between *what is acceptable and what is not.* As soon as we begin discussing these questions, whether in private or in public, we are engaging in ethical discussion – discussion in which we seek to establish a substantial understanding of the concepts of good and right that can guide our choices when we are faced with opportunities whose acceptability appears uncertain.

The issue of ethical acceptability has closely shadowed developments within biotechnology over the past 30 years, not least when it comes to animal biotechnology. A range of possibilities including reproductive technologies, genetic modification and cloning has prompted concern about the ethical limits of our use of animals. It is probably an understatement to say that discussion has so far led to no consensus in the public sphere, but it would also be an overstatement to say that the debate has been futile. What *has* emerged, among other things, is a clearer understanding of the basic ethical assumptions behind the different viewpoints, together with greater attention to our ethical duties to animals.

What is animal biotechnology?

Animal biotechnology has developed rapidly over the past 20 to 25 years. The production of genetically modified animals began in the early 1980s, and cloning took off with the experiments by Steen Willadsen in the mid-1980s in which cloned sheep were produced by embryonic cell transfer (Willadsen, 1986). However, cloning technology only came to public prominence through work, lead by Ian Wilmut, in which somatic cell nuclear transfer was used to produce the cloned sheep, Dolly, in 1996 (Wilmut et al., 1997). Most work within animal biotechnology has been carried out on laboratory mice, sheep and cattle, but more recently the technologies have been adapted to other species such as pigs, goats, horses and cats. It should be noted that methodologies and success rates vary from species to species.

Animal biotechnology is used primarily for two purposes: to produce animals that can be employed in basic biological research into biological development and function, and to produce disease models that mimic human diseases and can therefore be utilised both in the study of disease (such as Parkinson's, cancer, cystic fibrosis, etc.) and to test new drugs. Increasingly, since the early 1990s, researchers have sought to develop animals with special traits making them useful within pharmaceutical production (bioreactors) and to create production animals with traits offering improved production, better animal health and/or reduced environmental impact. None of these applications has reached the market yet, but reports indicate that the first pharmaceuticals based on human proteins produced in animals are to be released in 2006 (CeBRA, 2005a). Similarly, some observers expect the first cloned animals to reach the agricultural production system in a few years; others anticipate that genetically modified animals will also enter the system within the foreseeable future (NAS, 2002).

Animal biotechnology can be defined in a number of ways. Which definition is used is of some importance, because the definition determines what should be considered a biotechnological novelty and what should be considered an established practice. Thus some people believe that only the new possibilities with genetic engineering and cloning should be categorised as animal biotechnology, while others wish to include well-established breeding technologies such as artificial insemination and even some older breeding practices (AICE, 1995; NAS, 2002). From an argumentative viewpoint, there are various reasons for including as much, or as little, as possible under the heading *animal biotechnology,* but we shall not discuss the merits of the contrasting definitions here. The more the new technologies can be seen as a natural extension of well-established practices the more it can be argued that there is nothing new under the sun and that, for example, regulation can be based on existing regulation and that the ethical concerns are no different from those arising from already established technologies – and vice versa (Lane, 1996). In this chapter we will arrive at a fairly broad view, but our starting point will be modern biotechnological applications such as genetic engineering and cloning. We are proceeding in this way in order to demonstrate how the ethical debate about these novel possibilities might shed light on established practices within animal breeding. These established practices can be traced back to the rediscovery of Mendelian theories at the beginning of the 20th century and the development of modern selective breeding practices from the 1920s onwards.

The possible applications of the new technologies can be divided up on the basis of the reason for using the technology. The applications that are mentioned in this and the following section are the ones usually mentioned in scientific articles on animal biotechnology. This does not mean that they have come to fruition, but only that researchers believe that they will be achievable in the light of anticipated scientific and technological expertise (CeBRA, 2005). Thus some animals are used within basic research and as disease models (research animals). Here genetically modified animals are produced to investigate the function of genes and gene products and to create animals that mimic human diseases such as cancer or Parkinson's disease. The aim is to facilitate research into the diseases and test possible treatments (Khanna and Hunter, 2005; Emborg, 2004; Swanson et al., 2004). In this area, cloning is mainly used as a tool to produce the GM animals and to study abnormalities in reproduction (Olsson and Sandøe, 2005). Other animals are used as bioreactors that produce biological compounds not naturally occurring in them (so-called "pharm animals"). Typically a gene of human origin is introduced in the animal genome. This might be done to cause the animal to produce a specific protein in its milk that can be used in producing medicine to cure or alleviate human disease. For example, a sheep produced by the company PPL Therapeutics has been genetically modified to express a human protein in its milk called alpha-1-antitrypsin, which can be used in the treatment of lung disorders (NAS, 2002).

A third application involves animals used within the agricultural sector (farm animals). In principle animals with desirable traits could be cloned to speed up the dissemination of the desired genotypes; and animals could perhaps be genetically modified to increase productivity (growth rates, feedstuff utilisation, disease resistance, etc.), to develop new products (leaner meat, functional foods, etc.) or to reduce negative impact on the environment (Kues and Niemann, 2004). Finally, there is a range of more or less "exotic" applications of biotechnologies. The first genetically modified pet hit the market in 2003. It is a luminescent fish for aquariums called GloFish(tm) (Caplan, 2004, see also www.glofish.com). An American company – Genetic Savings and Clone, Inc. – offers to save genetic material from pets and clone them later. The company has so far only produced cloned cats, but it hopes to begin cloning dogs soon (CGS, 2005). There is also speculation that cloning may be used to save endangered species or recreate extinct species (Holt et al., 2004). Serious attempts to clone *Bos gaurus,* an endangered large wild ox, have been made but so far no successful results, in the form of viable animals, have been reported (Lanza et al., 2000). Other, more fanciful, projects in cloning, for example, Tasmanian tigers and mammoths are frequently reported in the media but no results of this kind have as yet been confirmed.

It should be noted that a prerequisite of ethical thinking on a specific human practice, such as animal biotechnology, is sound understanding of the technologies involved, the science behind them and the objectives of the applications. Although it has been questioned to what extent this kind of factual information is necessary to be able to pass ethical judgment, there is no doubt that more than superficial understanding is needed (Thompson, 1997). This, however, should not point to the erroneous conclusion that *all* that is needed to convert sceptics about biotechnology is information. Although widely assumed within the scientific community (CeBRA, 2005d), the so-called "knowledge deficit" of lay people does not explain the discrepancy between the often very positive conception of biotechnology that scientists bring to the debate and the far more sceptical attitude of the public. Studies have shown that the more information people have, the more likely they are to make up their minds and form an opinion; but they have also shown that this opinion will not necessarily be positive. Thus the Danish population proved to be one of the most informed about biotechnology in the 1999 Eurobarometer survey, but at the same time came out as one of the most sceptical (INRA, 2000; Lassen et al., 2006a).

Potential effects on animal welfare

The use of biotechnology on animals may cause welfare problems, and the present section provides a short list of examples. GM animals have so far mainly been used within biological research and as disease models. Usually the goal of modification is to produce animals that either under- or over-express certain genes, or that express a mutated, disease-causing human gene. In all these cases body function in the organism is in some way disrupted. In principle, modifications can involve any part of the animal genome, and the effects on the animal's phenotype range from those that are lethal to those that have no detectable effect on the health of the animal. It is therefore impossible to generalise about the welfare effects of genetic modification (Olsson and Sandøe, 2004).

However, effects may be divided into two main categories: the intended and the unintended. Welfare problems stemming from intended genetic change are hard to avoid, since the very point of inducing the change is to affect the animal. Thus, the mouse carrying the human Huntington's disease gene will inevitably suffer welfare problems in developing the disease, including rapid progressive loss of neural control leading to premature death (Naver et al., 2003). Unintended effects are connected with the present inaccuracy of the technology and our insufficient understanding of the function of different genes in different organisms. Both of these kinds of factor operate to create the rather unpredictable nature of genetic modification at the phenotypic level. However, it is likely that at least some of the unintended welfare problems can be avoided as the technology and our scientific understanding develop. Where the intended consequences of genetic modification (for example, in creating a disease model) are concerned, it may be possible to predict welfare consequences using information about the effects of similar mutations in other species, including the human disease symptoms. Thus some studies try to evaluate welfare consequences beforehand. This potentially enables the producers of the animal to consider these consequences before the animal is actually produced (Dahl et al., 2003).

Animals are cloned either to produce genetically identical copies of desired individuals or as a tool to produce GM animals. Owing to the fact that some of the genetic material is located in the mitochondria and thus is provided by the egg cell that is used in cloning, and to certain epigenetic factors that are not yet well understood, the cloned animal will not be 100 % identical to the donor animal, either in genotype or phenotype (CeBRA, 2005c and 2005d). The importance of this for the different applications is still unclear. No matter what the purpose, the success rates of animal cloning are low (3-5%), and of the few individuals born, many suffer from impaired health and welfare. Problems include placental abnormalities, foetal overgrowth, prolonged gestation, stillbirth, hypoxia, respiratory failure and circulatory problems, malformations in the urogenital tract, malformations in liver and brain, immune dysfunction, lymphoid hypoplasia, anaemia and bacterial and viral infections (van Reenen et al., 2001). Some of these conditions are gathered under the term large offspring syndrome (LOS). LOS is often seen in cloned animals, but it also occurs when other reproductive technologies are employed. It is not yet clear whether the welfare problems experienced by cloned animals can be avoided through technological or methodological improvements or whether there are deeper epigenetic factors behind them (CeBRA, 2005c).

Two perspectives on animal welfare

There are two conceptions of the ethical concerns about animal welfare engendered by biotechnology: a narrow one and a broader one. We will describe these in more detail below. For the moment let us simply note that the first focuses on avoiding pain and other kinds of suffering in the animals, and on promoting positive experiences: in general this conception focuses on the subjective experiences of the animal. Besides these considerations the broader perspective also includes the animal's opportunity to engage in essential species-specific kinds of behaviour (Fraser et al., 1997; Duncan and Fraser, 1997; Appleby and Sandøe, 2002; Rollin, 1993). The broad perspective partly overlaps with a third category of concern in which animal biotechnology is questioned not because it poses any risks to animal welfare but because it is seen as violating animal integrity and basic concepts of naturalness. There is thus no consensus as to what should be counted as a welfare problem and what should not. Here we will simply describe in more detail some of the welfare problems that animal biotechnology might generate from the two main perspectives within the debate: the narrow perspective that looks at the subjective experiences of the animal and the broader perspective that also looks at the animal's ability to act according to its species-specific needs.

From a narrow perspective only the subjective experience of the animal has ethical importance. If the animal has negative experiences (for example, pain, suffering and anxiety), their cause (in this case biotechnology) is deemed ethically problematic. If the animal does not have any negative experiences, as for instance would a mouse with cancer in the early stages, it may have an incurable illness but it does not have a welfare problem (yet).

From the broader perspective the question of animal welfare is also about the extent to which the animal is allowed to fulfil what can be called its species-specific potential, regardless of its subjective experience. Very often the broader perspective will point to an additional group of considerations that has to be taken into account when we reflect on animal welfare. Being concerned with the opportunity of the animal to engage in certain kinds of behaviour does not prevent one from caring about the subjective experiences of the animal. Nevertheless, occasionally these two kinds of consideration are difficult to reconcile in practice; in that situation it becomes important to clarify what kind of perspective is in play. Considerations within the narrow perspective regarding the subjective experiences of the animal might be outweighed by the other considerations included in the broader perspective as we will illustrate in the following.

An illustrative dilemma – one not involving biotechnology but which highlights the difference between the narrow and the broad perspective – concerns the evaluation of the welfare of battery hens and free-range hens. From a narrow perspective, there is no ethical objection to denying the animal the opportunity to follow its instincts (as battery cage egg production does) as long as this does not affect the subjective welfare of the animal, that is, lead to negative experiences (Appleby and Sandøe, 2002). One can rarely prevent an animal from following its instincts without causing it suffering, but through breeding (either of the conventional sort or involving cloning and/or genetic engineering) changes could theoretically be induced in the animal that will make it more fit for the conditions under which it will have to live. And since this would have no negative subjective consequences for the individual hens, such a use of biotechnology would be seen as ethically unproblematic. This means that for instance the welfare problems caused by battery cage egg production could theoretically be solved through breeding chickens that did not suffer because of these conditions rather than changing the conditions (Rollin, 1995). In practice though, it is difficult to see how this can become a reality in the foreseeable future. Firstly, the trait to breed for would have a complex genetic background, since the objective must be an animal in which one has eradicated all motivations other than those that can be satisfied in a battery cage. Secondly, it will be a difficult challenge to ensure that one is indeed breeding for an animal with a restricted set of motivations rather than an animal that reacts passively, or even with apathy, to adverse conditions. This is not to say that breeding for behavioural traits cannot be used to improve animal welfare (problem behaviours such as feather pecking in hens have indeed been shown to be under genetic control), only that the objective of producing what Ben Mepham calls an "animal vegetable" does not seem to be easily obtainable.

From the broader perspective the very idea that we should breed hens to cope with battery cages raises serious worries and questions about what the natural life of a chicken is, and what experiences constitute such a life. Instead of changing the chicken, one would look for ways of allowing the chicken to fulfil its natural potential as far as possible through changes in the production system. Life as a free-range chicken is obviously less protected than life as a battery hen. Disease, feather pecking and cannibalism occur frequently within flocks of chickens (Kjær and Sørensen, 2002). Nevertheless, from a broader perspective this may be an acceptable situation, since it is counterbalanced by the fact that the chickens are living more naturally.

From a broad perspective the new animal biotechnologies raise concerns in two areas. First of all, they extend technological control over procreation – a control that is already widespread within animal breeding through the use of semen collection, artificial insemination, superovulation, embryo transfer, transvaginal ovum pick up, etc. This affects both the process (the sexual life of the animals) and the result (the offspring). In both cases it can be questioned whether this interference is ethically acceptable, since all the technologies mentioned can, in very general terms, be described as unnatural when compared to the "normal" life of animals. Secondly, however, the idea of naturalness as something valuable in itself raises questions about how naturalness should be understood. From animals used in basic research to farm animals bred for production, one can question if anything in their life is natural – at any rate, if "natural" means wild. The question should perhaps rather be about the extent to which the domesticated animal has an opportunity to fulfil its species-specific behaviour within the framework that the domestication process has built. Thus a laboratory mouse will live its life in a cage, but it might nonetheless fulfil certain species-specific behaviour (for example, digging or nest building) if given the chance.

Another case illustrating the difference between the narrow and the broad perspective is that of blind hens. Since genetically modified and/or cloned animals have not been introduced into the agricultural production system yet, we cannot draw on concrete examples but will highlight the envisioned ethical considerations by using realistic analogical examples. A Canadian scientist involved in poultry breeding has bred a blind egg-laying hen (Ali and Cheng, 1985). This variety of hen, according to the researcher, would help to reduce the welfare problems of free-range chickens. These birds harm one another by pecking, and sometimes even cannibalising, weaker members of the flock. Blindness apparently reduced these kinds of behaviour. It should be noted that the blindness was not inflicted on living chickens, but something they were born with. From a narrow welfare perspective the blind hens seem to be better off than their sighted peers.

At this point it is necessary to distinguish between two different viewpoints within the broad animal welfare perspective. To people taking the first viewpoint, both the notion of deliberately breeding chickens that have such limited potential as to be content with life as a battery cage hen and the aim of breeding blind hens to solve production problems in the agricultural sector are seen as ethically problematic in ways that might outweigh the advantages of these ideas as perceived from the narrow perspective. Something just seems to be amiss when you deliberately create an animal with less potential than normal (Lassen et al., 2006a), whether or not the animal has negative experiences as a result. Implicit in this version of the broader perspective is a certain respect for the natural state of the animal. Although it is intuitively compelling, it should be pointed out that this perspective suffers from an inherent ambiguity when domesticated animals are discussed, since it is almost impossible to point to a stage in the development of such animals that would constitute their natural state and thus be the developmental point that should be respected (Appleby and Sandøe, 2002).

This is a leading reason why other thinkers have suggested a different way of considering animal welfare problems within the broader perspective. They believe that the natural behaviour of the animal is to be respected, but the natural behaviour of the animal is not seen as something static. And just as domesticated animals have been bred to be better adapted to housing in confinement in the past, animals today can be bred, either conventionally or through genetic modification, to be better adapted for modern day production systems. Thus the fact that one can alter the nature of an animal by genetic modification does not constitute an ethical problem as long as one respects the nature that the animal ends up with (Rollin, 1995).

Whether we choose to look at animal welfare from a narrow perspective or one of the broader perspectives, two additional important issues must be borne in mind when evaluating the ethical dimensions of animal biotechnology. First of all, it is important to note that, from an animal welfare perspective, the difference between traditional breeding technologies and the new biotechnological tools seems to be more of a quantitative difference in the potential of applications than a qualitative difference that creates entirely new welfare issues.

The second issue is that the range of ethical concerns raised by animal biotechnology goes beyond questions of risks to animal welfare. An obvious group of considerations that we have only briefly mentioned concerns risks to human health. These considerations are usually treated within risk assessment frameworks. Then there is the familiar concern that one or other proposed uses of animal biotechnology might be the beginning of a "slippery slope" culminating in genetic modification and cloning of humans. The broadly social impact of animal biotechnology on agricultural structure, the economy and so on, is also an important ethical aspect to be considered in relation to animal biotechnology, as is the possible change that greater control of nature as such could induce in the overall relationship between humans and nature. We mention this only to emphasise that issues other than animal welfare – and issues of an equally complex kind – arise in connection with animal biotechnology. These are not covered in this article.

The challenges of animal biotechnology

Questions about the real difference between genetic engineering and animal cloning, on the one hand, and more conventional ways of "improving" animals by selective breeding and the creation of disease models through, for example, exposure to chemical compounds or radiation, on the other, are important – not least because the interconnectedness of the new technologies with the old is often used as an argument for the new biotechnologies. The argument runs roughly as follows. There is nothing new under the sun. We continue to change animals to suit our own needs. Only the precision and effectiveness of the methods has changed (Kues and Niemann, 2004). Hence animal biotechnology raises no unique ethical problems. As we have shown above, and as it has been argued in a number of publications in recent years (for example, Olsson and Sandøe, 2004; Buehr et al., 2004; NAS, 2002), the premises of this argument do seem to be true. At least, it is true that most of the welfare problems associated with cloning and genetic engineering can be found in more conventional technologies too. Large Offspring Syndrome is not only a problem within the cloning technology, but also when other kinds of biotechnology procedures are used (CeBRA, 2005c). The welfare problems that may arise from depriving animals of their natural procreative activity are also linked to other technologies. And welfare problems arising from the genetic engineering of animals can be found in selective breeding programmes as well, as for instance when an excessively narrow focus on productivity leads to leg disorders in broiler chickens, or to increased levels of mastitis in cows (Olsson and Sandøe, 2004). Ironically enough, the most eye-catching difference between the old and the new technologies may be uncertainty about the unintended side effects in the latter, and especially with genetic engineering, since this contradicts the biotechnologist's claim to work with greater precision.

However, it is not possible to dismiss criticism of animal biotechnology merely by pointing to the similarities between earlier and new uses of animal technology. The problem with this argument is that people will not necessarily have accepted the older techniques. Members of the public are largely unaware of the consequences of selective breeding. In general they are critical of confined housing systems, but in reality they were consulted on neither of these matters. We would therefore like to reverse the argument: public worries about new biotechnologies, and the genuine ethical concerns into which they can be translated, should be seen as a reason to critically analyse not only new biotechnologies but also existing technologies, and as a trigger for serious discussion of the limits to what it is ethically acceptable to do to animals (Olsson and Sandøe, 2005). Animal biotechnology might not be something radically new, but it can be the straw that broke the camel's back (Cooper, 1998).

What is evident today is that ethical questions raised about the regulation of the new biotechnologies used on animals are not concerned only with the question of welfare understood as mental states or experience. Today, all parties in the debate agree that there are limits to the amount of physical pain or mental stress that it is ethically justifiable to impose on an animal. But it is also becoming more and more widely recognised that other factors should influence the way we treat animals. These factors include the preservation of the naturalness of the animal, and the importance of giving an animal the opportunity to fulfil its species-specific potential. Such factors are becoming increasingly prominent within the regulatory debate. Of course, they are especially conspicuous when no traditional welfare problems are at stake.

As we have argued, there are two different conceptions of animal welfare in the ethical debate about animal biotechnology: one that focuses on the mental states of the animals and one that takes broader considerations into view. It is very seldom that one encounters the view that animal welfare is irrelevant to the evaluation of the biotechnological possibilities. This situation, though, should be compared with the situation only 15 to 20 years ago. At that time, only a minority defended what is today considered the narrow perspective (Matheny, 2005). This shift in attitudes can also be detected in the regulatory framework. Consider Article 3 of the Protocol of Amendment to the European Convention for the Protection of Animals kept for Farming Purposes adopted by the Council of Europe in 1992:

> "Natural or artificial breeding or breeding procedures which cause or are likely to cause suffering or injury to any of the animals involved shall not be practised; no animal shall be kept for farming purposes unless it can be reasonably expected, on the basis of its phenotype or genotype, that it can be kept without detrimental effects on its health or welfare."[1]

It should be noted that even though this article of the amending protocol focuses "only" on the narrow conception of animal welfare, it has proved difficult to transpose the convention into European legislation. At any rate, this excerpt can be compared with recently passed legislation on cloned animals in Denmark. In this legislation it is explicitly stated that animals may be cloned only if an independent research approval committee deems the purpose of this procedure useful (Danish Ministry of Justice, 2005). What is most noteworthy here is that the law limits certain applications of animal cloning regardless of its effect on animal welfare. This means that even if no welfare problems are involved, it is still necessary to demonstrate the perceived usefulness of the technology to show that it is ethically acceptable. This justification involves balancing the perceived goal of the process (research, medicine, agriculture, etc.) and the ethically problematic features inherent in the technology. The underlying motive for this strict regulation of animal cloning is not stated in the Danish legislation, but it is evident from the report prepared as foundation for the legislative work that the concept of animal integrity is one of the major factors (Danish Ministry for Science, Technology and Development, 2003). In December 2002 the Folketinget [Danish parliament] decided to encourage the government to appoint a preparatory committee to follow up the Folketinget motion for adjournment of May 1997 with a view to establishing rules for research regarding animal cloning and accompanying technologies. The result of this work can be seen in The Danish Ministry for Science, Technology and Development 2003.

1.
ETS No. 145.

Animal integrity can perhaps best be understood as an inherent limit in the relationship between humans and nature governing what is ethically acceptable for humans to do to animals. In other words, integrity is a limit based on an understanding or experience of animals as beings surrounded by an impenetrable aura that may be violated only if the reasons are adequate from an ethical perspective (Gjerris, 2005). It should be noted here that this is only a rough outline for one interpretation of the concept of integrity. Nevertheless, it should be clear that the idea of animal integrity both broadens the concept of animal welfare beyond the narrow perspective and rejects the notion that the naturalness of an animal is something that should only be respected in the individual animal – thus permitting humans to change the nature of animals in general, as was the case in the second version of the broader perspective.

The balancing of commercial and scientific interests against the "interests" of the animals raises a set of challenges. These challenges arise both for proponents of the broader approach (who will have to argue convincingly that a concept such as integrity should be respected) and in the political and regulatory process that follows in the wake of the different applications of biotechnology on animals. What is clear from a number of European surveys is that concepts such as integrity and naturalness play a significant and growing role in the general perception of legitimate use of biotechnology on animals (Lassen et al., 2006a).

This situation could lead to a growing discrepancy between the very scientific and individualistic way of evaluating the ethical consequences of animal biotechnology that is implicit in risk-based studies of human health and animal welfare which have traditionally guided the regulatory process and a wider evaluation, involving notions of naturalness and integrity, for example. We do not mean to imply that there is something wrong with the scientific approach, but we do wish to point to the fact that the ethical concerns go deeper than that. As suggested, more general questions about the way in which animal biotechnology may contribute to change in the social world, about the possibility that animal cloning may facilitate reproductive cloning of humans, and about the perceived naturalness of the animals, are omitted in the scientific approach. This difference may also have a geographical and geopolitical dimension: where Europe and the EU are moving towards a broader understanding of animal welfare as the basis for regulation, the United States maintain a narrow understanding of animal welfare when they evaluate new biotechnology. This is evident in the emerging transatlantic discussion of the regulation of cloned animals and products derived from them or their offspring (CeBRA, 2005b).

Closer examination of what assumptions underlie the call for protection of the nature of animals could be a way of addressing some of these questions. These questions are usually dealt with rather superficially in the scientific literature, but they nonetheless play a significant role in forming public attitudes towards animal biotechnology (Lassen et al., 2006a, b). The fact that concepts such as naturalness or integrity are complex and not readily quantified does not mean that they are inappropriate subjects for rational discussion. It just means that they have to be discussed within a broader context than a narrow scientific one.

Any such discussion will reveal that there is more than one way to interpret such concepts. One way would be to claim that a concept such as naturalness tries to capture the distinction between the knowledge of the animal that is expressed through our understanding of its usefulness to humans and the knowledge that is expressed in our immediate experience of the animal. A cow is a producer of hide, milk and meat; it holds no surprises when experienced from a human perspective, where the fulfilment of human need is at the centre. But from another perspective, where the cow is understood as something independent of humans – as a life form with its own needs, history and importance – it becomes clear that we do not know all there is to know about cows just because we know how to use them. There is something more to cows: something that in a sense alienates them from us and that should prevent us from reducing them to merely a means to our ends.

Implicit in this distinction is a notion of the amount of control over the animal that we can exercise without violating its naturalness or integrity. In this sense, respect for naturalness can be understood as the polar opposite of total commodification of the animal as a natural resource. Although these notions are hardly of a scientific nature, they can be discussed meaningfully. They should not necessarily be dismissed offhand as either irrational or built upon elaborate religious or philosophical systems. They could also offer ways of describing very basic experiences of animals as something more than biological machines (Gjerris, 2005).

Whether considerations such as these should play a role in future regulation of animal biotechnology and more conventional ways of breeding animals is an open question. There can be no doubt, however, that failure to take them seriously will deepen the already existing gap concerning the ethical legitimacy of biotechnology, between science and industry, on the one hand, and the general public, on the other. We should seek socially robust solutions to the challenges that animal biotechnology raises. This may mean that we have to develop regulation that is based on something broader than empirical knowledge about physical risks to humans and animals. It may also mean not only that new possibilities will be rejected but also that existing practices within, say, animal breeding will need to be re-evaluated. But since the alternative scenario might very well be one in which growing public acceptance of the broader approach leads to even more negative public attitudes to new applications of animal biotechnology and conventional animal husbandry, this may be in the interests of all the stakeholders in the debate.

Acknowledgements: The authors would like to thank Gabor Vajta from the Danish Institute of Agricultural Sciences, Foulum, Denmark, Axel Kornerup Hansen from the Royal Veterinary and Agricultural University, Denmark, and Paul Robinson from Quercus for their valuable comments on an earlier draft of this article.

Bibliography

Ali, A. and Cheng, K.M., "Early egg production in genetically blind (rc/rc) chickens in comparison with sighted (Rc+/rc) controls", in *Poultry Science,* 64, 5, 1985, pp. 789-794.

American Israeli Cooperative Enterprise (AICE), *Breakthrough Dividend,* AICE, 1995. www.jewishvirtuallibrary.org/jsource/biotech/bdcontent.html

Appleby, M.C. and Sandøe, P., "Philosophical debate on the nature of well-being: Implications for animal welfare", in *Animal Welfare,* 11, 3, 2002, pp. 283-294.

Buehr, M., Hjorth, J.P., Kornerup Hansen, A. and Sandøe, P., "Genetically modified laboratory animals – What welfare problems do they face?", in *Journal of Applied Animal Welfare Science,* 6, 2004, pp. 319-338.

Caplan, A., "A dark side of glowing fish? More oversight of genetic engineering needed", in *Bioethics on MSNBC,* 2004, www.bioethics.net/articles.php?viewCat=2&articleId=16

Center for Genetics and Society (CGS), *The new industry of manufacturing pets,* Center for Genetics and Society, Oakland, United States, 2005, www.genetics-and-society.org/analysis/pet/industry.html#gsc

Cooper, D.E., "Intervention, humility and animal integrity", in Holland, A. and Johnson, A. (eds.), in *Animal Biotechnology and Ethics,* Chapman and Hall, 1998, pp. 145-155.

Council of Europe, *Protocol of Amendment to the European Convention for the Protection of Animals kept for Farming Purposes,* ETS No. 145, Strasbourg, 1992, http://conventions.coe.int/Treaty/EN/CadreListeTraites.htm

Dahl, K., Sandøe, P., Johnsen, P.F., Lassen, J. and Kornerup Hansen, A., "Outline of a risk assessment: the welfare of future xeno-donor pigs", in *Animal Welfare,* 12, 2003, pp. 219-237.

Danish Centre for Bioethics and Risk Assessment (CeBRA), *Animal Cloning: Technology, Applications and Ethics. Expert Workshop Conclusions,* prepared in co-operation with the Institute of Prospective Technological Studies (DG JRC-IPTS,

Sustainability in Agriculture, Food and Health Unit), 2005a, www.bioethics.kvl.dk/cloninginpublic.htm

Danish Centre for Bioethics and Risk Assessment (CeBRA), *Farm animal cloning: the current legislative framework. A review describing the existing law and its practical application within and beyond the EU*, report from the project "Cloning in public – A specific support action within the 6th framework programme", priority 5: Food quality and safety, 2005b, www.bioethics.kvl.dk/cloninginpublic.htm

Danish Centre for Bioethics and Risk Assessment (CeBRA), *The science and technology of farm animal cloning: a review of the state of the art of the science, the technology, the problems and the possibilities*, report from the project "Cloning in public – A specific support action within the 6th framework programme", priority 5: Food quality and safety, 2005c, www.bioethics.kvl.dk/cloninginpublic.htm

Danish Centre for Bioethics and Risk Assessment (CeBRA), *Why clone farm animals? Goals, motives, assumptions, values and concerns among European scientists working with cloning of farm animals*, report from the project "Cloning in public – A specific support action within the 6th framework programme", priority 5: Food quality and safety, 2005d, www.bioethics.kvl.dk/cloninginpublic.htm

Danish Ministry of Justice, *L8 Lov om kloning og genmodificering af dyr m.v. af 14. Juni 2005* (Animal cloning and genetic modification act of 14 June 2005), Copenhagen, 2005.

Danish Ministry of Science, Technology and Development, *Genmodificerede og klonede dyr* (Genetically modified and cloned animals), Copenhagen, 2003.

Duncan, I.J.H. and Fraser, D., "Understanding animal welfare", in Appleby, M.C. and Hughes, B.O. (eds.), in *Animal Welfare*, CAB International, Wallingford, UK, 1997, pp. 19-31.

Emborg, M., "Evaluation of animal models of Parkinson's disease for neuroprotective strategies", in *Journal of Neuroscience Methods*, 139, 2004, pp. 121-143.

Fraser, D., Weary, D.M., Pajor, E.A. and Milligan, B.N., "A scientific conception of animal welfare that reflects ethical concerns", in *Animal Welfare, 6*, 1997, pp.187-205.

Gjerris, M., "Ethical aspects of animal cloning", Association Européenne de Transfert Embryonnaire, 2005, submitted.

Hansen, J., Holm, L., Frewer, L., Robinson, P. and Sandøe, P., "Beyond the knowledge deficit. Recent research into lay and expert attitudes to food risks", in *Appetite*, 41, 2003, pp. 11-121.

Holt, W.V., Pickard, A.R. and Prather, R.S., "Wildlife conservation and reproductive cloning", in *Reproduction*, 127, 2004, pp. 317-324.

INRA (Europe) – ECOSA, *Eurobarometer 52.1. The Europeans and biotechnology*, 15 March 2000, http://europa.eu.int/comm/public_opinion/archives/ebs/ebs_134_fr.pdf

Khanna, C. and Hunter, K., "Modeling metastasis in vivo", in *Carcinogenesis*, 26, 3, 2005, pp. 513-523.

Kjaer, J.B. and Sørensen, P., " Feather pecking and cannibalism in free-range laying hens as affected by genotype, dietary level of methionine + cystine, light intensity during rearing and age at first access to the range area", in *Appl. Anim. Behav. Sci.,* 76, 2002, pp. 21-39.

Kues, W.A. and Niemann, H., "The contribution of farm animals to human health", in *Trends in biotechnology,* 22, 6, 2004, pp. 286-294.

Lane, M., "Invention or contrivance? Biotechnology, intellectual property rights and regulation", report prepared for the second meeting of the Conference of the Parties to the Convention on Biological Diversity, Jakarta, Indonesia, November 1995, rev. January 1996. Washington DC, Community Nutrition Institute (CNI), 1996. www.acephale.org/bio-safety/IoC-indx.htm

Lanza, P., Cibelli, J., Diaz, F., Moraes, C., Farin, P., Farin, C., Hammer, C., West, M. and Damiani, P., "Cloning of an endangered species (*Bos gaurus*) using interspecies nuclear transfer", in *Cloning,* Vol. 2, No. 2, 2000, pp. 79-90.

Lassen, J., Gjerris, M. and Sandøe, P., "After Dolly – ethical limits to the use of biotechnology on farm animals", in *Theriogenology*, 65, 5, 2006a, pp. 992-1004.

Lassen, J., Sandøe, P. and Forkman, B., *Happy pigs are dirty! – Conflicting perspectives on animal welfare,* Life Stock Production Science, 2006b, in press.

Matheny, Gaverick, "Utilitarianism and animals", in Singer, Peter (ed.), *In defense of animals – The second wave,* Blackwell Publishing, London, 2005.

National Academy of Sciences (NAS), *Animal biotechnology: science based concerns,* National Academy of Sciences, Washington DC, 2002.

National Academy of Sciences (NAS), *Safety of genetically engineered foods: approaches to assessing unintended health effects,* National Academy of Sciences, Washington DC, 2004.

Naver, B., Stub, C., Moller, M., Fenger, K., Hansen, A.K., Hasholt, L. and Sorensen, S.A., "Molecular and behavioral analysis of the R6/1 Huntington's disease transgenic mouse", in *Neuroscience*, 122, 4, 2003, pp. 1049-1057.

Olsson, A. and Sandøe, P., "Ethical decisions concerning animal biotechnology: what is the role of animal welfare science?", in *Animal Welfare,* 13, 2004, pp. 139-144.

Olsson, A. and Sandøe, P., "Biotechnology and the animal issue", in *Global Bioethics,* 2005, in press.

Rollin, B.E., "Animal production and the new social ethics for animals" in Purdue Research Foundation (ed.), *Food animal well-being. Conference Proceedings and Deliberations,* US department of Agriculture and Purdue University Office of Agricultural Research Programs, West Lafayette, 1993.

Rollin, B.E., *Frankenstein Syndrome: ethical and social issues in the genetic engineering of animals,* Cambridge University Press, Cambridge, 1995.

Swanson, K.S., Mazur, M.J., Vashisht, K., Rund, L.A, Beever, J.E, Counter, C.M and Schook, L.B., "Genomics and clinical medicine: Rationale for creating and effectively evaluating animal models", in *Experimental Biology and Medicine,* 229, 9, 2004, pp. 866-875.

Takahashi, S. and Ito, Y., "Evaluation of meat products from cloned cattle: biological and biochemical properties", in *Cloning and Stem Cells,* 6, 2, 2005, pp. 165-171.

Thompson, P.B., *Food biotechnology in ethical perspective,* Blackie Academic and Professional, London, 1997.

Van Reenen, C.G., Meuwissen, T.H.E., Hopster, H., Oldenbroek, K., Kruip, T.A.M. and Blokhuis, H.J. "Transgenesis may affect farm animal welfare: A case for systematic risk assessment", in *J. Anim. Sci.,* 79, 2001, pp. 1763-1779.

Willadsen, S.M. "Nuclear transplantation in sheep embryos", in *Nature,* 320, 1986, pp. 63-65.

Wilmut, I., Schnieke, A.E., McWhir, J., Kind, A.J. and Campbell, K.H., "Viable offspring derived from fetal and adult mammalian cells", in *Nature,* 385, 1997, pp. 810-813.

Wilmut, I., Beaujean, N., De Sousa, P.A., Dinnyes, A., King, T., Paterson, L., Wells, D. and Young, L., "Somatic cell nuclear transfer", in *Nature,* 419, 2002, pp. 583-587.

Pet animals: housing, breeding and welfare

by Andreas Steiger

The term "pet animal" is used in various ways, sometimes including, sometimes excluding the usual "companion animals" such as dogs and cats. The Council of Europe's Convention for the Protection of Pet Animals gives the following definition in a broad sense:

> "By pet animal is meant any animal kept or intended to be kept by man, in particular in his household, for private enjoyment and companionship."[1]

According to the explanatory report to this convention, the definition of a pet animal covers animals sharing man's companionship and in particular living in his household, animals intended for this purpose, animals kept to breed animals for this purpose, and stray animals and the first generation of animals born of stray animals. Excluded from this definition are, for instance, animals kept for the production of food, wool, skin or fur or for other farming purposes, those kept in zoos and circuses for exhibition and those kept for experimental or other scientific purposes. It was admitted that the inclusion of wild animals in the convention might be considered as recognition of the possibility of using these animals as pet animals, on the other hand, it was realised that to leave out wild animals would create a legal lacuna and that these animals would not be protected at all.

The growing importance of pet and companion animals

Worldwide the importance of pet and companion animals has grown. High percentages of the population are owners of pet and companion animals, in particular in towns, with different percentages from country to country. The industry of animal feed and pet animal equipment as well as the number of pet animal shops is growing. The great majority of veterinarians in practice are working in mixed practices with small and large animals or in small animal practices (Unshelm, 1997, 2002).

1.
European Convention for the Protection of Pet Animals (ETS No. 125), signed on 13 November 1987 in Strasbourg, Article 1.

Specialisations in small pet animal and exotic animal medicine (including treatment of reptiles) and in behavioural medicine (treatment of behavioural problems in particular of dogs and cats) are gaining in importance, both in veterinary practice and in veterinary schools of universities.

Animal welfare problems in housing of pet animals

There are numerous popular books, booklets and brochures on housing of many pet and companion animals on the market. Often the requirements of housing, in particular measures for boxes and cages, are taken over uncritically from source to source over many years, or the state of practice is taken as a minimal norm or as a recommendation without being questioned and without any scientific examination. From the experiences of animal welfare organisations, animal welfare authorities and veterinarians it is known that in practice often pet animals are not kept according to their biological needs and to scientific knowledge. Frequent faults in housing conditions of pet animals are boxes or cages which are too small, therefore a lifelong lack of movement of the animals, unstructured boxes for small pet mammals, insufficient hiding possibilities for various pet species, single housing of very social animals such as guinea pigs, many pet birds and parrots, furthermore insufficiently structured boxes for cats in cat shelters, inadequate feeding, including overfeeding, and many other conditions. Many diseases in pet animals are the consequences of faults in housing (Hollmann, 1988, 1997). Species-specific locomotion in most birds means flying, and not only hopping from perch to perch, and in small rodents running, climbing, jumping and digging, and not only walking some steps along a wall from edge to edge of a box; it also means behaviours such as exploring, marking, hiding, nesting and other activities, which are often very restricted in cages (Hollmann, 1997). Nevertheless measurements of boxes and cages are not the only factor of housing, other important factors are a good microclimate and location of the cage, adequate structures and accessories, good feeding in quality and quantity, and careful treatment by the owner (Hollmann, 1997). For pet birds, negative factors of housing are, for example, anthropomorphism, wrong judgement of the well-being of the animals, the role of the animal as status symbol or as object for representation, insufficient knowledge on behaviour, housing and feeding requirements, insufficient climate, additionally problems of adaptation of wild-caught birds (Kummerfeld, 1997).

The main problems pet owners have with their animals were analysed by Falbesaner (1991) from 3 000 letters to a pet magazine in 1987 and 1988: 14% of the questions concerned housing problems, 12% health problems and 11% behaviour problems; 29% of the letters concerned birds, 26% small pets (mammals, for example, rodents), 16% dogs, 15% cats, 5% horses, 5% reptiles and the others further species. Behaviour problems most commonly appeared in dogs, birds, small pets, and cats, in this order. The main problem in birds was the acclimatisation of members of the same species. In dogs most problems arised with the human-animal bond, particularly with the dominance of hierarchical consideration. The main problem with cats was the house-training, and in birds and small pet animals difficulties due to lack of tameness were often reported.

For pet animals, many inadequate and even hazardous equipments and accessories are on the market. A list of such materials, which are in contradiction with the principles of animal protection, was published recently (TVT, 1998, 1999) and includes, for example, bowls for hamsters, animal boxes closed on all sides, synthetic cotton for hamsters, running wheels with broad spaces between rods, litter with odorous or colouring substances, feed troughs without cover plates; for pet birds round cages, cages with white lattice, cages with lattice with plastic or lacquer for psittacides, plastic perches, perches and floors with sandpaper, inadequate toys, or chains for parrots on perches. Inadequate accessories for fish are, for example, goldfish bowls, mini aquariums, tower aquariums and inadequate gravel, for reptiles, for example, mini terrariums with isles for water tortoises, or leather jackets for iguanas. Inadequate accessories are also on the market for dogs and cats (TVT, 1999).

Some circumstances are enhancing the risk of faults and animal welfare problems in pet animal housing, more than in farm animal housing, in animal experimentation and in other categories of animal housing (Steiger, 1999, 2005a): for pet animals there are no or very few state regulations on animal welfare, no special education is required for keeping animals in a private household, often there is no "public control" of private housing conditions for animals, there is also less "public pressure" compared to farm animal housing and animal experimentation, there are no procedures of authorisation as, for example, for animal experimentation and sometimes for keeping wild animals, the market for equipment and accessories for pet animals is mostly free, and finally in research on housing of most pet animals there are more gaps than in research on other species.

Animal welfare problems in breeding of pet animals

For thousands of years man has caused animals to change by domestication (farm animals, horses, companion animals), by breeding and rearing wild animals for special purposes (such as the production of meat, milk, eggs and fur), by using animals in performance sports (horses, dogs, pigeons), by selecting animals for special appearance or behaviour (dogs, cats, rabbits, poultry, small pet rodents, pet birds, ornamental fish), and by using laboratory animals and developing models for disease research. Animal welfarists and scientists have criticised several pedigree breeds of farm animals and companion animals. They are considered to be "defective breeds" or "extreme breeds" (in German *Qualzuchten*), since they have extreme morphological, physiological or behavioural characteristics. It is claimed or assumed that these characteristics lead to unnecessary suffering and to unacceptable restrictions in the life of these animals. This applies to certain breeds of cattle, swine, horses, dogs, cats, rabbits, pet rodents, poultry, turkeys, ducks, pigeons, pet birds, reptiles, amphibians and ornamental fish (Wegner, 1993, 1995, 1997; Bechtel, 1995; Peyer, 1997; Wegner, 1997; Bartels and Wegner, 1998; Not ,1998; Peyer and Steiger, 1998; Stucki, 1998; McGreevy and Nicholas, 1999; Expert Group Germany, 2000; Bartels, 2002). The most active discussion on adverse breeding effects in companion animals has been in the German-speaking community, but discussion is also evident in the English-speaking community where the term "animal illfare" has been used (Ott, 1996). Reviews on extreme breed types in domestic animals are presented by Bartels and Wegner (1998), in companion animals by a report of an Expert Group in Germany (2000), in dogs by Peyer (1997), in cats by Wegner (1995), Stucki (1998) and Steiger (2005), in exhibition poultry and cage birds by Stucki (1998), Not (1998) and Bartels (2002), and in small pet mammals, pet birds, reptiles and ornamental fish by Not (1998).

The Federation of Veterinarians of Europe (FVE) has issued a resolution on breeding and animal welfare which:

> "urges its member countries and the European Commission to consider the introduction of measures designed to safeguard the welfare of animals with respect to the risks inherent in selective breeding programmes, while preserving the unique characteristics and genetic advantages of European breeds.
>
> Selective breeding programmes may cause animal welfare problems. It may become difficult or impossible for natural copulation or parturition to occur; offspring produced by selective breeding for certain specific, characteristics may be unable to express their natural behaviour; or they may be predisposed to hereditary, congenital, metabolic or infectious disease, disability or early death. The introduction and continuation of such selective breeding programmes may make it impossible for the breed to be maintained by natural means (...)
>
> The FVE believes that it is the function of the veterinary profession not only to treat sick and injured animals, but to promote and safeguard animal health and welfare. Its members believe that selective breeding of animals should not be used to introduce a welfare deficit into a species or breed, or to impair the ability of a breed or individual to express its natural behaviour throughout its natural lifespan.
>
> Furthermore, where selective breeding has already resulted in welfare disadvantages being introduced into any species or breed, the FVE urges veterinarians not only to treat individual animals humanely, but also to bring to the attention of the breeding organisations and the competent authorities in their countries the need for action to alleviate the welfare problems caused by selective breeding."[2]

The European Convention for the Protection of Pet Animals includes general rules on breeding of pet animals and an additional resolution concerning breeding of dogs and cats (see below).

2.
Federation of Veterinarians of Europe, 1999, resolution "Breeding and Animal Welfare", FVE/99/010; see website at: www.fve.org

Information and education on housing of pet animals

Reasons for insufficient housing conditions of pet animals are often the lack of knowledge. This is recognised by authorities of animal welfare regulations in many countries. The importance of information means for owners of pet animals was shown by a survey by phone to 730 owners of various pet animals (Bhagwanani, 1995; Steiger 1999, 2005). Amongst many other questions they were asked if their animals are social animals and how they were keeping them. The owners knew quite well about the social requirements of their animals, but these were housed to a lower percentage in social conditions than according to the answers. There was an obvious lack between own knowledge and own handling (Table 1).

Table 1 – Questions to pet animal owners (Bhagwanini, 1995)		
Answers of pet owners Interviewed owners of pet animals	**Animals declared as social animals**	**Own animals are housed in groups**
Guinea pigs (64 people)	81%	58%
Pet birds (76 people)	75%	62%
Rabbits (70 people)	69%	58%
Hamsters (34 people)	24%	27%

The European Convention for the Protection of Pet Animals also deals with the matter, the Council of Europe acknowledged the importance of information and education on housing of pet animals and in Article 14 on information and education programmes gives some general rules:

"The Parties undertake to encourage the development of information and education programmes so as to promote awareness and knowledge amongst organizations and individuals concerned with the keeping, breeding, training, trading and boarding of pet animals of the provisions and the principles in this Convention. In these programmes, attention shall be drawn in particular to the following subjects:

a. the need for training of pet animals for any commercial or competitive purpose to be carried out by persons with adequate knowledge and ability;

b. the need to discourage gifts of pet animals to persons under the age of 16 without the express consent of their parents or other persons exercising parental responsibilities, gifts of pet animals as prizes, awards or bonuses, unplanned breeding of pet animals;

c. the possible negative consequences for the health and well-being of wild animals if they were to be acquired or introduced as pet animals;

d. the risks of irresponsible acquisition of pet animals leading to an increase in the number of unwanted and abandoned animals."

This article aims at ensuring that publicity is given to the provisions of the convention amongst private persons who are directly concerned by the implementation of some of the articles. It was agreed that on a number of issues, such as the training of animals by persons with adequate knowledge and ability, giving pet animals to children as presents or as prizes, the unplanned breeding of pet animals, the introduction of wild animals as pets and the irresponsible acquisition of pet animals, effective results could be obtained only by informing and educating private organisations and individuals and that accordingly contracting parties should encourage the development of information and education programmes.

The elaboration and distribution of adequate, modern information means on pet animal housing and breeding is an important and promising task for animal welfare organisations, animal welfare authorities and animal housing and breeding associations.

Research on housing and breeding of pet animals

At an international level, there is a lack of research results on housing and breeding of pet animals, and much more is known on the most common farm animals cattle, pig and poultry, on laboratory rodents and alternatives to animal experimentation, and on stunning of slaughter animals, than on pet animals. Research on pet animals, at least small pets, is not frequent, due perhaps to less attractiveness of such research and fewer financial sources in this field compared to research on farm and laboratory animals or dogs (Table 2).

Table 2 – Numbers of scientific publications according to search in Pubmed (March 2005)	
Species	**Number of publications**
Rat	790
Mouse	469
Poultry	266
Pig	206
Cattle	149
Dog	62
Hamster	48
Cat	47
Rabbit	32
Sheep	31
Horse	30
Guinea pig	29
Fish	27
(Pet)	25
Turkey	22
Gerbil	19
(Reptiles)	13
Goat	7
(Psittacines)	7
Ferret	5
Parrot	4
Ground squirrel	4
(Pet bird)	4
Canary	2
Tortoise	2
Budgerigar	1
Chinchilla	0
Degu	0

Methods in research on housing are mainly: a. comparison of animals kept in various housing forms (with clinical, morphological, ethological and physiological parameters); b. preference tests with animals (choice tests with free access to various housing forms or elements); c. operant-tests with animals (assessment of the degree of preference, of the strength of motivation for certain housing forms or elements, for example, measurable by work or time for reaching a certain aim), and d. epidemiological investigations.

Some results of recent research on housing of pet animals concern the following aspects (Steiger, 2005): with a "cat-stress-score" Kessler (1997) investigated the stress effects of high density in cat groups, single housing versus group housing, small cage size, and lack of socialisation in cats; other authors showed the stress effects of lack of hiding places for cats (Carlstead et al., 1993). Contributions on welfare of cats are presented by various authors (Mertens,1997; Turner and Bateson, 2000; Wöhr, 2002; Rochlitz, 2002, 2005). In guinea pigs it was shown by preference tests that guinea pigs together clearly prefer conspecifics versus dwarf rabbits as social partners (Sachser, 1998). Gerbils need a dark nest with a tunnel and should not be separated too early from their offspring (Wiedenmayer, 1995; Waiblinger, 2002, 2004; Waiblinger and König, 2004). Hamsters can use adequate big running wheels in a reasonable way and show less stereotypies in deep litter and on big litter surfaces (Vonlanthen, 2002; Gebhardt et al., 2004, 2005; Fischer, 2005; Hauzenberger, 2005; Hauzenberger et al., 2005). Running wheels for mice and hamsters may be constructed in various forms and are not always adequate for the animals (Mrosovsky et al., 1998; Banjanin and Mrosovsky, 2000). In hand-reared, parent-reared and wild-caught grey parrots it was shown that the breeding method, also the method of hand feeding and the human contact, has an influence on the behaviour and health of the animals (Schmid 2004; Schmid et al., 2004; Schmid et al., 2005).

Methods of research on extreme breeds of companion and pet animals include the comparison of animals with extreme characteristics with other, less extreme or "normal" breeding types, or the comparison of various breed types, by using the parameters morphology, behaviour, physiology, clinics, morbidity and mortality (as an example, research on crested ducks with radiography, computer-assisted tomography, magnetic resonance imaging, and behaviour studies (Bartels, 2002)).

Some results of recent research on breeding of pet animals are dealing with brachycephaly and respiration difficulties in dogs (Balli, 2004), with deafness in cats (Keller, 1997), with anomalies of crane and brain in crested ducks (Bartels and Wegner, 1998; Bartels, 2002), with the behaviour of plumage care in pigeons (Bartels et al., 1994), and with alterations of eyes in canaries (Steinmetz et al., 2002; Wriedt et al., 2002). Critical aspects, which should be investigated, concern, for example, long hairs in the guinea pig, hamster and dwarf rabbit, impairing probably temperature regulation and fur hygiene, the restriction of locomotion in the gibber canary, special feather forms in canaries, and breeding types in goldfish and telescope fish, which restrict their feeding and locomotion behaviour. Many aspects of extreme breeding types are open for research.

National animal welfare legislations on pet animals

National animal welfare legislations pay little attention to housing and breeding of pet animals. Some countries, such as Germany, Sweden and Switzerland, introduced general articles on breeding. Detailed regulations on housing of small pet and on companion animals are provided in Switzerland. Germany has published several expert reports on housing of pet animals such as birds, parrots, ornamental fish, and on breeding of dogs, cats, rabbits and birds (BMVEL; Expert Group Germany, 2000).

Austria introduced in its new animal welfare law of 2004 (Bundesgesetz Österreich, 2004) the possibility of a type of "label" for housing and other equipment for pet and companion animals. According to Article 18, the Federal Minister of Health and Women is allowed to introduce at ordinance level, rules on labelling of series-produced housing systems and equipment for farm animals and of housing equipment and accessories for pet animals, if the requirements of the animal welfare law are fulfilled. These new and promising rules may in future provide the impetus for many research projects on housing of pet animals, including accessories for these animals.

European Convention for the Protection of Pet Animals

The European Convention for the Protection of Pet Animals includes general rules on keeping, breeding, training, trading, commercial boarding, animal sanctuaries, advertising, entertainment, exhibitions, competitions, surgical operations, killing, reduction of numbers, information and education programmes.

For breeding of pet animals the convention states in Article 5 the following basic principles:

"Any person who selects a pet animal for breeding shall be responsible for having regard to the anatomical, physiological and behavioural characteristics, which are likely to put at risk the health and welfare of either the offspring or the female parent."

The explanatory report of this convention comments on this rule as follows:

"Article 5 lays down the principle that, in the breeding of pet animals, care should be taken by those responsible for the breeding to ensure that the physical and mental health of the offspring and female parent are not put at risk.

In the selection of specimens for breeding, care should be taken to avoid the transmission of behavioural patterns such as abnormal aggressive tendencies and hereditary defects: for example progressive retinal atrophy (leading to blindness), oversized foetal heads (preventing normal birth), and other physical characteristics required by certain breed standards which predispose to clinical conditions such as entropion and soft-plate deformities."

On the basis of this convention and its general rules, an expert committee in the Council of Europe elaborated and adopted in 1995:

a. a resolution on the breeding of pet animals,

b. a resolution on surgical operations in pet animals, and

c. a resolution on wild animals kept as pet animals.[3]

3.
See the Multilateral Consultation of Parties to the European Convention for the Protection of Pet Animals, March 1995, in Strasbourg, Document CONS 125(95) 29, Council of Europe. See also website: www.coe.int/T/E/Leg al_affairs/Legal_coop eration/Biological_ safety%2C_use_of_ animals/Pet/A_texts_ documents.asp#Top OfPage

The resolution concerning breeding provides recommendations for the application and interpretation of the general rules of the convention. It includes detailed descriptions of extreme breed types of dogs and cats, with examples of various breeds, and it asks and encourages breeding associations, including breeders, judges and owners, to reconsider breeding standards, to select the animals not only taking into account aesthetic criteria, but to ensure, by good information and education, the interpretation of breeding standards in a responsible way and to raise public awareness to the breed problems. The resolution, which is not sufficiently widely known and applied, is presented in its full length in Appendix I to this chapter.

As a consequence of this resolution on the breeding of pet animals the parties involved in its elaboration, including four international breeding associations, also agreed on a declaration of intent at the Council of Europe in 1995. It was adopted at the same Multilateral Consultation of Parties to the European Convention for the Protection of Pet Animals on 10 March 1995. The declaration, which is also not sufficiently widely known and applied, is presented in Appendix II to this chapter.

Both the resolution on the breeding of pet animals of the Council of Europe and the declaration of intent emphasise the importance of contributions from several partners, such as breeding associations, breeders, judges and owners, the state and authorities, to improve aspects of animal welfare in breeding.

Appendix I – Resolution on the breeding of pet animals (adopted on 10 March 1995 at the Multilateral Consultation of Parties to the European Convention for the Protection of Pet Animals)

The Parties of the European Convention for the Protection of Pet Animals, by virtue of the terms of reference laid down in Article 15;

Recognising that these terms of reference imply the monitoring of the implementation of the provisions of the Convention and the development of common and co-ordinated programmes in the field of pet animal welfare;

Anxious to encourage full respect of the provisions of the Convention;

Recalling that Article 5 of the Convention provides for a selection of pet animal for breeding which takes account of the anatomical, physiological and behavioural characteristics which are likely to put at risk the health and welfare of either the offspring or the female parent;

Aware that problems are encountered with the implementation of these provisions, in particular with the development of extreme characteristics detrimental to the health and welfare of the animals;

Convinced that these problems are related for a large part to the way breeding standards are formulated and interpreted;

Considering therefore that a revision of these breeding standards is necessary in order to fulfil the requirements of Article 5 of the Convention;

Agreed:

1. to encourage breeding associations, in particular cat and dog breeding associations:

– to reconsider breeding standards in order, if appropriate, to amend those which can cause potential welfare problems, in particular in the light of the recommendations presented in the Appendix;

- to reconsider the standards and to select the animals taking into account not only aesthetic criteria but also behavioural characteristics (for instance with regard to problems of aggressiveness) and abilities;

- to ensure, by good information and education of breeders and judges, that breeding standards are interpreted in such a way as to counteract the development of extreme characteristics (hypertype) which can cause welfare problems;

- to raise public awareness to the problems related to some physical and behavioural characteristics of the animals;

2. if these measures are not sufficient, to consider the possibility of prohibiting the breeding and for phasing out the exhibition and the selling of certain types or breeds when characteristics of these animals correspond to harmful defects such as those presented in the appendix.

Appendix

The Parties are convinced that in the breeding of several breeds or types of pet animals, mammals and birds, insufficient account is taken of anatomical, physiological and behavioural characteristics which are likely to put at risk the animals' health and welfare. However, the Parties considered that problems connected with the breeding of cats and dogs should be addressed in priority.

The Parties strongly encourage cat and dog breeding associations to revise their breeding policies in the light of Article 5 of the Convention taking account in particular of the following guidelines:

Guidelines for the revision of breeding policies

- set maximum and minimum values for height or weight of very large or small dogs, respectively, to avoid skeleton and joint disorders (e.g. dysplasia of hip joints or elbows, fractures, luxation of elbow or patella, persistent fontanella) and collapse of trachea;

- set maximum values for the proportion between length and height of short-legged dogs (e.g. basset hound, dachshund) to avoid disorders of the vertebral column;

– set limits to the shortness of skull, respectively nose, so that breathing difficulties and blockage of lachrymal ducts are avoided, as well as disposition to birth difficulties (e.g. Persian cats, especially the "extreme type", bulldogs, Japan chin, King Charles spaniel, pug, Pekin palacedog);

– prevent the occurrence of:

- a persistent fontanella (e.g. chihuahua) to avoid brain damage;

- abnormal positions of legs (e.g. *very steep line of hind legs* in chow chow, Norwegian buhund, Swedish lapphund, Finnish spitz; *bow legs* in bassethound, Pekin palacedog, shi tzu) to avoid difficulties in movement and joint degeneration;

- abnormal positions of teeth (e.g. brachygnathia in boxers, bulldogs, Persian cats) to avoid difficulties in feeding and caring for the newborn;

- abnormal size and form of eyes or eyelids (e.g. ectropium: basset hound, bloodhound, St Bernard; *small deep lying eyes with disposition to entropium:* Airedale terrier, Australian terrier, Bedlington terrier, bull terrier, bloodhound, chow chow, English toy terrier, jagdterrier, Newfoundland, shar pei; *large, protruding eyes:* Boston terrier, Cavalier King Charles spaniel, Dandie Dinmont terrier, Brussels griffon, Japan chin, King Charles spaniel, pug, Pekin palacedog, shi tzu, Tibet terrier) to avoid irritation, inflammation and degeneration as well as prolapse of eyes;

- very long ears (e.g. English cocker spaniel, basset hound, bloodhound) to avoid disposition to injuries;

- markedly folded skin (e.g. basset hound, bulldog, bloodhound, pug, Pekin palacedog, shar pei) to avoid eczemas and, in the case of furrows around the eyes, irritation and inflammation of eyes;

– avoid or, if it is not possible to eliminate severe defects, discontinued breeding of:

- animals carrying semi-lethal factors (e.g. Entlebucher cattledog);

- animals carrying recessive defect-genes (e.g. homocygotic Scottish fold cat: short legs, vertebral column and tail defects);
- hairless dogs and cats (lack of protection against sun and chill, disposition to significant reduction of number of teeth, semi-lethal factor);
- Manx-cat (movement disorder, disposition to vertebral column defects, difficulties in elimination of urine and faeces, semi-lethal factor);
- cats carrying "dominant white" (significant disposition to deafness);
- dogs carrying "Merle factor" (significant disposition to deafness and eye disorders, e.g.: blue merle collie, merle sheltie, merle corgie, merle bobtail, tigerdogge, tigerteckel).

Appendix II – Declaration of intent
(adopted on 10 March 1995 at the Multilateral Consultation of Parties to the European Convention for the Protection of Pet Animals)

The Parties to the European Convention for the Protection of Pet Animals and the Fédération Cynologique Internationale, the Fédération Internationale Féline, the Governing Council of the Cat Fancy and the World Cat Federation agreed on the need to improve breeding and breeding standards of cats and dogs in accordance with the principles set out in the Convention.

In particular, they agreed:

- to contribute to the improvement of breeding standards, in particular with regard to surgical operations for aesthetic purposes, taking in account the welfare of the animals;

- to promote the respect of these standards by the judges and the breeders;

- to take necessary measures to control the breeding of animals with genetic or phenotypic characteristics harmful to the welfare of the animals in order to prevent suffering of such animals;

- to develop information to the public in order to achieve responsible ownership in accordance with the provisions of the Convention.

Bibliography

Balli, A., "Rhinometrische Parameter bei gesunden Hunden in Abhängigkeit vom radiologisch erfassten Brachycephaliegrad", in *Diss. med. vet.,* Vetsuisse-Fakultät, University of Zurich, 2004.

Banjanin, S. and Mrosovsky, N., "Preferences of mice, *mus musculus,* for different types of running wheel", in *Lab. Anim.* 34, 2000, pp. 313-318.

Bartels, T., Wittig I. and Löhmer R., "Gefiederpflegeverhalten bei Haustauben (columba livia f. dom.)", in *Zool. Anz.* 233, 1994, pp. 175-186.

Bartels, T. and Wegner W., *Fehlentwicklungen in der Haustierzucht,* Enke, Stuttgart, 1998.

Bartels, T., "Hereditary effects and predispositions in exhibition poultry and cage birds – Erbschäden und Dispositionen bei Rassegeflügel und Ziervögeln", in *Habilitationsschrift Vet.-med.,* University of Bern, 2002.

Bechtel, H.B., *Reptile and amphibian variants – Colors, patterns and scales,* Krieger Publishing Co., Malabar, Florida, 1995.

Bhagwanani, S., "Öffentlichkeitsarbeit im Tierschutz in Europa – Der Stand heute und die Bedürfnisse morgen", in *Diss. med. vet.,* University of Bern, Bern, 1995, (Available at: Institut für Genetik, Ernährung und Haltung von Haustieren, Bremgartenstr. 109a, 3001 Bern)

BMVEL, Bundesministerium für Verbraucherschutz, Ernährung und Landwirtschaft, Gutachten über die Mindestanforderungen an die Haltung von Kleinvögeln, Zierfischen, Papageien, Reptilien, www.verbraucherministerium.de

Bundesgesetz über den Schutz der Tiere, Austria, 2004, www.vu-wien.ac.at/vetrecht

Carlstead K., Brown J. and Strawn W., "Behavioural and physiological correlates of stress in laboratory cats", in *Appl. Anim. Behav. Science* 38, 1993, pp. 143-158.

Expert Group Germany, Sachverständigengruppe BML, 2000, "Gutachten zur Auslegung von § 11b des Tierschutzgesetzes",

Bundesministerium für Ernährung, Landwirtschaft und Forsten BML, Rochusstr. 1, D 53107 Bonn, www.bml.de

Falbesaner, U., "Probleme in der Heimtierhaltung – Auswertung von Leseranfragen an eine Tierzeitschrift", in *Diss. med . vet.,* Ludwig-Maximilian University of Munich, 1991.

Fischer, K., "Behaviour of golden hamsters (*Mesocricetus auratus*) kept in four different cage sizes", in *Diss. med. vet.,* Vetsuisse Fakultät, University of Bern, 2005, www.vetmed.unibe.ch

Gebhardt, S., Vonlanthen, E. and Steiger, A., "Brauchen Goldhamster ein Laufrad?", KTBL-Bericht 36., Int. Tagung Angewandte Ethologie in Freiburg. i. Br., 2004, pp. 85-91.

Gebhardt, S., Vonlanthen, E. and Steiger, A., "How does the running wheel affect the behaviour and reproduction of golden hamsters kept as pets?", in *Applied Animal Behaviour Science,* 93, 3, 2005, pp. 199-204.

Hauzenberger, A., "The influence of bedding depth on behaviour in golden hamsters (*Mesocricetus auratus*)", in *Diss. med. vet.,* Vetsuisse Fakultät, University of Bern, 2005, www.vetmed. unibe.ch

Hauzenberger, A., Gebhardt, S. and Steiger A., "The influence of bedding depth on behaviour in golden hamsters (*Mesocricetus auratus*)", in *Appl. Anim. Behav. Sci.,* 2005.

Hollmann, P., "Tierschutzgerechte Unterbringung von Heimtieren – Tips für die Beratung in der Kleintierpraxis", in *Tierärztl. Praxis* 16, 1988, pp. 227-236.

Hollmann, P., "Verhaltensgerechte Unterbringung von Kleinnagern", in *Tierärztl. Umschau* 48,1993, pp. 123-134.

Hollmann, P., "Kleinsäuger als Heimtiere", in Sambraus H.H. and Steiger A. (eds.), *Das Buch vom Tierschutz,* Enke, Stuttgart, 1997, pp. 308-363.

Keller, P., "Untersuchungen zur Entwicklung der frühen akustisch evozierten Potentiale (FEP) bei der Katze für den Einsatz in der Grundlagenforschung und zur klinischen Anwendung", in *Diss. med. vet.,* University of Hanover, 1997.

Kessler, M., "Katzenhaltung im Tierheim – Analyse des Ist-Zustandes und ethologische Beurteilung von Haltungsformen", in *Diss. Naturwissensch.,* ETH Zurich, 1997.

Kummerfeld, N., "Ziervögel", in Sambraus H.H. and Steiger A. (eds.), *Das Buch vom Tierschutz,* Enke, Stuttgart, 1997, pp. 364-380.

McGreevy, P.D. and Nicholas, F.W., "Some practical solutions to welfare problems in dog breeding", in *Animal Welfare* 8, 1999, pp. 329-341.

Mertens, C., "Katze", in Sambraus H.H. and Steiger A. (eds.), *Das Buch vom Tierschutz,* Enke, Stuttgart, 1997, pp. 297-307.

Mrosovsky, N., Salmon, P. A. and Vrang, N., "Revolutionary science: an improved running wheel for hamsters", in *Chronob. Intern.* 15, 1998, pp. 147-158.

Not, I., "Beurteilung verschiedener Zuchtlinien von Ziervögeln, Kleinnagern, Zierfischen und Reptilien in tierschützerischer Hinsicht", in *Diss. med. vet.,* Univ. Zurich, Zurich, 1998, (Abteilung für Zoo-, Heim- und Wildtiere, Winterthurerstr. 268, CH 8057 Zürich, or Institut für Genetik, Ernährung und Haltung von Haustieren, Bremgartenstr. 109a, CH 3001 Bern)

Ott, R., "Animal selection and breeding techniques that create diseased populations and compromise welfare", in *J. American Veterinary Medical Association* 208, 1996, pp.1969-1974.

Peyer, N., "Die Beurteilung zuchtbedingter Defekte bei Rassehunden in tierschützer-ischer Hinsicht", in *Diss. med. vet.,* Univ. Bern, Bern, 1997, (Available at: Institut für Genetik, Ernährung und Haltung von Haustieren, Bremgartenstr. 109a, CH 3001 Bern)

Peyer, N. and Steiger, A., "Die Beurteilung zuchtbedingter Defekte bei Rassehunden in tierschützerischer Hinsicht", in *Schweizer Archiv für Tierheilkunde* 140, 1998, pp. 359-364.

Rochlitz, I., "Comfortable quarters for cats in research institutions", in Reinhardt V. and A. (eds.), *Comfortable quarters for laboratory animals,* pp. 50-55, Animal Welfare Institute, PO Box 3650, Washington DC, 2002, www.awionline.org

Rochlitz, I. (ed.), *The welfare of cats*, Springer, Heidelberg, 2005.

Sachser, N., "Was bringen Präferenztests?", in *KTBL-Bericht 29*. Int. Tagung Angewandte Ethologie 1997 in Freiburg. i. Br., 1998, pp. 9-20.

Schmid, R., "The influence of the breeding method on the behaviour of adult African grey parrots", in *Diss. med. vet.*, Vet-suisse Fakultät, University of Bern, 2004, www.vetmed.unibe.ch

Schmid, R., Steiger A. and Doherr M. G., "Der Einfluss der Auzuchtmethode auf das Verhalten von erwachsenen Grau papageien", *KTBL-Bericht 36*. Int. Tagung Angewandte Ethologie in Freiburg. i. Br., 2004, pp. 99-106.

Schmid, R., Steiger A. and Doherr M.G., "The influence of the breeding method on the behaviour of adult African grey parrots (*Psittacus erithacus*)", in *Applied Animal Behaviour Science*, 98, 1, 2005, pp. 293-307.

Steiger, A., "Informationsquellen und Beratungskonzepte für Heimtierhaltende", Tagungsbericht "Heimtierhaltung – menschliche Motive und Anliegen des Tierschutzes", Tagung Evangelische Akademie Bad Boll, D-73087 Bad Boll, 1999, pp. 117-129.

Steiger A., "Breeding and welfare of cats", in Rochlitz I. (ed.), *The welfare of cats*, Springer, Heidelberg, 2005, pp. 259-276.

Steiger, A., "Tierschutzprobleme in der Heimtierhaltung – was trägt die Forschung bei?", Tagungsbericht DVG-Tagung "Ethologie und Tierschutz", Munich, 2005a.

Steinmetz, A., Krautwald-Junghanns M.-E. and Bartels T., "Vergleichende erste ophthalmologische Untersuchungen des äußeren Auges und zur Sehfähigkeit von Positurkanarienvögeln der Rasse Norwich und Farbkanarienvögeln", in *Tierärztl. Prax.* 30 (K), 2002, pp. 461-466.

Stucki, F., "Die Beurteilung zuchtbedingter Defekte bei Rassegeflügel, Rassetaube, Rassekaninchen und Rassekatzen in tierschützerischer Hinsicht", in *Diss. med. vet.*, University of Bern, 1998, (available at: Institut für Genetik, Ernährung und Haltung von Haustieren, Bremgartenstr. 109a, 3001 CH Bern).

Turner, D. and Bateson P., *The domestic cat – Its biology and behaviour*, Cambridge University Press, Cambridge, 2000.

TVT, "Tierschutzwidriges Zubehör in der Heimtierhaltung", in *Merkblatt* 62, 1998, www.tvt.de

TVT, "Tierschutzwidriges Zubehör in der Hunde- und Katzenhaltung", in *Merkblatt* 70, 1999, www.tvt.de

Unshelm, J., "Animal hygiene in the field of small and companion animals", *Proc. 9th Internat. Congress in Animal Hygiene,* Helsinki, 1997, pp. 811-815.

Unshelm, J.,"Schwerpunkte der tiergerechten Haltung von Heim- und Begleittieren", in Methling W. and Unshelm J. (eds.), *Umwelt- und tiergerechte Haltung von Nutz-, Heim- und Begleittieren,* Parey, Berlin, 2002, pp. 515-524.

Vonlanthen, E., "Einflüsse der Laufradnutzung auf ausgewählte ethologische, morphologische und reproduktionsbiologische Parameter beim Syrischen Goldhamster (*Mesocricetus auratus*)", in *Diss. med. vet.,* Vetsuisse Fakultät, University of Bern, 2003, www.vetmed.unibe.ch

Waiblinger, E., "Comfortable quarters for gerbils in research institutions" in Reinhardt V. and A. (eds.), *Comfortable quarters for laboratory animals,* Animal Welfare Institute, PO Box 3650, Washington DC, 2002, pp. 18-25, www.awionline.org

Waiblinger, E. and König B., "Refinement of pet and laboratory gerbil housing and husbandry", in *KTBL-Bericht* 36. Int. Tagung Angewandte Ethologie in Freiburg. i. Br., 2004, pp. 124-134.

Waiblinger E., "Behavioural stereotypies in laboratory gerbils – causes and solutions", in *Diss. Math.-naturwissensch.,* University of Zurich, 2004.

Wegner, W., "Tierschutzrelevante Missstände in der Kleintierzucht – der §11b des Tierschutzgesetzes greift nicht", in *Tierärztliche Umschau* 48, 1993, pp. 213-222.

Wegner, W., *Kleine Kynologie* (with appendix on cat breeding, Terra Verlag, Konstanz, Germany, 1995, pp. 353-400.

Wegner, W., "Tierschutzaspekte in der Tierzucht", in Sambraus H.H. and Steiger A. (eds.), *Das Buch vom Tierschutz*, Enke, Stuttgart, 1997, pp. 556-569.

Wiedenmayer, C.., "The ontogeny of stereotypies in gerbils", in *Diss. phil. nat.*, University of Zurich, 1995.

Wöhr, C., "Tiergerechte Haltung von Katzen", in Methling W. and Unshelm J. (eds.), *Umwelt- und tiergerechte Haltung von Nutz-, Heim- und Begleittieren*, Parey, Berlin, 2002, pp. 572-595.

Wriedt, A., Hamann H., Distl O., Werner F. and Bartels T., "Häufigkeit von Katarakten und Irisveränderungen bei Japanischen Mövchen (*Lonchura striata [Linnaeus, 1766] f. domestica*)", in *Tierärztl. Prax.* 30 (K), 2002, pp. 220-225.

Religious viewpoints

Buddhism

by Daniel Chevassut

To understand the position of Buddhism on animal rights, we must first take a look at various basic points of Buddhist doctrine: compassion coupled with wisdom, the six realms of existence, non-aggressiveness and the principle of interdependence and of the mandala.

Compassion and wisdom play a decisive part in the attitude to be adopted towards animals. Compassion can be defined as a state of great receptiveness to the suffering of others or as a complete absence of indifference to the suffering of others. It is also a profound and sincere wish that others should be released from their suffering and from the causes that trigger it. Animals, like human beings, possess the Buddha nature. But their mental structure and various physiological and anatomical components do not allow them to achieve it. The Tibetan master Kalu Rimpoche felt great compassion for animals:

> "Mental darkness, attachment, aversion: the three poisons cause them many sufferings. In body and mind, just like us, they experience suffering and fear. However, they have few means of shielding themselves from this and no one thinks of protecting them: their mode of existence is the consequence of a very poor karma[1] accumulated during past lives. So protecting them is an act of great compassion."[2]

It also seems that our lack of wisdom and insight prevents us from understanding all the aspects of reality and the many consequences that may stem from it in ethical terms. This is demonstrated by the story of Katayana, one of the Buddha Shakyamoni's direct disciples:

> "Katayana had reached the state of *arhat* and therefore possessed a number of psychic powers.[3] One day, when he was begging for food, he saw a young woman sitting on her doorstep eating fish. When she had finished her meal, she threw the fishbone to a bitch who was looking out for a bite to eat and shouted to chase her away. Thanks to his powers, Katayana was able to see the karmic ties binding these four beings together: the woman, the baby, the fish and the bitch. The fish was none other than the young woman's father, who

1.
Karma: law of cause and effect.

2.
Paroles et visages de Kalou Rimpotché, Editions Claire Lumière, Eguilles, 1986.

3.
Arhat: who has mastered conflicting emotions and concentration. Psychic powers: the results of contemplative practice: clairaudience, clairvoyance, knowledge of the mind of others, knowledge of beings' births and deaths, etc.

had died a few years earlier. The baby was someone with whom she had had a relationship of mutual hatred and who had also died a few years earlier. As for the bitch, she was the reincarnation of the woman's mother. The woman could not possibly be aware of these relationships. She was far from realising that she was hugging her enemy to her, eating her father and violently rejecting her mother. Katayana exclaimed, "Eating one's father, ill-treating one's mother and cherishing one's enemy, what a strange sight *samsara* is".[4] And he burst out laughing."[5]

Thus, the combination of wisdom and compassion is symbolised in some tantric divinities by the *mudra* of both hands joined on a level with the heart.[6] The other human qualities naturally and spontaneously derive from these first two, including the sense of ethics, of universal responsibility and of solidarity.

As regards the six realms of existence, from a Buddhist point of view, death is an extension of life and simply a change in our level of perception, an entry into unknown territory. We no longer perceive the same things, but we still perceive them with the same mental structure. What is experienced after death is precisely the continuity of the karma accumulated earlier, which then reaches maturity.

Depending on the nature of this karma, rebirth can be experienced in one of the six worlds described by the Buddha: the world of gods (dominant characteristic: pride), the world of jealous gods (jealousy), the world of humans (desire), the world of animals (ignorance), the world of hungry ghosts (craving) and the world of hell (anger). Buddhism thus accepts that it is possible to experience a new form of life in the shape of an animal, due to the unwholesome acts committed in past lives. The great yogi and Buddhist ascetic Milarepa expressed this quite clearly in his songs:

4.
Samsara: the cycle of conditioned lives.

5.
See above, note 2.

6.
Tantric divinities: manifestations of the pure nature of the spirit; *mudra*: a symbolic gesture.

> "Narrow-minded ignorance and dark stupidity
> Lead most fools to rebirth as animals.
> Weighed down by their karma and their unawareness,
> They have no idea of the doctrine, in truth,
> And do not distinguish good from evil.
> As explanation alone is not enough for a sound grasp

Of the karma that leads you to animals,
Train your mind and bend your head."[7]

Lastly, non-aggressiveness means harming neither others (including animals) nor oneself. Interdependence means understanding that our own happiness is bound up with that of other living beings. The word mandala has several meanings. One of them is "centre periphery", in other words the idea that there is always interdependence between a centre and a periphery. To take the case of human beings, it is easy to see that they have an impact on their environment and that the environment has an impact on them: an interactive process links the two in practical terms. Thus, any disturbance to the animal realm affects human beings and vice versa. This is a law of life and a general principle that can be observed in many practical situations. Respecting and protecting animals therefore means respecting and protecting human beings.

To conclude, over and above the ethical approach, I think it is important, and indeed essential, to aim for greater depth in the debate. Besides being entitled to a happy life, animals, just like nature, have the power to make human beings experience "rapture" – in the etymological sense of the word – in which we "forget ourselves"; the superficial part of us disappears, allowing our real nature to show through. At the end of his life, Mircéa Eliade, that great visionary of the 20th century, said he believed the key element of the human condition was the sense of the sacred.[8] Nature and animals have that capacity to connect us to the sacred that lies at the core of our being, a dimension which is so cruelly lacking in today's modern world. So the failure to take care of animals and respect them, and the fact of making them suffer or massacring them for fun or profit, should also be viewed in evolutionary terms: it quite simply amounts to working against the evolution of the human species.

7.
Milarépa, *Les cent mille chants*, Editions Fayard, Paris, 1993.

8.
Mircéa Eliade, *Testament spirituel*, in *Source* No. 17, August 1988.

Catholicism

by Brother Maurizio Pietro Faggioni

The Catholic Church approaches the subject of animals and man's relationship with them from the particular point of view of Christian faith in God, creator of heaven and earth and all that dwells thereon. Everything was created in Christ and through Christ, everything exists for the glory of God, everything exists primarily to show the goodness and beauty of God. Man, as a creature amongst others, was made in the image and likeness of God and that likeness is the foundation of man's dignity and excellence and determines his supremacy on a purely material and biological level.[1] As he has been created in the image of the Lord, man has been given genuine dominion over all created things, but this is a ministerial and participatory dominion, which must be exercised with wisdom and love, and which cannot be disloyal to the will of the Creator whose every work is for the good and who keeps everything in harmony. It is true that creatures have been entrusted to the stewardship of man so that he may make use of them, but man cannot forget that these creatures exist first and foremost for the glory of God and only subsequently to be useful to man.

On this basis, the Catholic moral approach distances itself from two opposing and extreme views of man's relationship with animals. The first is that human and animal life both have equal dignity; the claim that man has special dignity is viewed as unfounded "speciesism" and the use of animals is viewed as illegitimate tyranny by man. At its most radical, this view holds that the instrumental use of animals cannot be justified even by the goal of sustaining human life and safeguarding human health. The other view, deriving from absolute anthropocentrism, holds that animals are objects of nature, devoid of any value, and therefore at the mercy of human arbitrariness, whereby man may use animals at his discretion, in accordance with his own desires and needs, without feeling subject to specific ethical limitations.

1.
See Genesis 1, 26-27.

Man's responsibility

The Catholic view is that animals, as creatures, have their own intrinsic value which man must acknowledge and respect because he, as a free being endowed with reason and placed as the steward of creation, must account to the Creator for everything, including the way he treats animals. The realities of the world are not the fruit of chance and necessity but are a gift; they are the culmination of an absolutely free and transcendent act of creation, motivated by pure love and intended to be fulfilled in love. Which is why the beings that make up the universe do not exist merely as objects, devoid of axiological value, of immanent teleology or of meaning; they are not mere instruments for human designs. The first chapter of Genesis repeats like a refrain, that the works accomplished each day were *tob,* good, in accordance with the purpose of the Almighty who had desired them, and therefore harmonious and beautiful.[2]

2.
See Höver-Johag, I., "*tob*", in *Theologisches Wörterbuch zum Alten Testament*, vol. 3, Stuttgart-Berlin-Köln 1982, col. 315-339 (especially 324). It should be noted that the LXX translated the six occurrences of *tob* in Genesis 1 (4.12.18. 21.25.31) not by *agathòn*, but by *kalòn*.

On the other hand, God placed the animals, together with all other non-human creatures, at the service of man, so that he should, through them, fully develop.[3] The fact that animals should be of service to man, in principle, is not in contrast with the order of creation. On the contrary, this represents for man an opportunity for creative responsibility in making reasonable use of the power which God has given him. "Man is the image of God partly through the mandate received from his Creator to subdue, to dominate, the earth. In carrying out this mandate, man, every human being, reflects the very action of the Creator of the universe".[4] "The dominion granted to man by the Creator is not an absolute power, nor can one speak of a freedom to 'use and misuse,' or to dispose of things as one pleases. The limitation imposed from the beginning by the Creator himself and expressed symbolically by the prohibition not to 'eat of the fruit of the tree'[5] shows clearly enough that, when it comes to the natural world, we are subject not only to biological laws but also to moral ones, which cannot be violated with impunity".[6] This, therefore, is the deeper meaning of man's domination vis-à-vis the created universe: not to reduce creatures to demeaning slavery, but to guide them through responsible action, the life he leads and that of what has been created,

3.
See Genesis 1, 26-28; Psalm 8, 7-9.

4.
John Paul II, Encyc. *Laborem exercens*, 14-12-1981, No. 4.

5.
See Genesis 2, 16-17.

6.
John Paul II, Encyc. *Sollicitudo rei socialis*, 30-12-1987, No. 34.

towards the fulfilment of God's design of love for the world. "To defend and promote life, to show reverence and love for it, is a task which God entrusts to every man, calling him as His living image to share in His own lordship over the world".[7]

Man, in using animals, must acknowledge the goodness of animal life and look after the welfare of the creatures which serve his existence, and with even greater attention when it comes to animals higher up on the zoological scale and, therefore, closer to him as regards the ability to feel pain and anxiety, to have interests and, above all, to have some degree of self-awareness. Even though animals may not be moral agents in so far as they are in essence devoid of the abilities normally acknowledged for such agents, especially freedom, they can be included in the category of moral patients, and can be treated justly or unjustly by moral agents. In Catholic bioethics, sensitive to the rights of the small and the weak, the category of moral patients is much vaster than that of moral agents: nobody, for example, would consider according less protection to the life and dignity of a person who has suffered brain damage or a foetus simply because they do not have the ability to act morally, since they are both an ethical centre, a moral subject. Once we have made the requisite distinctions and without losing sight of the intangible value of human existence, we can undoubtedly enlarge our moral consideration to encompass animal life. *Moral duty is not linked to the other's ability to express or defend his/her own interests, but to our ability to respond to the appeal, often unspoken, which emerges from his/her existence.*

These fundamental principles guide our behaviour towards animals: the use and even the sacrifice of animals may be justified, but only if necessary for the substantial good of mankind not attainable in any other way. Man therefore has the right to make use of animals for food, work, clothing, but must avoid unnecessary suffering and pointless slaughter of the animals he is rearing and which labour alongside and help sustain him. Man can avail himself of the company of animals and involve them in sport and recreation, but always with due regard for the characteristic behavioural patterns, dignity and well-being of the various animals. Man, as custodian of creation, must respect and look after wildlife, limit senseless

7.
John Paul II, Encyc. *Evangelium Vitae*, 25-3-1995, No. 42.

hunting and fishing, not endanger through his behaviour, the delicate environmental balance, but strive to preserve natural habitats and endangered species. Man can make use of animals for research and experiments when this is genuinely necessary; he can avail himself of them with all due caution as sources of organs and tissues for transplants; he may even genetically modify animals to improve their characteristics for lawful purposes, but always with due regard for the quality and dignity of animal life. Here too, Catholic ethics, contrary to the view so typical of modern times of science seeking to control nature and contrary to the myth of progress at any cost or price, puts forward the idea of science for the whole good of the person, which cannot be divorced from the good of those creatures that co-exist with us on this planet and which the Creator has placed in our custody.

The archetypal example of Saint Francis of Assisi, quite rightly proclaimed patron saint of ecologists, clearly expresses the Christian ideal of the relationship with the natural world, and especially animals. Saint Francis regards the animals as brothers and sisters, created by one and the same Father, invites them to praise God, and freed from any yearning for possession or exploitation, looks at them with a renewed heart. He is the model of a man who:

> "redeemed by Christ and made a new creature in the Holy Spirit, man is able to love the things themselves created by God, and ought to do so. He can receive them from God and respect and reverence them as flowing constantly from the hand of God. Grateful to his Benefactor for these creatures, using and enjoying them in detachment and liberty of spirit, man is led forward into a true possession of them, as having nothing, yet possessing all things. 'All are yours, and you are Christ's, and Christ is God's.' "[8]

8.
Second Vatican Ecumenical Council, Pastoral Constitution. *Gaudium et Spes*, No. 37.

Islam

by Raoutsi Hadj Eddine Sari Ali

> "No creature is there crawling on the earth, no bird flying with
> its wings, but they are nations like unto yourselves. We have
> neglected nothing in the Book; then to their Lord they shall be
> gathered."
>
> Koran, 6, 38

Ever since the 7th century Koranic teaching has been one of
the driving forces behind the development of natural sciences
among Arabs and in the Islamic lands in general. This teaching
describes animals as *ummas* (translated as "nations"), which
means that Arabs developed genuine empathy towards these
creatures, to which the Creator attributes the soul and conscience of an *umma*. The *umma* is more than just a nation, in
the usual meaning of the word. It is the essential (*umm* =
essence) relationship among individuals, which necessitates
awareness of others and responsibility towards them. Furthermore, the Koran teaches[1] that the heavens, minerals and vegetables all participate in the needful harmony of lives on earth:

> "It is incumbent upon man, as he himself has demanded, to
> keep watch over knowledge and fairness in safeguarding this
> harmony, for generations have vanished because of their cor-
> ruption ... corruption has appeared in the land and the sea on
> account of what the hands of men have wrought."[2]

This means that the believer has an attitude of complete
respect for all creatures, without any preconceptions, which
duty is in fact decreed by the Prophet in laying down the obligation of knowledge.[3] The responsibility of a human being
endowed with *aql* and *rouh*, that is to say reason and spirit, lies
in his capacity for impairing his nature through passion, exal-
tation of the ego or *nefs*. The consequences of such degrada-
tion by human acts are disasters on a local or even global scale,
as in the "butterfly effect" described by the great master Rumi
in his "Methnawi". The Koran teaches that Moses (Musa)
invited his people to eat and drink of the provisions of the
earth, although he added "do not act corruptly in the land,
making mischief";[4] the twelve sources of knowledge are the

1.
Koran, 16, 3-18; 22,
18.

2.
Koran 7, 172; 33, 72;
24, 40-45; 30, 22; 41.

3.
Koran, 10, 36-39.

4.
Koran, 2, 60.

five sensory organs, the five cerebral areas corresponding to these organs, desire and will (Ibn Arabi). All good fortune that befalls you comes from the Creator; and all adversity that strikes you comes from yourself.[5]

Attar, a 13th century author who gained renown for his famous "Conference of the Birds", or "*Mantiq O Tayr*", stresses the harmony of creation, the *Qaf-Tuba-Simorg* triad. *Qaf* is the mountain, which is capable of reacting to damage caused by human beings and of moving, even though the ignorant suppose them fixed".[6] *Tuba* is the ecological habitat of the human being, the necessary return to an awareness of his environment.[7] *Simorg* is the bird through which life continues on earth, a symbol of airborne winged beings, angels, or elevation.

The Prophet taught that plants should be considered as our kith and kin, because "your aunt the palm-tree was begotten of the clay of Adam ..." (Bokhari). According to a tradition reported by Al-Jâhiz, Solomon spoke with the flowers of the Temple.

Belief and science: animals and wisdom

The geographical extension of Arabian Islam into Persia, India, China, Africa and the Mediterranean led to acculturation and the development of canon (Sharia) law jurisprudence. The ways and customs of the various Muslim peoples have in fact always absorbed their own traditional beliefs unless they stood in formal contradiction to Islamic morality, or *ihsàn*, as has been demonstrated by the historians and geographers El Bekri, Ibn Battuta and Ibn Khaldun. Thus the popular beliefs concerning animals as conveyed by the epics, myths and legends of the Muslim peoples from the 7th century to the present day have been echoed in the verses of the Koran and the words of the Prophet. From the dove as the harbinger of peace (the end of Noah's Flood) to the men who were changed into apes for flouting the Law,[8] all the extant examples show animals participating in every sphere of the human being's terrestrial life.

The Bedouins' knowledge of desert or steppe ecosystems was a major factor in the acculturation of nomads and settled peoples in Africa and Asia: animals as remedies, adornments,

5.
Koran, 2, 79; 99, 1-8.

6.
Koran, 50, 1-45.

7.
Koran, 42, 25-42.

8.
Those exceeding the limits of the Sabbath, Koran, 2, 65 and 66.

companions, guardians, sources of food, mounts, or even examples of moral conduct (the raven in the Koranic version of the crime of Cain shows the latter that he has a duty to bury his brother Abel by scratching earth to cover a dead raven).[9] Ibn Tufayl, who was Averroës' master, expands on this in "*Hayy Ibn Yaqzàn*": the child raised by a gazelle; the spider which secures protection by spinning a web at the entrance to the cave in which the Prophet and Abu Kekr have taken refugee from the Mecca idolaters;[10] the toad which is protected because it put out the fire on to which Abraham had been cast; Solomon entrusting the hoopoe with messages of peace for the Queen of Sheba and respecting the ants which he hears fleeing the horses' hooves;[11] four birds symbolising human nature (peacock = self-satisfaction; cockerel = sense of duty done; raven = moral sense; dove = desire for peace) were analysed and trained to follow Abraham in order to soothe his mind (life is accepting oneself as one is).[12] These examples have been incorporated into the oral traditions of Muslim peoples worldwide.

The famous treatises by Al-Jâhiz and Damiry in the 8th and 14th centuries develop a holistic approach to animal behaviour, dealing with all the aspects of evolution, adaptation and animal psychology. Another equally famous book, *Kalila and Dimna* written by Ibn Muqaffa in Baghdad in the 8th century, was a work on which La Fontaine largely drew for his *Fables*. Suyuti's *The Medicine of the Prophet*, written in the 15th century, shows the importance of animals in medication: the use of cowpats or *alyah* as a poultice for treating sciatica, grasshoppers as a source of protein, butter, milk and many more examples besides, encouraged this empathy with animals.

Sharia law and animals

Islam urges believers to act with the Last Judgment in mind. Each act is written in a book *(mektoub)* which the human being will present on that day. In terms of justice, an act is primarily defined in accordance with the underlying intention *(nya)*; scientific acts designed to improve life are in conformity with the Creator's will.[13] Muslim scientists do not consider themselves

9.
Koran, 5, 30-32.

10.
Koran, 9, 40.

11.
Koran, 27, 17-22.

12.
Commentary by Ibn Arabi, Koran, 2, 260; 26.

13.
Koran, 2, 225 and 255.

as creators when they work on genes, as this would be blasphemous; they are aware of changing things for the better with tools placed at their disposal, an ability granted by the Creator, as exemplified by Noah.[14] Al-Jâhiz stresses the process of natural changes in creatures.

To both Shiah and Sunni Muslims, the Sharia is based essentially on the Koran and the words of the Prophet *(hadith)*, and this has led to a legal consensus on non-political subjects. Bokhari reports that the Prophet spoke of two cases of duties and rights vis-à-vis animals: a very pious person was condemned for refusing to feed a cat, while another person of loose morals was admitted to Paradise for drawing water from a well to quench a dog's thirst. Caliph Omar sentenced an unscrupulous road mender to a severe penalty for leaving sharp stones scattered on a road, because this was liable to injure load-bearing mules. Abu Huraira, one of the ten companions of the Prophet, was known among people as "Abu Hurrah" ("the kitten's father") because he tore off a strip of his coat for a cat when it settled on it to kitten.

Sacrificing animals, namely sheep, cows, camels, etc. requires compassion and gentleness: the main preconditions for producing consumable *(hallal)* meat are avoiding undue stress or suffering for the animal, cleansing it ritually and meticulously positioning it in the direction of Mecca. The Koran explains that in Abraham's sacrifice the flesh is not supposed to be offered up to Allah,[15] it is no offering; rather, according to Ibn Arabi's commentary, the act symbolises the sacrifice of the ego, the father's secret son, as epitomised by Abraham. This is *hosion* (from the Greek *hosios, teqwa* in Arabic), that is, reverential piety.

One of the reasons for the disappearance of the troglodytic Thamud people of Arabia was their cruel ill-treatment of camels: they mutilated and starved them and refused to share their water with them[16] (manipulations of animals for man's pleasure are condemned, although genetic manipulation is permitted if it constitutes a "good deed").[17]

14.
Koran, 9, 36-39.

15.
Koran, 22, 37.

16.
Koran, 26, 141-159; 15, 82; 11, 64; 7, 77; 7, 56 and 85; Koranic prohibition: 4, 119.

17.
Koran, 4, 122-125.

So the rights of animals are part of an ethical system *(ihsàn)* embracing human rules of conduct vis-à-vis all creatures, whereby the Sharia considers corruption of ecosystems as a crime against humanity: "civilisations were exterminated because *mufsidyn fi el ard*".[18]

18.
Koran, 2, 27 and 60; 5, 33, 64 and 85; 7, 56 and 74; 26, 101 and 102; 47, 22.

Bibliography

Attar, *Mantiq O Tayr,* Sindbad, Paris, 1970.

Bekri, *L'Afrique septentrionale,* translation De Slane, Maisonneuve, Paris, 1965.

Bokhari, *Les traditions islamiques,* translation O. Houdas , Volume IV, Maisonneuve Paris,1977.

Coran, translation and commentary, H. Boubeker, Fayard, Paris, 1985.

Hadj Eddine Sari Ali, Raoutsi, "Evaluation sous l'angle de la morale musulmane", in *Ethique et médecine des catastrophes,* Editions du Conseil de l'Europe, Strasbourg, 2002, pp. 73-81.

Hossein Nasr, Sciences et savoir en Islam, Sindbad, Paris, 1979.

Ibn Ajiba, *Autobiographie,* translation J-L. Michon, Ed. Arché, Milan, 1982.

Ibn Arabi, *La sagesse des prophètes,* translation T. Burkhardt, Albin Michel, Paris, 1974.

Ibn Battuta, *Voyages,* translation C. Defremery, Maspéro, Paris, 1982.

Ibn al-Muqaffa, *Kalila et Dimna,* translation A. Miquel, Ed. Klincksiek, Paris, 1980.

Ibn Tufayl, *Hayy bin Yaqzàn,* translation L. Gauthier, Ed. Papyrus, Paris, 1983.

Jàhiz, *Anthologie du Livre des animaux,* translation L. Souami, Sindbad, Paris, 1988.

Rumi, *Le Methnawi,* translation Eva de Vitray, Sindbad, Paris, 1998.

Suyúti, *La médecine du Prophète,* Ed. Al Bustane, Paris, 1997.

Judaism

by Albert Guigui

Jewish law lays down the principle, of divine origin, that animals must not be made to suffer. This prohibition is to be found in the Talmud, expressed in the following terms: "It is forbidden, as a Torah precept, to cause pain to animals."[1]

Not only must animals not be beaten, but, like human beings, they are entitled to a weekly rest. "Six days shalt thou labour and do all thy work. But the seventh day is the sabbath of the Lord thy God: in it thou shalt not do any work, thou, ... nor thy cattle ...."[2] "Six days thou shalt do thy work, and on the seventh day thou shalt rest, that thine ox and thine ass may rest ..."[3]

It is forbidden to inflict any kind of suffering on animals. The Scriptures add "Thou shalt not plough with an ox and an ass harnessed together"[4] this is because their paces and their strengths are different and one animal will tire more than the other. "Thou shalt not muzzle the ox when he treadeth out the grain",[5] in other words the ox has a right to eat the corn that it is threshing for human consumption, and it would be cruel to whet the animal's appetite without satisfying it.

Relieving the suffering of animals is also compulsory. "Thou shalt not see thy brother's ass or his ox fall down by the way, and hide thyself from them: thou shalt surely help him to lift them up again."[6]

It is also forbidden to remove birds from the nest.[7]

When a calf, a lamb or a goat is born, it must be left with its mother for seven days.[8] Nor must an animal and its young be slaughtered on the same day.[9] According to Maimonides, this rule is designed to spare the mother's feelings, since animals are attached to their young to the same extent as human beings.[10]

Humans must not eat their own meal before having fed their animals.[11] A heart-rending tale shows how Jews apply this principle in practice. In a station in Slovakia a train was stopped on the tracks en route for Auschwitz. From the window of one of

1.
Shabbat 128b; Baba Metsia 36b.

2.
Exodus XX, 10

3.
Exodus XXIII, 12

4.
Deuteronomy XXII, 10

5.
Deuteronomy XXV, 4.

6.
Deuteronomy XXII, 4

7.
Deuteronomy XXII, 6-7.

8.
Leviticus XXII, 27.

9.
Leviticus XXII, 28.

10.
Guide of the Perplexed, III, 48.

11.
Deuteronomy XI, 15 reads first "And I will give grass in thy fields for thy cattle [and only second] and thou shalt eat and be full."

the wagons full of men and women condemned to die a voice called out. It was a man saying to a friend on the platform: "I left some chickens in the house. They've had nothing to eat since this morning. Do me a big favour and go to feed and water them. It is forbidden to make them suffer." No comment.

It is a religious duty to rescue an animal that has suffered an accident or is in danger. When an animal has fallen into a ditch and cannot easily be lifted out, it should be brought food and drink and bedding.[12]

An animal's tail must not be cut off, since that prevents the animal from chasing away the flies and thus causes it to suffer.[13]

The same considerations underlie the Talmudic prohibition on hunting.

The Jewish religion also expressly prohibits castration.[14]

Moses and his sheep

The Talmud also emphasises these tenets of the Torah. Two stories are instructive in this connection.

One day, while looking after a flock of sheep, Moses followed a runaway lamb, which on reaching a stream stopped to drink. "I didn't know you ran away because you were thirsty," said Moses, "now you must be tired.". And he hoisted the lamb onto his shoulders to carry it back to the flock. God then said to him "Because you showed compassion in tending the flock in your care, you truly deserve to become the shepherd of Israel."[15]

The Talmud also tells a story about Rabbi Yehuda HaNasi,[16] who was on his way to the slaughterhouse. A calf that had escaped ran up to him and hid under his cloak. But the rabbi pushed it away saying "Go to your destiny." Shortly afterwards the rabbi fell ill, and the doctors could not cure him. Some time later a servant was cleaning his room and found a nest of white mice under his sickbed. She wanted to kill them, but the rabbi said "Let them live." From that point on the rabbi recovered completely.[17]

12.
Shabbat, 128b.

13.
Sefer Hasidim, 589.

14.
Even Ha-ezer, V, 14.

15.
Midrash, Shemoth Rabba, LXXXII.

16.
135-220.

17.
Baba Metsia, 85a.

Hasidic literature follows in the footsteps of the Talmudic writings.

It tells how Rabbi Naftali Tzvi Berlin, the author of the Haemek Davar, came home from the synagogue on the day of Rosh Hashanah, when he had fasted as required by tradition. Despite his hunger, he waited until the chickens had been fed before sitting down to eat.

Some fundamental rules

It goes without saying that, in Judaism, any law that may improve an animal's quality of life is desirable and approved. Technical advances that may relieve animals' suffering or prevent unnecessary pain and distress have been adopted in our slaughterhouses, particularly regarding methods of restraint.

That is also why slaughter according to the religious rite is performed solely by a *shohet*,[18] who, apart from having the necessary theoretical and practical knowledge, must also display moral qualities, even to the point of feeling scruples.

After several years' study in a Talmudic school a student with a sound theoretical grounding may decide, as a specialisation, to undergo training as a *shohet*, which lasts two years on average and is dispensed by a qualified fellow scholar. During this period he learns the theory and practice of slaughter. He is required to perform a number of practice killings and to learn to sharpen the knife and must not lose his self-control when shedding the animal's blood. When the teacher considers that the pupil is sufficiently skilful, the latter undergoes a theoretical and practical examination before a rabbinical tribunal, made up of three rabbis. If he passes, he is issued with a diploma, authorising him to become a practising slaughterer. He is required to revise the theoretical rules throughout his career and is also subject to stringent supervision by the rabbi of the community he serves. The probity of the *shohet*, as shown by his moral and religious conduct, must also be verified. In view of the responsibilities incumbent on him, his behaviour must be beyond criticism.

18.
Ritual slaughterer.

There are many laws on the slaughtering of animals according to the religious rite. These govern, *inter alia*, the choice of the slaughterer, his appointment, the required qualities, the choice of the instrument,[19] and the operating method.[20] The *shohet* must be a man in good health and in full possession of his physical capacities. In particular, he must not suffer from nervous trembling of the hands, so as to ensure that his movements will be swift and sure.

Animals are slaughtered by being cut across the throat with a knife whose blade is razor-sharp and perfectly even. The quick stroke inflicted, without hesitation and without exerting pressure on the large vessels, makes the method virtually painless and causes a massive haemorrhage, ensuring complete drainage of the blood, and cerebral anaemia, leading to unconsciousness and total loss of the capacity to feel pain within a few seconds. Many medical authorities consider that *shechitah* (or ritual slaughter) is the fastest method of removing conscious life. The effectiveness of the traditional, non-ritual method, using a bolt gun to stun the animal, depends on the point of impact and the angle of entrance, and accordingly on the slaughterer's skills. If only the cortex or the brain's motor centre is destroyed, the animal's limbs will be paralysed but it will remain conscious. In view of the profitability criteria to be met, doubts subsist as to whether the animal is systematically rendered unconscious.

Furthermore, anyone who has cut themselves deeply with a very sharp object (a razor blade, a sheet of paper or a blade of grass for instance) will agree that the pain is felt only some time later. Sometimes we notice that we are hurt only on seeing or feeling the blood or when a third party brings the injury to our attention. The knife used in ritual slaughter is extremely sharp, without the slightest nick or unevenness, and is moreover honed and handled by an expert, who inflicts a stroke without any superfluous pressure. No pain can therefore be felt during the first six to ten seconds, after which the animal is already unconscious. What is more, after two seconds hypoxia sets in, and from that point on the animal is already scarcely conscious.

19.
The knife used must be particularly sharp, and its blade must not be nicked. "The point and both edges of the knife must be tested with the finger and nail." (Hullin, 17b).

20.
The killing takes one or two seconds, and the blood flow is at first abundant before gradually decreasing.

What do the scientists say?

We attach considerable importance to scientists' opinion, since it is objective and disinterested.

In 1978, Professor Schultz measured the brain activity of two groups of sheep and calves slaughtered according to the two different methods. When the *shechitah* method was used, brain activity dropped to zero level after 13 seconds in the case of the sheep and 23 in the cattle, compared with respectively 10 or more and 28 seconds for animals slaughtered after stunning.[21]

In 1982 Dr Alain Koginski of the French National Veterinary School in Maisons-Alfort reported that adrenaline and glycaemia – both signs of stress – were lower in animals killed by throat cutting than in those slaughtered after being stunned.[22]

During ritual slaughter the vagal nerve is severed, which speeds up the heart beat, with the result that the blood drains away faster and more completely. The blood flow to the cells is accordingly quickly cut off.[23]

The opinion expressed in 1991 by Professor R. Dantzer, director of the neurobiology laboratory of the French agricultural research institute, INRA, can also be cited:[24]

> "The debate on the possible suffering caused by ritual slaughter must be resituated in a more pragmatic context, that of the efforts made by the competent authorities to improve slaughtering conditions, and in particular restraint of animals, while respecting the rite. This is a field where technological progress allows significant improvements, beneficial for both the animal and the slaughterer, in the short term.
>
> In sum, there are no serious scientific grounds for the position regarding ritual slaughter adopted by certain members of the Veterinary Scientific Committee, which is not conducive to the efforts currently being made to improve conditions while observing religious requirements. One is accordingly tempted to view this as a stratagem, serving objectives that are not humanitarian in nature."

21.
See Fison, B., "L'abattage rituel: une garantie incomparable" published in *Le Cachère Magazine*", No. 57, pp. 44-45.

22.
Ibid.

23.
Ibid.

24.
Veterinary doctor, doctor of science, head of the INRA neurobiology laboratory and member of the European Commission's Veterinary Scientific Committee.

Orthodox Church

by Alexandre M. Stavropoulos

The general position of the Orthodox Church on the protection of nature in general, and animals in particular, is rooted in the commandment originally given man by God, who, in creating him "took the man, and put him into the Garden of Eden to dress it and to keep it".[1] Of course, Adam's naming of the animals may seem to imply human domination of animals and the world: "... have dominion over every living thing that moveth upon the earth".[2] However, protecting and conserving the Creation and all creatures is also part of this commandment.

In the story of the Flood, Noah also protects and perpetuates the species in a special way, by saving two of each kind, so that they can reproduce when the waters subside ("And they went in unto Noah into the ark, two and two of all flesh, wherein is the breath of life").[3]

The rules embodied in the Old and New Testaments are concerned with human welfare, but they also take a benevolent view of animals. This appears in the rules on keeping the Sabbath: most normal activities are prohibited – but caring for animals and watering them are excepted. The Sabbath was made for animals too, not animals for the Sabbath!

Obviously, man's harmonious relationship with animals and nature was disturbed when his "first disobedience" disrupted his relationship with God.[4] It is true that he sacrificed animals to God as an act of expiation (the "scapegoat", symbolically loaded with the sins of the people and driven into the desert, is one example)[5] – but God's indirect aversion to sacrifices, including animal sacrifices, appears when He declares that "mercy, and not sacrifice"[6] is what He wants of man, for "the sacrifices of God are a broken spirit and a contrite heart".[7] A 7th-century saint, Isaac the Syrian, tells us that a "merciful heart" is "a heart which burns for the entire creation, that is, for men, birds, animals and demons, and every creature".[8]

1.
Genesis 2, 15.

2.
Genesis 1, 28; 2, 19.

3.
Genesis 7, 15.

4.
Genesis 3, 17-18.

5.
Leviticus 16, 10.

6.
Matthew 9, 13.

7.
Psalm 51, 17.

8.
Discourse 81.

Most important of all is a "clean heart",[9] that is, steadfast sense that man was created in the image of God and in His likeness, and acquires it through ascetic living and sanctity.

The Orthodox Church looks to this sanctity to restore the troubled relationship between nature, animals and man. Our tradition tells us of men who, having achieved a harmonious relationship with God, achieve an equally harmonious relationship with animals (particularly wild animals) and are able to speak to them, tame them and make them serve them. The animals respond admirably.[10]

We have a whole series of examples: Saint Gerassimos, who lived close to the River Jordan (4 March), Saint Copris (24 September), Saint Aninas the Wonder Worker (16 March), Saint Luke (6 November), Saint Makarios the Roman (23 October), Saint Eleutheria (15 December).

At the time of the great persecutions and at other times when the Church came under attack, some animals even refused to obey their masters' orders and harm the martyrs. For example, Saint Alexander the Martyr, Archbishop of Jerusalem (12 December) was sentenced to death and thrown to the wild beasts, but they, instead of devouring him, prostrated themselves in veneration before him! The lives of the martyrs Artemon (24 March) and Zoticos (31 December) offer similar examples. In those cases, the animals spoke and rebuked the executioners "by God's order".

The lives of the saints, and particularly those contained in the official liturgical books of the Church, contain a host of such examples.

These stories are presented to the faithful as examples of the exceptional favours which God's grace may occasionally bestow on human beings – but the Church also has many saints who, during their lives, treated animals with special kindness and cared for them. These are the saints whom it has chosen as the patron saints of animals, and whom it honours on special occasions and on their feast days.

Examples include Saint Modestos, Archbishop of Jerusalem (16 December) and Saint Mamas the Martyr (2 September), whose

9.
Psalm 51, 10.

10.
All the stories from the lives of the saints and the names mentioned in this article are taken from the "Synaxaristis", a compendium of the lives of the saints ("synaxaria"), which are read when the Christian community gathers to honour a martyr or a saint. Most of these "lives" are also contained in the Minaia – the books giving the offices for the saints of each month. There are several editions. In what follows, the date of the saint's feast is given in brackets after his/her name.

prayers for animals – even sick animals – and blessings for flocks are included in the Orthodox missal.

At Assi Gonia on the island of Crete, shepherds still assemble with their flocks before the Church of Saint George on his feast day (23 April), and are blessed by the parish priest. Also typical is the ceremony which takes place at a monastery on Mount Athos on the feast of Saint Modestos: when the holy office has been recited, all the monastery's mules file past the chapel door, and the priest sprinkles them with holy water. When a new mule arrives at the monastery, the monk who has charge of it presents it to the prior, who blesses it by making the sign of the cross over it and gives it a name (not, however, a Christian name!) – an action which recalls the naming of the animals by the first man, Adam.[11] The strange thing is that, from that moment on, the animal answers only to that name.

The same benevolence towards animals is reflected elsewhere too: for example, canon law forbids the bringing of animals into churches, except in cases of great danger (storms, etc.), when a man may take shelter there with his beast.[12] If he does so otherwise, he – and not the animal – is punished.

We may also note that, although canon law punishes humans who have sexual congress with animals,[13] the animal is not put to death, as provided for in the Old Testament,[14] or punished in any other way. Nor are animals judged in court, as reported in other traditions.

Two crucial and sensitive points which must be mentioned are the use of animals for scientific research (laboratory animals), and hunting. To my knowledge at least, the Orthodox Church has no fixed doctrine on either. This is not to say that the Church may favour the uncontrolled use of laboratory animals, even in research designed to protect human health. The time has come for humans to face up to their responsibilities in this area, and stop seeing themselves as the centre of creation. Animals also have rights – and humans themselves are the threat to nature today.

As for hunting, I remember how strongly one of our contemporary spiritual fathers, Father Porphyrios, urged me to propose a restriction or even a ban on hunting to a minister of

11.
Genesis 2, 19.

12.
88th Canon of the Ecumenical Council of 692 AD (the Concilium Quinisextum).

13.
7th Canon of Basil the Great, 4th Canon of Saint Gregory of Nyssa.

14.
Leviticus 20, 15-16.

agriculture, declaring that "taking innocent lives for mere amusement's sake is irresponsible".

The Church still protects animals today. A special prayer of blessing has even been composed for those who love animals, celebrating their devotion to them. It will be sent, as an example to be followed, to all the international animal welfare associations.[15]

In conclusion, we can say that the position of the Christian churches in general, and the Orthodox Church in particular, is summed up in the bold symbolic image of Jesus Christ as Lamb of God. He unshrinkingly takes upon himself the fate of all those who cannot defend or protect themselves – a fate illustrated by that of the innocent lambs – and identifies with them. But he also portrays himself as the Good Shepherd, speaking out, amid the silence of the lambs, as Lord and Protector, upholding the rights of all creatures and willing their protection.

At all events, we must read or reread the ecclesiastical texts which deal with animal protection and welfare, since this will help to dispel any misunderstandings which may come between us and a sound bioethical grasp of past and present issues in this area.

15.
This prayer was composed by the present Archbishop of Athens and All Greece, Monsignor Christodoulos, when he was Metropolitan of Volos in 1988.

Bibliography

Christinaki-Glarou, I.P., *The ecclesiastical crime of bringing an animal into a temple,* Athens, 2002 (in Greek).

Psariotis, T., *The natural environment in Orthodox belief,* with a preface by A.M. Stavropoulos, Grigori, Athens, 2001 (in Greek).

Psariotis, T., *Ecological synaxarion,* Tinos, Athens, 2001 (in Greek).

Stavropoulos, A.M., "Animal stories", two articles published in the journal, *O Ephimerios* (The parish priest), Athens, 1992, pp. 376-378; 1998, pp. 128-130 (in Greek).

Protestantism

by Karsten Lehmküler

> *"A righteous man regardeth the life of his beast [...]"*
>
> Proverbs 12, 10
>
> *"And God said, Let us make man in our image, after our likeness: and let them have dominion over the fish of the sea, and over the fowl of the air, and over the cattle, and over all the earth, and over every creeping thing that creepeth upon the earth."*
>
> Genesis 1, 26

Theological thinking on animal rights is based on two major principles:

- Animals, like human beings, are God's creatures. This status confers dignity on animals and requires human beings to protect them from all forms of ill-treatment.

- Only human beings are created in God's image. The consequence of this special destiny is that when an ethical conflict arises and interests are weighed up, human beings take precedence over animals.

The dignity of animals

The dignity of animals, the duty to protect them and the prohibition of all forms of cruelty to animals should be obvious rules for Christian ethics.

The Bible bears witness to the dignity of animals in its very first pages: after creating animals, God brings them to Adam so that he may name them. This naming of animals by Man admittedly demonstrates the superiority of human beings. At the same time, however, this act includes a close relationship between human and other living beings – a relationship which also makes human beings responsible for their fellow-creatures. The legislation of the people of Israel, which expressly provides for the good of animals,[1] lends further weight to this view. Profound respect for animals is particularly apparent in biblical passages about the future fate of the world: the

1.
See Exodus 20, 10; 23, 11; Deuteronomy 25, 4.

prophet Isaiah envisions a world in which human beings and animals will be able to live in peace,[2] and the Apostle Paul states in his Epistle to the Romans[3] that "the creature" will be delivered from corruption.

A number of 20th century Protestant theologians paid special attention to animals in ethics and theological doctrine, foremost among them Karl Barth and Albert Schweitzer. In his famous *Dogmatics*, Karl Barth, the theologian from Basle, criticises anthropocentrism and its derogatory approach to other creatures. In the creation he distinguishes between an inner circle (human beings) and an outer circle (other creatures). We are not in a position to assert that the outer circle exists only for the benefit of the inner circle, he says. "How do we know that these two sectors do not each have their own autonomy and value and their specific way of existing with God?"[4] In any case, animals can be regarded as human beings' "companions",[5] and as a result of this status, human beings have an ethical duty to animals. Albert Schweitzer's ethics of "respect for life" particularly implies respect for animal life. Albert Schweitzer criticises the omission of animals from the history of ethics:

> "Just as a housewife who has just cleaned her room makes sure to shut the door properly for fear the dog might rush in with its dirty paws and spoil her work, European thinkers also make sure that no animals disrupt their ethics."[6]

He therefore advocates ethical devotion to all forms of life, which entails completely eliminating all animal suffering. In cases where taking an animal's life is put across as an "unavoidable sacrifice", Albert Schweitzer first requires us to ask ourselves whether such damage to the animal is truly necessary. If such cases exist, it is essential to ensure that the animal's suffering is reduced to an absolute minimum.

The difference between human beings and animals

As human beings are created in God's image, human life is untouchable.[7] The same cannot be said of animals. The difference becomes clear when the issue of active euthanasia is raised: the great majority of ethicists oppose the active putting to death of a human nearing the end of his or her life. Con-

2.
Isaiah 11, 6-9.

3.
Romans 8, 19-21.

4.
Barth, Karl, *Dogmatique*, III, 2 (1), Labor et Fides, Geneva, 1961, p. 151.

5.
Barth, Karl, *Dogmatique*, III,1, Labor et Fides, Geneva, 1960, p. 190.

6.
Schweitzer, Albert, *La civilisation et l'éthique,* translated into French by Madeleine Horst, Editions Alsatia, Colmar, 1976, p. 147 ff.

7.
See Genesis 9, 6.

versely, we consider it an ethical duty to put to death a dying animal which is suffering a great deal. Whereas human life is in God's hands, animal life is at least in some cases in human hands. Since human beings have a responsibility towards the creation, they must be regarded as the "stewards" who take care of all creatures.

This difference is also apparent in connection with the killing of animals to feed human beings. It must admittedly be stated, as Karl Barth does, that the Bible does not mention permission to eat animals until the Flood.[8] So this state of affairs may be regarded as part of a world marked by sin. Neither the Creator's original plan[9] nor the eschatological vision of a new life[10] include this killing of animals in the interests of human beings. So a vegetarian lifestyle would be a possible way of looking ahead to that future life. However, Christian ethics concern the current state of the world and do not allow us to lay down a general rule.

Animal experimentation is a related issue in which ethics is required to weigh up different interests. If animal experiments prove absolutely necessary and unavoidable for the benefit of human beings, particularly where they are conducted for the purpose of developing medicines, the value of human health takes precedence over that of animal integrity. However, this is admittedly a grey area which is difficult to address and calls for meticulous scrutiny of each individual case.

Theological ethics states the following principles on animal rights:

- All animals have intrinsic dignity because they are creatures and must be respected as such. A key element of respect for animals is recognition of their right to life and to physical integrity.

- Human beings are responsible for protecting animal habitats (preserving the creation).

- Domesticated animals have the right to be fed and cared for.

8.
Genesis 9, 2 and 3.

9.
Genesis 1, 29.

10.
Isaiah 11, 6-9.

- Human beings have a duty to avoid inflicting suffering on animals as far as possible. In so doing, they demonstrate the compassion which is an integral part of the Christian faith.

- Any arbitrary killing of an animal infringes animal rights.

- It is possible to put an animal to death or damage its integrity only:

  - if the animal endangers human health or life;

  - to provide human beings with food;

  - if an animal experiment proves necessary and unavoidable for the purposes of research to preserve human health.

- In these cases, human beings must as far as possible avoid inflicting suffering on the animal in question.

Given these basic rules, some of the current practices involved in the treatment of animals are distinctly questionable.

Despite all attempts to improve the situation, many animals are still bred, transported from one country to another and slaughtered in appalling conditions. Christian theology can only stand up for animals, forcefully pointing out that ill-treatment of animals goes against the Creator's will.

While accepting the possibility of animal experiments as a lesser evil, theology must always remind people that the scope of such experiments must remain very restricted. In particular, we must refuse all experiments which could be replaced by other techniques (even if these are more costly and more time consuming) and experiments conducted for purposes other than human health.

These principles also apply to biotechnology research projects (such as the creation of genetically modified animals). This kind of research is justified only if it aims to provide medical treatment for animals or human beings.

11.
Church of the Confession d'Augsbourg et réfomée d'Alsace et de Lorraine, "Nature menacée et responsabilité chrétienne", 1979.

With this in mind, the Protestant Churches are working for a rediscovery of the biblical ethos in the treatment of animals. The authors of a paper entitled "Nature under threat and Christian responsibility" *(Nature menacée et responsabilité chrétienne)*[11] condemn "the objective barbarity of human beings in their treatment of farm animals bred for food purposes and in a number of notoriously useless animal experiments". These practices must be tackled with a reminder of the actual mission of humankind:

> "Dominance over nature implies respect for nature and its fundamental equilibria, even during the cultivation process. Our mission as human beings is to manage nature, which was created by God and belongs to God; we are answerable to God for our management."[12]

12.
www.protestants.org/
faq/ethique/htm/ecol
ogie.htm

Bibliography

Müller, D. and Poltier, H. (eds.), "La dignité de l'animal. Quel statut pour les animaux à l'heure des technosciences?" in *Le champ éthique,* No. 36, Labor and Fides, Geneva, 2000.

Protestant Churches (Germany), *Zur Verantwortung des Menschen für das Tier als Mitgeschöpf. Ein Diskussionsbeitrag des Wissenschaftlichen Beirats des Beauftragen für Umweltfragen des Rates der EKD,* 1991, EKD-Text 41, (available at: www.ekd.de/EKD-Texte/2086_tier_1991_welcome.html).

Röhrig, E., "Mitgeschöpflichkeit. Die Mensch-Tierbeziehung als ethische Herausforderung im biblischen Zeugnis, in der Theologiegeschichte seit der Reformation und in schöpfungstheologischen Aussagen der Gegenwar", European University Publications Series XXIII, vol. 706, Peter Lang, Frankfurt, 2000.

Situation in Europe

From animal suffering to animal welfare: the progressive attainment of animal rights in Europe

by Elisabeth Hardouin-Fugier

Of the many thinkers of the Enlightenment who, from Benjamin Franklin in America to Jean-Jacques Rousseau in Europe, called for rights to be granted to the oppressed, England's Jeremy Bentham, was one of the few who expressed a desire to protect animals through legislation:

> "Cock fights and bull fights, the chase of the hare and the fox, fishing, and other amusements of the same kind, necessarily suppose a want of reflection or a want of humanity; since these sports inflict upon sensitive beings the most lively sufferings, and the most lingering and painful death that can be imagined. ... Why should the law refuse its protection to any sensitive being? A time will come when humanity will spread its mantle over everything that breathes. The lot of slaves has begun to excite pity; we shall end by softening the lot of the animals which labour for us and supply our wants."[1]

Have two centuries of unremitting perseverance been enough to win animals the right to well-being? This short essay describes some of the main advances that have been made on this long road.

Protecting animals from barbarity

Old and new forms of cruelty

Many 18th-century accounts talk of brotherly intimacy between stockbreeders and their animals. All the more surprising, then, that festivals prominently exhibiting torture of domestic animals were always so successful. Folklorists report examples in England, Spain and France of live fowl having their heads ripped off, rabbits were stoned, cats being burnt to death in midsummer bonfires and bulls having their eyes and genitals riddled with darts. Three of the most popular spectacles, which became mass leisure pursuits at the time, subjected animals to imitations of the harshest types of criminal punish-

1.
See Bentham, J., *The theory of legislation*, edited by C.K. Ogden, London, 1931, pp. 428-429.

ment. The phases of the bullfight were identical to those of public execution with torture, horse racing condemned horses to lifelong hard labour and zoological gardens imprisoned exotic animals for life. The ruling classes had their own forms of cruel sport, including hunting and cockfighting, while Hogarth's engravings show street urchins torturing small animals. In Spain[2] and (post-1950) in Portugal, legislation to prohibit scalding of animals and "burning [them] in oil" is evidence of a cruelty that had been tolerated and taught.

The industrial revolution's need for motive power and urbanisation's need for meat led to increased and more obvious abuse in the cities. The spectacle of horses being whipped half to death and the horrors of animal transport and slaughter drew scandalised comment. Soon larger numbers of beasts had to be killed and slaughter systematised, with increased suffering as live animals were hung up prior to being butchered.

Livestock transported by rail were mistreated, animal fighting continued for many years and bullfighting and certain other cruel shows continue today. The expansion of vivisection in the mid-19th century added its own distinctive type of cruelty. Animal welfarism was an uphill battle.

Animal protectors and legal specialists object to the worst excesses

In the 18th century came new systems (written and detailed) of criminal law, providing the citizen with guarantees of fair treatment which customary law had all too often lacked. Renowned jurists and thinkers like Montesquieu contributed to an unprecedented Europe-wide law-making boom set in train by political events. The 1789 revolutionary Constituent Assembly's declaration of human rights, then Napoleon Bonaparte's conquests, albeit unpopular, disseminated France's legal codes. Most of the kingdoms of Europe adopted criminal codes, into which animal welfarists attempted to introduce animal protection separate from the provisions governing property rights (animals having always been regarded as items of property). The Criminal Code of Saxony[3] was one of the first to punish animal abuse. In addition, some of the provisions in rural codes, and in particular many local regulations, dealt with

2.
Royal Decree of 31 July 1929.

3.
Article 310 of the Criminal Code of Saxony, 30 March 1838.

specific matters such as slaughter. Although ad hoc, such rules, particularly in Germany, built up an important body of case law that helped judges to interpret often very abstract legal principles.

At that time the welfarists in touch with the law makers were sometimes committed individuals like the Scotsman Lord Thomas Erskine, but for the most part they were representatives of animal protection associations and mainly lawyers. The first association for the protection of animals was founded in England by Arthur Broome, in 1824, following a debate in parliament on prohibiting bull-baiting, a debate which had begun in 1809 and spread to the continent through various publications. Similar associations began to be established throughout Europe. The work of spreading the word was taken up in Munich, in 1842, by a polyglot legal scholar, Ignaz Perner, in Russia by the aristocracy, and then progressively by women, who proved to be extremely efficient in this new sphere of activism. By 1861 the various legislative proposals were being co-ordinated at international congresses.

The first legal victory in Britain (1822)

In Britain there arose a "culture of kindness" that took a stand against the widespread abuse of animals. The parliamentary system made it possible for individuals to seek legal prohibition of bull-baiting, an activity very popular in the industrial suburbs in which a bull was tethered and dogs or wild animals let loose on it. In ten years of debate on the subject three successive campaigners brought about the prohibition of bull-baiting. With the support of William Wilberforce's slave trade abolitionists, they secured passage of the Martin's Act on 22 July 1822. After this, similar debate took place in parliaments throughout Europe. The ruling classes (in the British House of Lords) tried to protect their privileges of cockfighting and fox-hunting, and hunting was supported by the war minister, William Windham, as useful combat training. A recurring objection was "Why not cockroaches?", as if the question of how far to go was unique to animal welfare. Paradoxically, Darwinism, particularly outside England, aggravated anthropocentrism to such an extent that mistreating animals was regarded by some as an indication of human superiority which had to be preserved.

The Martin's Act of 1822 surpassed its initial aim and on 31 July 1854 animal fighting was prohibited once and for all in Britain, and afterwards in France. In keeping with the English legal approach, which was resistant to abstraction, the 1822 Act simply listed specific cases of prohibition, making no attempt to tie these into a general concept. This casuistic method posed no threat to legal institutions, with the result that new legislation was more readily accepted. Animal welfare campaigners soon gained the support of Queen Victoria and saw to it that laws were passed in specific areas such as rail transport or the slaughter of animals for food (9 August 1844). A consolidating act of 1 August 1849 increased prison sentences for cruelty to animals to three months and was much admired in Europe.

So-called direct, or disinterested, legislation of this type was widely adopted in North America after 1865 but only a few European countries achieved as much. Examples were Luxembourg, Belgium (the criminal code of 8 June 1867) and Italy (the Zanardelli draft criminal code),[4] whereas Spain, which was just as Catholic, regarded animals as outside the scope of the law until Francesco Silvela's draft law of 29 December 1884. Animal protectionists took emergency action to avoid the worst, having to make do with the limited animal protection that Parliament was prepared to offer.

Circumventing "the cruel right of ownership" (Beccaria)

Use and abuse of animals

According to an ancient belief, cruelty to animals primes men for violent crime. For some people, who may have been influenced by Kant, the punishment of ill-treatment was more of a moral issue than a legal one. Since torturing animals was more dangerous for society than for individuals, only public ill-treatment would be punished because it was "contagious". This theory of "publicity" *(Öffentlichkeit)* also attempted to inculcate morality, requiring the people to witness and condemn, while

4.
Article 173, 15 May 1875.

judges were to investigate the morals of the accused, determining whether they were evil or negligent before imposing the punishment, which could be a fine of varying amounts according to the country or a prison sentence of up to five days in France and Belgium, 10 in Hungary, 14 in Austria, Basle and Vaud, and 20 in Chile, and more severe penalties for repeat offenders.

However, the real and main purpose of publicity was to protect what Beccaria described as the "cruel right of ownership", which reduced animals to the status of objects. Animals were considered *res propria*, drawing their identity solely from their status as an item in someone's possession. If no one was in charge of them, they hardly existed at all, amounting to *res nullius*. The principle of publicity allowed animals to be tortured with impunity. Horses working down the mines were still totally unprotected. In 1931, a Belgian association attempting to improve their conditions was not able to take its case to court. Hidden away in forests, hunters welcomed the publicity principle as it meant their activities were safe.

France's so-called Grammont law illustrates how animal protectionists were forced to accept the publicity principle. On 14 June 1850, General Philippe Delmas de Grammont tabled a bill in the French national assembly punishing "anyone guilty of an act of cruelty to animals". On 2 July 1850, another member of the assembly replied: "I wish ... only to punish offences which, by their seriousness and their public nature, pose a threat to public morals ... in adopting [my proposal], you will afford animals sufficient protection without undermining the right to property, which amounts to a right to use and abuse". In reply, Grammont said: "You are destroying this entire piece of legislation". In its final version the act punished "all those publicly and improperly mistreating animals". The final draft of the Criminal Code of Saxony seems in the end to have been similarly watered down.

Various approaches in Europe

Taking their lead from the University of Leipzig, which was something of a laboratory of animal rights law, the newly emerged nations of Italy and Germany equipped themselves in turn with criminal codes that included provisions on animal protection. The Criminal Code of the Second German Reich[5] punished "anyone publicly or scandalously torturing animals or grossly mistreating them" and was much imitated in Europe. Examples of laws inspired by it were those of Austria-Hungary (1874), Serbia and some Swiss cantons. The equivalent Russian law[6] prohibited "shameful, indecent treatment causing scandal in a public place". The Scandinavian countries were strongly attached to their property rights but made a tentative attempt to bend the rules as early as 1812, in the Norwegian Criminal Code. The Swedish Criminal Code of 29 June 1890 insisted on publicity but protected wild animals.

Breaking away from the concept of publicity

There was great criticism of the publicity principle by animal rights campaigners in Germany at the time of the much awaited reframing of the 1871 criminal code. A legal survey was conducted throughout the world and in 1891 a criminal law jurist, Robert von Hippel, published papers on animal law. Associations, countless law theses and renowned lawyers such as Radbruch examined countless animal protection proposals, but the new criminal code had not been completed by the time the Nazis came to power in January 1933. The Nazi propaganda machine was clever enough to formalise and publish the animal protectionists' proposals with the clear intention of "bringing them into line". This gave rise to the law of 24 November 1933, which was outside the criminal code and whose origins are fully documented by Eberstein. It was a gift to the Nazi propaganda machine and met with enthusiastic response from as far as way as America; the Nazis stole all the credit for doing away with the publicity clause as if it was some kind of innovation. The fact was that on 22 March 1929 the Belgians had pre-empted the Germans, adopting a law prohibiting "acts of cruelty and excessive ill-treatment of animals". The German law involved the highly vague concept of use of suffering whereas the Belgian law referred to "excessive ill-treatment". But at least some animal suffering was recognised and penalised, and the casuistic German law satisfied campaigners' long-standing demands, except where vivisection

5.
Article 370, No. 13, Criminal Code of the Second Reich, Germany, 11 July 1871.

6.
1864, paragraph 43.

was concerned. The 1933 law remained in force until 1972, whereas France waited until 1959 to remove the publicity clause from the Grammont law, which had already been undermined on 2 July 1951 through the legalisation of bull-fighting in the name of tradition.

Vivisection

Vivisection had a long tradition – and, above all, caused atrocious suffering before the introduction of anaesthetics in around 1850 – but in the 19th century it took on a new scope which opponents first began to become aware of in about 1850. J. Burden Sanderson's professional handbook was published in 1873 and illustrated with detailed drawings showing his experiments. It triggered a huge outcry from British campaigners, which soon spread to the rest of Europe and the world. Following consultations with specialists, an act to amend the law on cruelty to animals was adopted (on 15 August 1876). It laid down regulatory principles, required competence, certification and supervision of experimenters, and introduced rules on choice and anaesthesia of animals, avoidance of wasteful practices and training for experimenters. Neither side was satisfied by this. Most subsequent European laws were based on the British act but controls seem to have been non-existent or impracticable except in Geneva, where experiments were restricted to supervised establishments, and perhaps in Italy. The British legislation was a particular source of inspiration for Prussia's Gossler decree of 1885, which formed the basis of the law of 24 November 1933 but was never completed by an implementing act. Italy's "Rocco" Criminal Code[7] banned animal experiments in public while the Scandinavian countries prohibited laboratories from using cats and dogs.

Opponents of vivisection, who are now constantly disparaged, nonetheless put the right question, which was whether it was legitimate to inflict suffering on living beings. At the start of the 20th century the vivisection issue repolarised the social situation. Now it was not the proletarian cart driver who was cruel, but the academic and the scientist. However reasonable, the legal framework that had been established had no effect on the ground because it was never applied. Its attempt to employ

7.
19 October 1930,
Article 727.

the criteria of usefulness to set legal limits on the pain inflicted on animals was to no avail. Matadors, people who made the screws for garrottes, experimenters and hunters never lacked arguments to deny or justify the pain they inflicted. The negativity of "avoid all pointless suffering" was guilty conscience on the part of a law maker who was actually referring to "useful suffering", but that form of words did implicitly allow a degree of argument, enabling doubt to creep in. Even so, the convenience of humans could still be used as legal justification for inflicting pain on animals.

From punitive law to calls for animal welfare

Europe as the crow flies

Disinterested defence of wild animals, including moles, birds of prey, vermin and ants, spread beyond hunting circles to small local associations and entomologists, but all the attempts of the French society for the protection of animals to protect non-domestic animals failed.[8] Aristocratic aficionados of cruelty still kept a tight grip on their exclusive rights to game. For instance, some 30000 quail intended for shooting by "sportsmen" were unloaded at the port of Genoa in 1930. In Belgium, a ban on shooting live pigeons was at last introduced into law in 1956.[9] Nothing, however, could prevent worldwide extermination of exotic species by animal trappers working for zoos and circuses.

A Europe for migratory birds came about long before political Europe. In 1868, Germany obtained an Austro-Hungarian, then an Austro-Italian agreement, which was soon signed by France and Spain. Ornithological congresses, held from 1884 onwards, resulted in a European convention in 1902. Each country progressively did away with its cruel traditions, including bird netting in Belgium and the universal blinding of songbirds with red-hot irons. When the League of Nations was founded in 1932, a motion on animal protection was passed unanimously and, following this, it was attempted to replace the transport of live animals by that of animal carcasses in refrigerated lorries.

8.
Senate, 17 April 1866.

9.
Decree of 18 June 1956.

A code of ethics, the declaration of animal rights

At the end of the 19th century the humanitarian, Henry Salt, said that the forthcoming attainment of human rights would result, in turn, in the attainment of animal rights. In England, then in France,[10] a Declaration of Animal Rights was adopted, based on the famous French revolutionary text and putting forward a code of ethics rather than a legal instrument. Animal rights associations were set up throughout the world and in particular, at the instigation of a group of scientists and research workers, in France. The contents of this declaration established parallels between animals and humans without treating them as alike – an approach which had the backing of discoveries in molecular genetics, ecology and ethology, all showing a common biological heritage that had to be acknowledged.

In 1920 a new legal strategy began to emerge. Punitive law, which was still crucial, began to be combined with more positive methods. Among the first was a proposal by a Dutch judge to create a new legal status for animals, removing them from the category of property – a status called, for want of a better term, the legal personality of animals. Around 1930 a more disinterested form of animal protection was included in many landmark laws, in Holland (18 June 1931), Belgium (22 March 1929), Poland (22 March 1928, including provisions on captive wild animals), Portugal (11 April 1928, banning bullfighting), Spain (31 July 1929, strangely, also protecting plants), Norway (12 June 1929, rules on the slaughter of domestic reindeer), Austria (on birds) and Scotland (3 August 1928, so-called humane animal slaughter techniques). Animal protection associations could now take cases to court. The legislation often contained case-based reasoning (Poland) together with a general punitive principle such as: "in a word [it is prohibited] to cause suffering to animals without any reasonable need" (Poland). This genuine new impetus in Europe was interrupted by the Second World War.

Around 1957, of the 30 or so European criminal codes in force, one fifth contained provisions on animals, which most often related to property rights (Austria, the Netherlands, Norway, Belgium). The Luxembourg code prohibited fighting[11] while

10.
UNESCO, 1978.

11.
Chapter III, Summary Offences.

Finland's[12] and Italy's, which still closely resembled the Rocco Code of 1930 – imitated by Turkey – prohibited all cruelty, as did the code drawn up for Greenland by an eminent Danish lawyer, Verner Goldschmidt. After the fall of the Berlin Wall in 1989, it became clear that the Marxist regime had ruled out any protection for animals – to such an extent in fact that campaigners had had to conceal their activities, claiming to protect nature in general. In the 1957 Treaty of Rome animals were still defined as "agricultural products" – a fact which provoked the indignation of the MEP Gianfranco Amendola in 1994. This was the time when the practice of factory farming gained official approval, with a 1970 rationalisation plan that definitively cut battery animals off from humans and the natural environment. At the same time, the decision to use the Draize test in laboratories, more than any other, condemned rabbits to long periods restrained in stocks, during which their eyes were slowly burnt out by the cosmetic products being tested. It was only when the 7th amendment to Directive 2003/15/EC was introduced that cosmetic testing on animals was banned – a measure to which France objected.

From "agricultural products" to sensitive beings

Paradoxically, after 1970, legal instruments began to include provisions paying renewed attention to animals. A German law of 24 July 1972 replacing the 1933 law said that it was "dedicated to protecting the lives and welfare of animals". A French law of 10 July 1976[13] drew the link between sensitivity and welfare: "since all animals are sensitive beings, their owners must keep them in conditions in keeping with the biological requirements of the species". Among others, a draft law in Romania (1999) described animals as "sensitive beings, capable of physical and mental suffering, which also have intrinsic value over and above their purely utilitarian value". While this met ethical requirements it opened cracks in law systems. According to J.P. Marguénaud,[14] the legal recognition of animals as sensitive beings meant that animal abuse had to be incorporated into a specific category of French law (covering neither property nor persons), which brought the formerly implicit contradiction between property law (animals are property) and criminal law

12.
X/III, paragraph 5.

13.
Article 9.

14.
Author of *L'animal en droit privé*, (Animals in private law), Presses universitaires de Limoges, Limoges, 2006.

(ill-treatment of animals will be punished) into stark relief and, therefore, amounted to a significant legal advance.

Welfare or factory farming?

Throughout Europe, this new definition of animals was at variance with many practices, one example of which was intensive farming, a method which so disgusted one farmer in Hampshire, Peter Roberts, that he founded the association Compassion in World Farming in 1967, which has been represented in France since 1994 by the association *Protection mondiale des animaux de ferme* (World Farm Animal Protection). English animal protection associations laid down the law of the "five freedoms", that is, freedom from hunger, disease, stress and fear, and freedom to behave naturally. In 1980, they founded the Eurogroup for Animal Welfare.

The Brambell Committee was formally entrusted with the task of defining animal welfare. Several countries, like Belgium (14 August 1986), established an animal welfare council, and a German law of 25 May 1998[15] defined animal welfare as physical and mental harmony between animals and their environment. A flagrant contradiction arose between this now official concept and intensive farming. The pollution from intensive farming deprived whole areas like Brittany of drinking water. Animal suffering went on and on, as attested by behavioural anomalies such as stereotypical and inappropriate movements (cage bar licking, for example) and cannibalism. To mutilations carried out without anaesthetic (dismemberment, castration of pigs, pulling of teeth, severing of tails) were added physical deformities (particularly of the legs), wounding and frequent disease (despite massive doses of antibiotics), all of which were telling evidence of ill-treatment.

Yet French scientists maintained that appraisals of animal welfare required us to look beyond the appearance of suffering and they established a working hypothesis that animals were capable of adjustments that would cancel out the effect of trauma. Stress theory was based on analysis of hormone secretions, while theories on psychological adjustment (or coping theory) were said to be "difficult to reduce to mere physiological or behavioural matters". The European Commission's scien-

15.
Paragraph 2.

tific committee on animal welfare (1995, 1999) condemned research based on human criteria and the lack of simple documentary data on mortality and disease in off-the-ground stock-raising complexes or during transport or the force-feeding of poultry. Armand Farrachi took a sentence from a report by a French scientist sent to the French Ministry of Agriculture and used it ironically as the title of his book against intensive farming "Chickens prefer cages". Shortly before his election as pope, Cardinal Ratzinger told a journalist that battery hens were "caricatures of birds".[16] Admittedly, there is a genuine problem with behavioural studies, but the French authorities readily lend an ear to powerful professional organisations, for instance by refusing to label eggs from off-the-ground stock-raising complexes as "battery farm eggs". As a result, it has every reason to fear the customer's verdict.

European animal protectionists believe that the peaceful method of consumer education and progressive implementation of legislation will eventually eliminate ill-treatment bordering on torture. In Italy, a million signatures and three years' campaigning led to the adoption of a law on 20 July 2004 which turns the offence of cruelty to animals from a minor offence into a serious one.

Politicians can no longer overlook the fact that animals have become a social issue affecting scientists themselves. The mad cow crisis shook many people's preconceptions once again – in fact, one time too many. 2002 saw an unprecedented step in the history of European law, when respect for animals was included in a constitutional text[17] and the German state declared itself responsible to future generations for the fundamental interests of animals and nature. It is a fact that there are countries in Europe where torturing an animal is considered an attraction and other countries, which used to be slave traders, where torturing an animal is now considered a crime. Two centuries of unceasing progress in favour of animals give us confidence in humankind and reason to believe that it is Italy's example that will be followed.

16.
Ratzinger, J., *Gott und die Welt* (God and the World), conversations with Peter Seewald, 28 April 2005.

17.
18 May 2002, Article 20a.

Bibliography

Ancel, M., *Les codes pénaux européens,* Centre Français de Droit comparé, Paris, 1957-1959.

Antoine, S. and Nouët, J.C., *La Fondation Ligue Française des Droits de l'Animal,* Paris, 2003.

Bulletin du Comité Juridique de la Protection animale, recueil trimestriel de Doctrine, de Législation et de Jurisprudence, CJIPA, Paris; particularly: Lespine, L., 1929 et al.

Burgat, F. and Dantzer, R., *Les animaux d'élevage ont-ils droit au bien-être?* INRA, Paris, 2001; particularly: Porcher, J., p.29; Dantzer, pp. 85-104.

Couret, A., *Homme, animal, société,* II, Presses de l'Institut d'études politiques, Toulouse, 1988; particularly: Samuel, Geoffroy, Angleterre, pp. 413-419.

Eberstein, W., Das Tierschutzrecht in *Deutschland bis zum Erlass des Reichs-Tierschutzgesetzes vom 24. November 1933,* Peter Lang, Frankfurt, 1999.

Farrachi, A., *Les poules préfèrent les cages. Quand la science et l'industrie nous font croire n'importe quoi,* Albin Michel, Paris, 2000.

Géraud, A., *Déclaration des droits de l'animal,* Port-Sainte Marie, first edition by the author, 1919.

Hardouin-Fugier, E., "La protection juridique de l'animal en Allemagne (1800-1933)", in *L'amour des animaux dans le monde germanique,* Cluet, Marc (ed.), Transdisciplinary Colloquy, 5-7 May 2004, Université Rennes 2, Rennes, Groupement de Recherches Autrichiennes et Allemandes (Graal), to be published, Presses universitaires de Rennes, 2006.

Hardouin-Fugier, E., *Histoire de la Corrida en Europe, XVIIIͤ-XXIͤ siècles,* preface by Maurice Agulhon, Connaissances et Savoirs, Paris, 2005.

Hardouin-Fugier, E. and Baratay, E., *Zoo, a history of zoological gardens in the West,* Reaktion Books, London, 2002, re-edited 2004.

Von Hippel, R., *Die Tierquälerei in der Strafgesetzgebung des In- und Auslandes,* Liebmann, Berlin, 1891.

Kean, H., *Animal rights,* Reaktion Books, London,1998.

Lorz, A. and Metzger, E., *Tierschutzgesetz,* Beck'sche, Munich, 1999.

Marguénaud, J.P. (ed.), *Les animaux et les droits européens,* Colloquy, 7 and 8 April 2005, Faculté de Droit et des Sciences économiques de Limoges, Limoges, 2005; proceedings of the conference, Pedone, Paris, 2006.

Le Moniteur Universel, No. 184, 3 July 1850, Assemblée nationale, deliberations of the Chambre des députés, examination of General de Grammont's proposal relative to the ill-treatments exerted towards animals, 3rd deliberation, 3 July 1850, pp. 2267-2269; Defontaine amendment, p. 2269.

Salt, Henry, *Animals' rights: considered in relation to social progress,* George Bell and Sons Ltd, London, 1892.

The Swedish approach

by Ingvar Ekesbo

The first national animal welfare laws were introduced in most countries, except for communist dictatorships, during the 1900s. However, the animal welfare matter goes all the way back to the beginning of the co-habitation of humans and domestic animals as it has to do with the human-animal relationship. The first Swedish Royal provisions regarding animal protection came in 1857. In 1921 they were modified but not until 1944 was a genuine animal welfare law enacted by the Swedish Parliament, the Riksdag. Compared to some other countries Sweden was late in approving an animal welfare law. Such laws had been inaugurated in England in 1911, in Denmark in 1916, in Germany in 1933, in Finland in 1934, and in Norway in 1935. However, already in the 1700s the Swedish courts punished persons who had commited acts of cruelty against horses or cattle (Cserhalmy, 2004).

This paper is subdivided according to the Council of Europe conventions for protection of animals. In addition, rules for animals in zoological parks, at circuses, deer in enclosures, and animals used for contests are included. For farm and pet animals, as for the animals in different situations, such as transport, slaughter, and experimental purposes, there have been great changes since the first Council of Europe convention was established in 1964. In the following, the focus will be kept on the Swedish practices and legislation that differ from other countries.

Farm animals have been exposed to more radical changes than any other of these groups in all countries. Therefore it has to be given the most space in this paper. Another reason for this is that Sweden, both in legislation and in animal husbandry, already chose during the 1960s to adopt a different strategy from other countries.

Pet animals

Each dog in Sweden must, unlike other countries, be identified by a microchip or tattoo in a central register for the country.

The reason for this is not only to demonstrate to owners their responsibility but also to register and prevent injuries and diseases caused by dogs.

Animals in zoological parks and at circuses, deer in enclosures

Each circus must, in order to get permission to keep animals, pass an inspection once a year.

For animals in zoological parks the space and other requirements are more far-reaching compared to most countries.

For deer kept in enclosures for hunting and slaughter there are detailed rules.

Animals used for experimental and other scientific purposes

Already by 1979 ethical review committees were established in Sweden regarding use of animals for scientific purposes. There are seven such committees each one with a chairman and vice-chairman, lawyers, scientists, and staff caring for the experimental animals. Laymen are also included of which half shall represent local animal welfare organisations. For several experimental animals Swedish rules are more stringent than in most other countries.

Animals for slaughter

All animals in Sweden must be efficiently stunned and unconscious before slaughter, including ritual slaughter.

Animal transport

Although large parts of Sweden are characterised by long distances, slaughter animals shall not be transported longer than eight hours. Vehicles must undergo inspection and be approved before use. Since the 1970s pregnant animals shall not be transported later than three weeks before parturition. However, the maximum time for dogs and cats is two weeks.

Animals at training or competition

Animals must not be given any substance in order to increase the capacity for training or competition. Strict withdrawal periods are stipulated after different veterinary treatments before training or competition is allowed.

Farm animals

From animal husbandry to animal production

In Sweden, as in other industrialised countries, the time after the Second World War, especially during the 1950s, meant the beginning of a radical change in farm animal husbandry. A new and unique period in the last 12 000 years of joint history of humankind and farm animals began, with greater changes than during any other period in the mutual history of humankind and farm animals. "Animal husbandry" became "animal production".

Changing the animal material

In traditional animal husbandry, breeding several characteristics, such as calm temperament, good health, maternal quality, etc., were very important. From the 1950s onwards breeding was more and more taken over by organisations or private firms which have developed systematic programmes where the focus as a rule is concentrated on just one characteristic, increased productivity. Poultry is the most extreme example. In most commercial egg-laying hen and broiler flocks all over the world, only a few breeds and hybrids, all originating from a few parent generations and owned by international firms, remained by the end of the 1900s. The introduction of artificial insemination, AI, after the Second World War had the effect that decisions on cattle breeding were moved from farm level to the AI organisations, which successively also became breeding associations. A similar development came later for pigs. The Swedish dairy cow breeding programmes were internationally very successful. In 2000 the Swedish Red Breed and Swedish Holstein Breed had increased their average annual milk production from 1955 by 117% and 102% to 8 356 and 9 204 kg, respectively. The back fat thickness for Swedish fattening pigs decreased by 31% from 1955 to 1988. Growth rate increased rapidly and feed requirement per kg pig growth decreased by 22% from 1955 to 1994. The annual average egg production increased by 153% to 22.5 kg from 1955 to 2000, and the broiler growth rate increased by 38% from 1955 to 1995.

However, the increased production figures are a result not only of genetic achievements but also of feed compositions aimed at increased production.

Changing the animal environment

From the 1950s farmers were advised by state and agricultural colleges to mimic the industries' principles and thus specialise in one species per farm. The old tradition of keeping a limited number of several species on each farm (horses, cattle, pigs, poultry, sometimes also sheep and geese, plus cats and a dog) was replaced by only one species, and often just one age category. New animal housing design and management methods were introduced, for example, cages for hens, tying and cage and stall confinement of sows, loose housing for dairy cattle, liquid manure handling, slatted or perforated floors, mechanical ventilation, and reduction or total elimination of bedding material for cows, pigs and poultry. Few countries had such fast changes in farm animal husbandry as in Sweden from the end of the 1950s.

Changing biological knowledge

In the old peasant society where children accompanied and assisted their parents in the care of animals, they learned the normal behaviour of several species and the differences between the species. They knew how a cow behaves when getting up or laying down, that pigs do not put their droppings on their laying area but cows do, how the hen took care of her chickens, etc. By transferring the older generation's biological experience to the children, most farm people had a "silent" but profound knowledge of the animals' biology. This biological knowledge also created the basis for several unwritten rules regarding animal housing, management and the relationship between man and farm animal. This knowledge and rules involved a fairly certain guarantee for animals' health and welfare. The fast changes in society, and the specialisation and rationalisation of animal husbandry made this "silent" biological knowledge deteriorate very fast in Sweden. Mechanisation reduced manual labour and the time children spent with the animals. Most young boys and girls preferred sitting on the tractor instead of caring for the cattle or pigs. In addition, specialisation in one species on the farm eliminated the possibility of getting experience of more than one species. Some examples of this lack of biological knowledge during the 1960s, not only among farmers but also among their advisers, are: in an agricultural journal earlier generations of farmers were carped at for "not understanding that sows could be kept tied"; in another that "within a few generations sows would be adapted to confinement", and that "our geneticists will create cows adapted to standing with their hind feet on gratings without getting

hoof injuries". Experienced farmers who questioned or criticised new, non-biological methods were brushed aside as "reactionaries".

Changing farm animal disease panorama and incidences

According to annual veterinary reports in the late 1950s a new disease panorama and an increase of disease frequencies appeared in many dairy herds where new methods of housing and management had been introduced. The veterinarians could not eliminate the cause of the disorders, but only treat the symptoms, and they were worried for the animals' welfare. They also reported that hygienic conditions had deteriorated. Therefore in 1959 the Veterinary Association wrote to the then Royal Veterinary College demanding research on how the new methods influenced dairy cow health and welfare, in order to increase the scientific knowledge necessary to improve veterinary diagnostics and advice to farmers.

Research on the connection between environmental factors and animal health

As a result of this demand research started in 1960 at the then Royal Veterinary College's Animal Hygiene Department, now the Veterinary Faculty's Department of Environment and Health (HMH-Dept) at the Swedish Agricultural College, Skara. Instead of using the traditional method of carrying out research on just one experimental farm, this unique epidemiological study comprised monthly reports from the farms of all disorders, and a complete description of housing and management in about 700 dairy herds with about 20 000 cows. The health status in the herds during pasture served as a control facilitating the analysis of different risk factors compared with a "natural" environment. The results presented a total picture of the health situation in dairy herds considering a great number of factors in the animals, housing and management (Ekesbo, 1966). Risk factors for different disorders were defined by statistically significant association between disease incidences and risk factors, for example, breed or production intensity, loose or tied system, liquid or solid manure handling, bedding or not, keeping cows on pasture in the summer or not, etc. It was also possible to study and identify least risk factors for different disorders among factors in animals, housing or management. The veterinarians and many farmers were very fast to utilise the results. In 1965 similar research was started for sows and piglets (Bäckström, 1973) and in the 1970s for fattening pigs (Lindqvist, 1974), egg-laying hens and broilers (Svedberg, 1976) and again for dairy cattle (for example, Bendixen et al., 1986).

From the 1970s the epidemiological research at the HMH-Dept was combined with ethological methods (for example, Jensen, 1983; Lidfors, 1992). As a result, the causal reasons for the associations between disease frequencies and the risk factors could be better analysed and explained (for example, Algers, 1989). The experiences from the combination of epidemiological and ethological research facilitated further clarification of environmentally evoked farm animal diseases. Later a chair in ethology was created at the HMH-Dept. Cost-benefit studies were also performed, such as the costs of conventional and improved animal environment or transport correlated with the costs of injuries, diseases and deaths.Results from these studies confirm that optimal economy is achieved when herd environment and transport are adapted to the animals' health and welfare needs (Ekesbo, 1973; Ekesbo and Lund, 1994).

Carefully prepared animal welfare legislation is also preventive veterinary medicine

Introduction of new husbandry methods often involved attempts to adapt the animals to the technique. In connection with the publication of the dairy cow research results in 1966, the author instead emphasised the necessity to replace such strategy with an adaptation of the technique to the animals. He proposed four measures to change and canalise the technical developments for improved animal health and welfare:

1. improved animal health and welfare legislation;

2. the one-sided technical advisory service to farmers wanting to build or remodel their farm animal housing to be supplemented by veterinary advice and drawings and plans to be checked;

3. education of specialised veterinarians for this purpose, and

4. new techniques or methods which when subjected to veterinary checks could be regarded as risk factors, should be animal health and welfare tested before being accepted for general use.

As a result, in 1969, the Swedish government summoned 48 selected veterinarians, two in each province, to get further education on the connection between animal keeping and animal health at the then Animal Hygiene Department. Then, in addition to their usual duties, two were appointed as animal welfare specialists in each province. Next, the Riksdag amended the animal welfare law in 1970 to require all plans and drawings for new or remodelled farm animal buildings to be checked in advance by such a veterinarian. Also, new techniques and methods had to be tested for health and welfare before general use. In 2005, Sweden was still the only country to have mandatory animal health and welfare checks of farm animal housing plans. However, after the Swedish model, Switzerland in 1980 and later other countries, for example, the

Netherlands, chose to follow the principle of legal animal health and welfare testing of new techniques.

Between 1973 and 1978 the veterinary administration required all veterinarians in farm animal practice to take a two-week course in animal environment and health at the HMH-Dept. Nowadays, courses are regularly arranged for veterinarians responsible for checks of building plans, animal welfare inspections, etc. From the 1990s education of animal welfare inspectors has been located at the department where a section for animal welfare was created. The Swedish government created a chair in animal welfare at the HMH-Dept in 2002.

In 1988 a new animal welfare law was introduced in Sweden which demanded that "animals ... shall be protected from ... suffering *and disease*" and "shall be kept ... to *promote their health and allow natural behaviour*". These formulations, internationally unique in 1988, prescribe that their environment must be adapted to the animals' biological and health needs. The 1996 Finnish law has similar formulations. The 1991 Danish law does not mention the health aspect, but, inspired by the Council of Europe convention, prescribes "animals shall be treated with regard to their physiological, behavioural and health-related needs". In Norway a committee is finalising a proposal for a new law to be introduced on 1 July 2005.

The following are some examples of other differences between Sweden and one or more Nordic countries and the rest of Europe: since 1986 it has been prohibited in Sweden to use drugs as growth promoters, later also in Norway and Finland. This means that diseases caused by deficiencies in animal environment can not be concealed by drugs. Sweden like Norway demands windows in animals' houses, also required in Finland, but with exception of poultry houses. In Sweden since 1988, cows must be kept at pasture during the summer, in Finland from 2006. After a study of early weaning and cage keeping of piglets (Algers, 1984*a* and *b*) pigs in Sweden shall not be either kept in conventional piglet cages, nor be weaned before four weeks of age. In most European and other countries early weaning and cage keeping is the predominant method. Sows in Sweden must be provided with straw in the bedding area, other countries deem it sufficient to provide access to material for rooting. Tail docking is banned only in Sweden, Norway, and Finland. Sweden and Finland do not accept mechanical noise exceeding 65 dB(A) whereas other European countries accept 85 dB(A). For a 90 kg pig the area in Sweden must be 0.90 sq.m, in the rest of Europe 0.65 sq.m. Debeaking of poultry is banned in Sweden, Finland and Norway but allowed in the rest of Europe. This exemplifies that modern animal welfare legislation can also serve as animal health legislation, as more than 95% of farm animal disorders are partly or entirely caused by risk factors in their housing or management.

Swedish farmers choose a different route for their cattle and pigs than the rest of Europe

The results from the comprehensive cattle and pig studies gave farmers and veterinarians information on how to avoid risk factors in animal husbandry. Instead, an increasing number of the cow and sow herds had their environmental standard improved, some already during the second part of the 1960s. Thereby, and from the 1970s to a great extent through the mandatory checks of plans for new or remodelled animal houses and the animal health and welfare tests of new methods, the trend toward increased use of risk factors was halted in Sweden. This meant that laying areas without bedding, totally slatted flooring, keeping cows indoors all year round, tying or other confinement of sows, keeping piglets in cages (which started to be more and more common in Europe in the 1960s), use of liquid manure handling inside barns, and other risk factors were eliminated. These, and other similar measures, resulted in healthier animals and improved animal welfare. Remarkably, the initiative in banning growth promoters came in 1985 from the Swedish farmers' union. The good standard in their husbandry had resulted in healthy animals in no need of antibiotics as compensation for bad housing and management. Without the animal welfare achievements in the farm animal environment from the 1960s this initiative would never have been taken.

However, Swedish poultry farmers were not as prepared to accept the research results on egg-laying hens as their cattle and pig colleagues. The poultry industry had already in the 1970s been greatly influenced by the technical advice from international firms. Thus, the authorities had great difficulty in enforcing even slight improvements, such as a reduced number of hens in the cages. Not until 2005 were all hens given limited access to perches and sand baths in cages or were kept loose housed, where such facilities are provided for all hens.

It was easier to get the research results on broiler environment and health accepted (Ekstrand, Algers et al., 1997; Ekstrand, Carpenter et al., 1997). Thus a system was established for using injury frequencies found at slaughter to determine the number of chicken per square area. In order to prevent the spreading of salmonella and similar contagious diseases via feed, a programme for improved hygiene in the chain from the feed factory to the moment the chickens left the flock was introduced with great success (Svedberg, 1988). It resulted in Swedish broiler flocks being uniquely regarded as salmonella-free as early as the 1990s, and now also in Norway and Finland.

Scientific research during the 1960s, and confirmed in the early 1970s, had shown breed differences in diseases (Ekesbo, 1966; Bendixen et al., 1988). Therefore, unlike in other countries, from the early 1970s Swedish breeding programmes have also considered genetic disposition to some diseases. The risk that increased production might be accompanied by an increase in the frequency of some diseases was thereby diminished.

The intensive pig growth rate from the end of the 1950s was accompanied by increased spontaneous bone fractures especially in young pregnant sows. However, after the veterinarians brought this to the attention of the geneticists in the early 1970s, the breeding programmes were changed, and after some years this type of fracture practically disappeared.

Misuse of free trade – A threat to farm animal welfare

Some products originating from farm animals, for example, untreated meat, must, according to EU and Swedish legislation, be labelled with the name of the country of origin. However, if a primary product is in any way treated in Sweden, for example, poultry or pork meat by injection of salt water or nitrate, it is only labelled "processed in Sweden". The primary product might originate from a country where the animal husbandry has a very low standard because of a lack of animal welfare legislation. But the average consumer thinks that the label "processed in Sweden" means that the animal originates from Sweden and has been kept under Swedish conditions. This is a threat against not only Swedish farmers but against farmers in all countries aiming at good animal welfare standards. Therefore the free trade rules must be changed so that the average consumer will have a free choice between products from animals kept under good or not good conditions.

An independent animal welfare agency strengthens animal protection

Since 2004, after a decision in the Riksdag, the overall responsibility for animal welfare in accordance with the Swedish Animal Welfare Act has been given to a new agency, the National Animal Welfare Agency. For the time being it is without parallel internationally.

Almost one third of its budget is made up of research funds. Most of these go into research on alternatives to animal experiments, that is, methods that refine, reduce, or replace the use of laboratory animals. It also supports research on measures to promote animal welfare in other areas, such as ethological studies aimed at producing techniques to solve problems related to farm animal welfare. The agency is charged with strengthening the supervision of animal welfare in Sweden. The goal is to provide competent support and guidance to local and regional supervisory agencies with the aim of obtaining uniformity, legal certainty, and quality in the supervision of animal welfare. There are about 100000 different objects for supervision, from farms, plants for experimental animals or fish breeding, to kennels and reindeer herds and if there are no problems, each of these gets a visit every 4.5 years. Animal transport is controlled at departure, on the road or on arrival. Slaughter animals are controlled on arrival at the slaughterhouse under the responsibility of a veterinarian.

Besides an administrative unit, the agency has one unit for supervision, information and education, another for pets, a third for laboratory animal issues, and a fourth, the largest, for agricultural animals, fur-bearing animals, fish, slaughter, and animal transport. The laboratory animal unit also hosts Sweden's seven ethical review committees.

There are few conflicts about animal welfare in Swedish society. The farmers' organisations, representatives for experimental animal research, and other interested parties promote, with few exceptions, animal welfare. The main reason for this is probably that the law and the legislation are based on scientific evidence and practical experience, and those who have to discharge the official duties as a rule have been educated for the tasks.

Bibliography

Algers, B., Thesis, Swedish University of Agricultural Sciences, Department of Animal Hygiene, Skara, Report 25, 1989.

Algers, B., in *ZBL. Vet. Med. A.*, 31, 1984a, pp. 1-13.

Algers, B., in *ZBL. Vet. Med. A.*, 31, 1984b, pp. 14-24.

Bäckström, L., Thesis, *Acta Vet. Scand.*, suppl. 41, 1973, p. 240.

Bendixen, P., Vilson, B. and Ekesbo, I., in *Prev. Vet. Med.*, 4, 1986, pp. 291-306.

Berg, C., *Acta Univ. Agr. Sueciae, Veterinaria* 36, 1998.

Cserhalmy, N., *Djuromsorg och djurmisshandel,* Gidlunds, Hedemora, 2004.

Ekesbo, I., *Acta Agr. Scand.* Suppl. 15, 1966.

Ekesbo, I., *Vet. Rec.* 1973, 93, pp. 36-40.

Ekesbo, I. and Lund, V., Proc. 8th ISAH Congress, St Paul, 1994, pp. 1-5.

Ekstrand, L., Algers, B. and Svedberg, J., *Prev. Vet. Med.*, 31, 1997, pp. 167-174.

Ekstrand, C., Carpenter, T. and Algers, B., ISVEE International Congress, Paris, AEEMA, 1997, pp. 31-32.

Jensen, P., Thesis, Swedish University of. Agricultural Sciences, Department of Animal Hygiene, Skara, Report 8, 1983.

Lidfors, L., Thesis, Swedish University of Agricultural Sciences, Department of Animal Hygiene, Skara, Report 30, 1992.

Lindqvist, J-O., *Acta Vet. Scand.* suppl. 51, 1974.

Svedberg, J., *Proceedings,* ISAH-Congress, Zagreb 1976, pp. 282-286.

Svedberg, J., *Proceedings,* 6th International Animal Hygiene Congress, Skara, 1988, pp. 826-830.

Vilson, B., *Proceedings,* ISAH-Congress, Zagreb 1976, pp. 135-140.

The example of Slovenia

by Aleš Brecelj

Slovenia gained independence in June 1991, only six months after a successful referendum with the majority of Slovenians opting for independence from the then Socialist Federative Republic of Yugoslavia (SFRY). Along with changes in the political system, other changes evolved in practically all the spheres of everyday life, including the economy, culture, social life, ethics, and many more. The new democratic approach changed the system of values. Some matters deemed less important in the past suddenly got much more attention. Thus, animal welfare is an area deriving benefits from these democratic changes. The public has become much more sensitive to animal welfare issues and willing to openly express their feelings against the unnecessary suffering of animals in the intensive farming systems, live animal transport, experiments on animals, animal slaughter as well as other situations involving animal suffering.

It would be inappropriate to conclude that public perception of animal suffering had been triggered by political changes alone. Nevertheless, the possibilities of expressing freely one's views in public or in the media had been rather limited. These limitations had been clearly evident from the media coverage of animal welfare concerns, dedicating almost exclusive attention to the welfare of pet animals and practically no attention to livestock and other food production animals. This may be due to the public property of livestock in the past socialist system, and any criticism of circumstances in which livestock had been kept might easily have been interpreted as criticism of the political system itself, and that would definitely not have been a welcome attitude in those days.

All due criticism of the past socialist system put aside, it is fair to acknowledge that Slovenia had always been intolerant of animal suffering. The appropriate legislation governing several important aspects of protection of animals against unnecessary suffering and cruelty had been in place within the legal order of the SFRY. Although there was no general framework law on animal welfare, the Yugoslav Federal Act on the Protection of Animals against Contagious Diseases, applicable throughout the SFRY since 1976, provided an adequate legal basis for the adoption of a regulation in 1978, the so-called Rules, laying down the most important animal welfare provisions applicable to live animal transport. The Rules of 1978 were amended in 1983 and recast in 1990, and according to my judgment, some provisions of those Rules were way ahead of their time.

Animal slaughter procedures were laid down by a law passed in 1978 governing the health suitability of foodstuffs, and providing the basis for a regulation governing veterinary-sanitary inspection and control also passed in 1978, and laying down in particular compulsory stunning prior to slaughter to be carried out professionally and by humane methods under the supervision of slaughterhouse veterinarians.

As early as 1985, the Animal Health Act was passed by the then Socialist Republic of Slovenia, part of the SFRY, defining in two of its articles "cruelty to animals". These two articles constituted a legal basis for issuing two implementing regulations, the Rules on the protection of animals during veterinary procedures, issued in 1985, and the Rules on conditions for granting authorisations of animal experiments, issued in 1987. The above Animal Health Act also stipulated sanctions to be imposed in case of violations of legal provisions. The latter two implementing regulations incorporated some important aspects of protection of animals against suffering, for instance, the compulsory anaesthesia in all veterinary procedures on animals in order to avoid unnecessary suffering, and in procedures on experimental animals. Detailed reports had to be kept on all procedures involving experimental animals, specifying the conditions and purposes authorised for such experiments.

In 1990, the SFRY ratified the European Convention for the Protection of Animals kept for Farming Purposes (ETS No. 87), and the European Convention for the Protection of Animals for Slaughter (ETS No. 102), which were also legally binding on Slovenia as part of the SFRY.

Development of animal welfare legislation in Slovenia after 1991

On gaining independence in 1991, Slovenia assumed all the legal acts governing animal welfare that had been in force in the SFRY.

The new Constitution of the Republic of Slovenia of 1991 lays down in its Article 72(4) that "The protection of animals against cruelty shall be regulated by law", and this provision has served as the basis of the currently applicable Animal Protection Act, passed on 18 November 1999.

Protection of animals against suffering has been regulated also by the Penal Code of the Republic of Slovenia, in force since 1994, laying down in its Article 342 that "Everyone handling an animal with cruelty, or causing avoidable pain to an animal, shall be imposed a fine, or a penalty of imprisonment of up to three months."

The Veterinary Practice Act of 1994 laid down in detail the competence of supervision and control of implementation of the laws, regulations and administrative provisions governing the protection of animals against suffering, authorising the veterinary inspection services, established within the Veterinary Administration of the Republic of Slovenia (VARS), for carrying out the tasks and obligations of such supervision and control.

In 1994, two draft animal welfare laws were put into parliamentary procedure. In 1995, the parliament found one thereof a good basis for a future animal welfare law and approved of its second reading. Under the stress of circumstances and possibly due to a lack of political will, the second reading was put off to be resumed as late as 1998, simultaneously with the negotiations on the accession of Slovenia to the EU, and it was finally adopted in November 1999.

The Animal Protection Act was the first framework act regulating all animal welfare issues and was considered a big step towards an animal welfare friendly regulation in Slovenia. The act lays down public responsibility for the protection of animals, comprising the protection of their life, health and welfare; it provides the principles of good practice in handling animals; it defines the practices which are considered as cruelty to animals, and the types of handling or procedures on animals which are prohibited; it lays down the conditions to be ensured in the rearing of animals, transport, carrying out of certain procedures and experiments on animals, at the time of slaughter and killing of animals; it regulates the procedure, the rights and obligations in the cases of abandoned animals; it lays down the conditions for societies active in the protection of animals in the public interest; it lays down the awards and acknowledgements in the field of protection of animals; it regulates control over the implementation of criminal law sanctions in the case of a violation of provisions. It applies to all animals disposing of senses responsive to external stimuli, and of a developed nervous system able to feel painful external influences, with a particular focus on vertebrate animals and other animals in proportion to the level of their sensitivity, in accordance with the established experience and scientific knowledge.

In addition to the protection of animals against unnecessary suffering and cruelty, the aim of the act is to obligate enforcement and implementation of the declaration on the rights and protection of animals by all the legal and natural persons that are involved with animals in any way, and in particular animal keepers, local communities and the State, veterinary organisations, livestock breeding associations, scientific, research and pedagogic institutions, hunting and cynological associations, other animal breeders' organisations and associations, animal welfare organisations and other associations.

The act is a sound basis for the implementation of some substantial structural, procedural and organisational changes in the area of protection of animals.

Under the act, the Expert Council for the Protection of Animals has been established within the Ministry of Agriculture, Forestry and Food (MAFF), comprising experts in the veterinary medicine, human medicine, biology, pharmaceutics and zootechnics, the representatives of non-governmental organisations active in the protection of animals against cruelty. The tasks of the Expert Council include:

- monitoring the situation in the country as regards animal welfare and proposing appropriate measures,

- defining criteria for granting authorisations for experiments, giving opinions on and proposals for draft animal welfare legislation, and opinions on animal welfare issues at the request of national authorities.

On establishing the Expert Council, the animal welfare NGOs have become formally involved in drafting animal welfare legislation and been able to formally express their opinions on animal welfare issues.

Established under the act was also the Ethical Commission, another most important body safeguarding animal welfare. Its tasks include giving opinions to the authorities on granting authorisations for individual experiments on animals, and consulting the competent authorities on other issues concerning animal experiments.

It needs to be pointed out with regard to experiments on animals that the act prohibits the use of animals in experiments with ethically unacceptable objectives, such as tests for military purposes, cosmetic preparations, tobacco or alcoholic products, or in experiments using muscle paralysing agents without the application of anaesthesia.

The new act prohibits, *inter alia,* animal mutilation, that is, removing claws in cats, removing the vocal cords, harmful shoeing of ungulates, beak trimming in poultry unless such a procedure should prevent major harm or disease within the flock, amputation or castration by elastic rings, ear cropping unless the procedure should benefit the animal, tail docking, excluding newborn pedigree dogs aged up to five days, provided that the docking is carried out in accordance with the pedigree and cynological standards and for the benefit of the animal concerned. Such procedures shall be carried out by doctors of veterinary medicine only.

A major step forward has been taken by laying down under the act the measures applicable to abandoned pet animals, animal shelters, and the responsibilities of the legal and natural persons concerning abandoned pet animals. The act stipulates that abandoned pet animals should be offered help, maintenance and accommodation in animal shelters. Provision of animal shelter facilities lies within the responsibility of the local authorities in the communities, and shelter activities shall be carried out as public service in the public interest; animal shelter capacity should be such as to provide a vacancy per each 800 registered dogs in a community. Operators of animal shelters may be the community or any natural or legal person complying with the prescribed requirements. The tasks of an animal shelter operator include, *inter alia:*

• providing for the capture, transfer, accommodation and care of abandoned animals in an animal shelter,

• providing the abandoned animals with all the necessary veterinary care, and

• locating the owners of abandoned animals.

The act lays down that certain funds should be earmarked within the national budget for co-financing the construction of animal shelters by local communities. Encouraged by this provision, local communities have been establishing animal shelters in most parts of Slovenia and thus rendering the problem of abandoned animals much less acute.

The requirement to compulsory microchip all the dogs born in Slovenia since 1 January 2003 has greatly improved the efficiency of abandoned animal management. The data gathered by microchipping are collected in a computerised central register of dogs, accessible via the web to veterinary inspection services controlling abandoned animals, and to all the veterinary clinics and animal shelters. Microchipping is funded from the national budget and thus free of charge for dog owners. This system of control of dogs in the country, which is linked to rabies control, has been extremely efficient in decreasing the number of lost and stray dogs and speeding up the recovery of dogs by their owners.

Important features of the act are also certain provisions constituting a legal basis for the adoption of several implementing regulations on different animal welfare issues that had previously not been regulated. In addition to national legislation, these implementing regulations include both provisions of the relevant EU legislation and of the Council of Europe.

By adopting and implementing appropriate legislation, some substantial structural, procedural and organisational changes have been brought about in Slovenia as regards animal welfare.

Transport of animals through Slovenia

Along with the *acquis*, Slovenia has transposed all the relevant EU animal welfare legislation into the Slovenian legal order. A particularly important segment, namely, animal welfare during transport, needs to be presented in greater detail.

Owing to its geographical position between the East and the West, Slovenia is transited by a number of vehicles carrying live animals on a daily basis. Before accession to the EU, Slovenia had been bordering on the EU and presenting a bottleneck for the so-called "Northern Route" from Lithuania through Poland, Czech Republic, Slovakia and Hungary to Slovenia, as well as the "Southern Route" from Romania through Hungary to Slovenia.

The two routes united at the border between Italy and Slovenia prior to entering the EU. Approximately 1.5 million animals transited Slovenia each year towards Italy and the other EU member states and, due to imperfect controls, animal welfare was frequently compromised.

Soon after adopting the Animal Protection Act, Slovenia adopted in 2000 the Rules on the Conditions and Methods of Transport of Animals, transposing the relevant EU legislation and authorising the border veterinary inspectors to perform the substantially more stringent controls of live animal consignments. Preparations for the full implementation of these rules took place several months before their entry into force, including training courses for border veterinarians and information campaigns for transporters. The governments of the countries involved in live animal transport through Slovenia and their respective veterinary services were informed well in advance of the intention of Slovenia to bring long distance animal transport in line with the relevant EU animal welfare legislation. The information materials clearly stated that all live animal consignments would be refused entry to Slovenia if they failed to comply with the relevant animal welfare requirements.

The new approach proved encouraging after a three-month period of giving warnings to transporters. A significant decrease in the violations of rules was noted by the border veterinary inspectors and the situation remained favourable until the accession of Slovenia to the EU.

As of 1 May 2004, veterinary inspectors have been withdrawn from all the internal borders of the new 25 EU member states, which rendered control of a large quantity of the long distance animal transport in transit through Slovenia rather difficult. An enquiry carried out by the Slovenian official veterinarians in the first three weeks upon accession of Slovenia to the EU showed a dramatic increase in the violations of transport rules, comprising the overloading of vehicles, feeding and watering requirements, and travelling times and resting periods.

In response to this insufferable situation and in order to reinstitute animal welfare standards that had been in place before the accession, Slovenia established a mobile unit of veterinary inspectors, specifically equipped and trained for the job and assisted by the police, to carry out regular non-discriminatory checks on animal consignments along the roads in Slovenia. These checks have soon yielded tangible results as the conditions in which animals are transported through Slovenia have improved and are currently at a satisfactory level.

Slovenia and the European Union

In the pre-accession period, Slovenia adopted all the relevant EU legislation, transposing the entire animal welfare *acquis* into the Slovenian legal order.

Implementing regulations included also the Rules on the protection of laying hens, transposing the provisions of the relevant EU legislation, with a derogation granted to Slovenia in the pre-accession negotiations with the EU, namely a transitional period to the end of 2009 for some systems of laying hen battery cages that at present fail to comply with the provisions concerning the minimum cage height and slope. A transitional period of an additional seven months was also granted concerning the space allowance, permitting an area of 450 sq.cm per hen.

Jointly with the other member states, Slovenia currently participates in drafting the EU animal welfare legislation proposed by the European Commission.

Slovenia and the Council of Europe

Slovenia became a member of the Council of Europe on 14 May 1993.

Slovenia ratified the European Convention for the Protection of Animals for Slaughter on 20 October 1992, and the European Convention for the Protection of Animals kept for Farming Purposes on the same day by the Notification of Succession Act. Slovenia signed the European Convention for the Protection of Vertebrate Animals used for Experimental and other Scientific Purposes (ETS No. 123) on 31 January 2001, which is awaiting ratification. Representatives of Slovenia participate in the meetings of the Standing Committee and working parties of the Council of Europe.

Animal welfare NGOs in Slovenia

Several societies and some individuals have been more or less involved in the protection of animals against suffering in Slovenia. Most societies and their members are doing their best to improve the living conditions of animals. A lack of interface between them is a weakness they have in common, preventing them from making a major impact on the developments and achieving a greater public response in resolving the key animal welfare issues.

Some societies had been founded in the former Yugoslavia, and some have come into existence after Slovenia's independence. Societies of the past system operated mainly in the pet animal sector, which is mostly the case to date. Some societies are active also in the livestock sector, dealing principally with singular cases of inappropriate handling or suffering of animals. As already pointed out, the societies lack interfaces so as to cover the different aspects of animal welfare, taking into account the problem areas in Slovenia and elsewhere in Europe that urgently need more focused attention. Nevertheless, some societies are covering the entire territory of Slovenia, mostly in conjunction with live animal transport.

Despite some deficiencies it needs to be pointed out that the NGOs have been must productive and exerted a most positive influence on the public, minors and adults alike, in particular as regards their activities in increasing public awareness and educating the public in all the aspects of animal welfare. A sign of public recognition of the NGOs is the fact that the Protection of Animals Act stipulates, in addition to their involvement in the Expert Council for the Protection of Animals, that the NGOs shall be funded from the national budget, provided they have been granted the status of a society operating in the public interest.

In its fourteen years of independence, Slovenia has made significant progress in all aspects of animal welfare, and the last seven years commencing with the pre-accession negotiations have been most intensive. In these seven years, with the Protection of Animals Act constituting a milestone, Slovenia has upgraded animal welfare standards to a level on a par with the most advanced countries giving a high priority to animal welfare. It is needless to say that many open tasks await us in the future as there is always ample space for improvement, and some areas in fact do need improvement.

Nevertheless, we are positive that fruitful collaboration with experts in the different bodies, institutions and organisations of the EU and worldwide, such as the Council of Europe, the OIE, the WHO and many more, will keep this progress going. We have realised the importance of the NGOs in the animal welfare sector, as they are frequently the ones triggering new developments in and approaches to animal welfare and bringing about changes in the welfare legislation.

Slovenia is resolved to continue its active participation in animal welfare nationally as well as internationally, implementing the legislation in practice and making the provisions work in real life. We know that public awareness of animal welfare problems needs much and continual training, and a particular focus on children, building their personalities through a humane and mindful attitude to animals.

Spain: a non-protectionist country

by Martin. R. Gamero

Historically, Spain belongs to the group of "non-protectionist" countries in Europe. Animal protection is not only alien to Spain but, in some respects it is even incompatible with the traditions of the Spanish people. There are many different reasons for this, but all lead back to a traditional lack of interest in, if not contempt for, protectionist movements. The picture has obviously changed considerably over the last 30 years, but history, traditions and people's feelings cannot easily be changed from one day to the next.

Reasons why Spain is not interested in animal protection

Spain is a traditionally Catholic country that was scarcely influenced by protestant reform, in which the roots of protectionist movements are to be found; Spain was even a leader of the counter-reformation.

For four centuries the country was either isolated or continually at war with most of the other European countries and its energies were focused on its vast American territories. When it lost its last colonies, it withdrew into itself and did not take part in either of the two world wars. Some of the negative consequences of its isolation were that hardly anyone spoke any foreign languages, society was very closed to outside influence and very few knew what animal protection meant.

In the second half of the 20th century we were subjected to a long period of dictatorship, which was by no means conducive to animal protection.

The Spanish look on some countries as champions of animal protection but, rightly or wrongly, also see a contradiction between their love of animals and their ethical and historical conduct in other spheres of life.

Events involving animals, in which the animals nearly always suffered, were a traditional form of entertainment deeply rooted in Spanish popular culture. It was not only bulls that were used, in a wide variety of ways, but also many other animals such as horses, ducks, cocks, goats and turkeys.

Until relatively recently, Spain was a poor, underdeveloped country with a high level of illiteracy. This is the least appropriate context for discussing animal protection.

Bullfights are always cited as the main cause or the prime example of Spanish people's insensitivity towards animals. It is not always possible to prove such a link, although people who are not familiar with our culture find this difficult to understand. What can be proved, however, is that both Spanish and foreign anti-bullfighting protesters have to some extent had a negative impact on animal protection as a whole by not treating this activity separately from other aspects of animal protection. Not only have they not made any progress in getting bullfights banned but bullfights are now governed by a law instead of by a decree as in the past.

Consequences of this non-protectionist policy

This longstanding ignorance of or contempt for animal protection has many political, legislative, administrative and social impacts, as well as consequences for cattle farmers and consumers. The following are some of the most noticeable.

None of the political parties have included animal protection in their programme (with the recent exception of a minority party). The main parties do not believe Spanish people are interested in animal protection or that including it in their programme or holding debates on the subject would influence the outcome of an election.

There is not the slightest reference to animal protection or animal welfare in either the Spanish Constitution or any of the statutes of the autonomous communities. No national law on animal protection has ever been passed.

The aim of the requirements set out in the (recently revoked) 1955 Epizootics Regulation, stipulating that animals must be given adequate water, living space and food, was not to protect animals but simply to improve output. EU directives were transposed word for word into decrees with no further comments concerning their specific application in Spain.

Until relatively recently there was no specific section at any level of the Ministry of Agriculture concerned with animal protection, only a minor branch of the animal health services that had no specialised staff. For many years Spain was absent from the Council of Europe's animal protection meetings precisely because there were no administrative bodies to represent it.

There are very few associations committed to protecting animals and any that do exist are not very firmly rooted in society.

Citizens often criticise animal protection groups and it is possible to hear the most varied and usually negative opinions: "it's all about protecting the interests of rich countries, which just happen to be those which protect animals", "protectionists care more about animals than people", "it is quite incongruous to worry about animals when thousands of people in the world are dying of hunger", "God put animals in the world to serve mankind not the opposite", "animal protection is typical of countries which have solved all their economic and social problems and need to relieve their boredom", are only some of the comments that can be heard. These arguments are all easily refuted, but we should not forget that only those who want to be convinced can be convinced.

Cattle breeders like to consider themselves animal protectors and their key argument is that only healthy, well cared for and well fed animals are productive. But when you talk to them about the distress caused to animals or the possibility that animals should be able to satisfy their ethological needs, or if they do not see a direct relationship between investment and economic yield, they no longer feel so protective.

Generally speaking, consumers are not concerned about how food is obtained unless there is an impact on its "quality", be it in terms of health, nutrition or taste.

Changes in the last thirty years

This is the traditional position in Spain with regard to animal protection, and although certain standpoints and opinions remain unaltered, the changes that have taken place in Spain over the last thirty years have been so profound that animal protection cannot continue to be ignored. A number of phenomena and events have taken place which have had a major influence on animal protection.

The emigration of Spanish workers to Europe in the 1950s, the massive influx of tourists from the 1960s onwards and, finally, Spain's entry into the EU in the 1980s put an end to Spain's centuries-old isolation.

We are living under a democratic regime which fully respects human rights and traditionally this goes hand in hand with respect for animal rights.

The economic and cultural standards of Spanish citizens have risen considerably and income is close (but not yet equal) to the average income of the former 15 EU member states. Illiteracy has virtually been eradicated.

The Catholic Church has lost much of its influence on society and although it is difficult to gauge the impact this may have had on animal protection, Spanish people have definitely become more open, in all spheres of life, to the influences of other cultures.

EU norms with regard to animal slaughter and transport, and above all the latest directives concerning the protection of farm animals, have made cattle farmers and consumers recognise the considerable importance of animal protection and welfare.

The extreme popularity of a naturalist, who met with an early death, had an unexpected influence on Spanish people's view of wild animals and radically changed their attitude to environmental issues. This change in attitudes has had an indirect impact on animal protection, particularly among young people who used to be enthusiastic bird hunters but now criticise all forms of hunting.

The drop in the size of the rural population and the corresponding increase in the urban population has also had an influence on the way animals are treated.

One of the results of the recent food crises is that consumers now tend to buy meat products which they believe are produced in a more "natural" fashion.

Following an incident in which dogs were savagely mutilated by a number of unidentified persons before being taken in by a rescue centre in Catalonia, Spain suffered a national trauma and there were calls from all sectors of society for tougher legislation to avoid a repetition of this sort of behaviour and exemplary punishment for repeat offenders. As a result of this incident the Spanish Criminal Code has been amended and the ill-treatment of animals has become a criminal offence subject to a prison sentence (something that would have been unimaginable in Spain only ten years ago).

Although the general mood is still one of hostility, for the first time people are willing to discuss and listen to others' views on the subject.

Positive evolutions

All of the above-mentioned circumstances have significantly altered traditional attitudes to animal protection.

Although there is still no national law on animal protection, all the autonomous communities have a law on the subject, enacted by their respective parliaments. The first of these laws was passed by the Catalonian parliament and the last by Andalusia – further proof that protectionist movements progress from north to south.

The Ministry of Agriculture, Fisheries and Food has separated animal welfare from animal health and set up a special department with its own staff, specialising in animal protection. As a result the relevant legislation has been widely disseminated, European directives are transposed in greater detail and reference is made to specific Spanish requirements, communication between the autonomous communities has improved and

Spain is represented at all international conferences on the subject.

Animal protection and ethology now play an important part in several closely related academic disciplines, after being virtually unheard of until recently. Training courses are continually organised at all levels by both the Ministry of Agriculture and the autonomous communities and other bodies, including some private organisations. Rapid advances have been made in this field to make up for lost time.

EU norms on animal slaughter and transport have shown cattle farmers and butchers not only that animal protection is not "a foreign philosophy" but also that it is worthwhile because of its impact on the quality of their products. Over the last few years there have been impressive improvements in transport conditions for livestock and in slaughterhouse conditions. It is still hard for Spanish cattle farmers to accept the new rules governing the protection of farm animals, given that for years everything was dependent on productivity and animals were considered to be mere machines. Nevertheless, they are making efforts to adjust to the new situation.

Although many grey areas remain, animal protection is beginning to impinge on the mentality of the average Spanish citizen. The situation differs considerably in the different sectors of the population; there is greater awareness of the problem among young people than among adults, in towns than in the country, among educated people than among those with a lower level of education, and in northern than in southern regions.

As in other European countries there are associations in Spain which protect animals and defend their rights but they have very little support from the population and limited political clout. There are also many more producers' organisations with far more members.

The enforcement of the financial penalties provided for in the laws of the autonomous communities, together with the amendment to the criminal code, have either made traditional events involving animals more humane or led to their disappearance.

There are therefore bright and dark sides to animal protection in Spain, but the bright sides give reason to hope that further progress will be made. Nevertheless, there is a sticking point, which is not likely to be resolved in the short or medium term: bullfights. The situation is not as simple as it appears to those who look at it solely from the standpoint of animal protection. Bullfighting has an impact on many spheres – the economy, the arts, journalism, society, politics, the environment, cattle breeding, agriculture, veterinary medicine, crafts, industry, tourism, tradition and sentiment – all of which are of major significance. Protesting against bullfighting without being familiar with its background and everything it stands for only provokes contempt, mockery or the opposite reaction on the part of its supporters, and even of those with no particular views on the subject, and leads to the opposite result from that which was intended.

Bullfights are not only governed by a law in Spain but also covered by the Treaty of Amsterdam (now incorporated into the draft European Constitution), which calls for full regard to be paid to animal welfare in drawing up various policies, but at the same time stipulates respect of cultural traditions

Foreign efforts to improve animal protection in Spain give rise to a nationalist reaction by Spanish people, even those who are not normally interested in the subject, and to curiosity among foreigners who are not aware of the complexity of the matter. There are continual anti-bullfighting campaigns and court proceedings but individuals and organisations should take account of all aspects of the situation before getting involved in the fight to ban an event, which may, in the eyes of many people, be cruel or primitive, but which is deeply rooted in the soul of many Spaniards.

From the above, a number of conclusions may be drawn about animal protection in Spain:

- the current situation needs to be carefully analysed without forgetting the historical background;

- in terms of legislation, administration, education and information, Spain has now attained the average level of other European countries;

- rapid progress has been made with regard to animal protection on farms, animal slaughter, transport and experiments and the care of pets, and these have now reached an acceptable level, with some shortcomings with regard to the treatment of pets;

- mental and cultural attitudes are changing at a slower pace, but the necessary foundations are being laid;

- in order to continue making progress, it is necessary to separate animal protection and its various aspects from the controversy over bullfighting to ensure that the whole anti-bullfighting movement does not act as a brake on animal protection as has been the case until now.

Given the nature of the Spanish mentality, which has geographical, historical and cultural roots in three continents, efforts to change it will always be more successful if they are aimed at convincing people rather than imposing ideas.

France and animal rights issues

by Nathalie Melik

A growing public concern relayed by animal protection movements and the media, animal protection has become an ineluctable feature of certain society debates, marking the fine detail of our day-to-day lives and even the agricultural production methods of tomorrow. As our predilection for pets grows, the notion of respect for the animal world is becoming part and parcel of our everyday lifestyle. So much so that the battery of laws and regulations linked to animal protection is constantly having to evolve within all the structures competent in this field.

In the course of history and different civilisations the notion of animal protection has not been viewed with the same importance or in the same light. It is closely linked, obviously enough, with mankind's self-image but also with political, economic and social priorities.

Since 1850, the year of the Grammont law, which, in France, punished those who ill-treated animals in public, successive phases have been necessary, both in France and internationally, to arrive at the current provisions for animal protection, reflecting a gradually growing awareness of animals as they were used on more of a mass (or even industrial) scale than before. If use is to be made of animals, whether for experimentation, livestock farming, shows, etc., and that use may inevitably engender their suffering, the duty of mankind, having control over the methods used, is to avoid any "unnecessary" cause of suffering and strive to provide animals with optimum conditions of existence. We must be guided by the realisation that all animals can feel stress and pain.

In France, animal rights, or in more accurate legal terms the obligations of owners and keepers in respect of their animals, have on the one hand followed trends in European law and on the other hand developed in a quite specific context at national level where pet animals are concerned, themselves a fairly characteristic feature of French society.

Structures responsible for animal protection

The Ministry of Agriculture is responsible for all problems linked to animal protection while the Ministry of Environment is tasked with the protection of species.

The *Bureau de la protection animale* (Animal protection bureau) set up in 1980 in the Directorate General of Food, draws up the texts of laws and regulations and also instructions for applying them. Within that process it consults representatives of professionals, associations and the other ministries concerned. It uses the findings of scientific studies on animal welfare. It co-ordinates the communication and supervisory activities of the departments. It represents France in community or international bodies for the negotiation of texts relating to any aspect of animal protection. It also serves as a forum for co-ordination and dialogue between professionals, animal protection associations and representatives of the scientific world with animal welfare concerns. It may fund the research efforts of technical or scientific institutes in this field. The *département* directorates of veterinary services, operating under the prefect, apply the texts at grassroots level, with the Rural Code clearly defining their tasks and powers:

> "[...] they shall be responsible for identifying and recording breaches of the provisions for animal protection, and [for that purpose] enjoy access to premises and facilities where animals are present, with the exception of those in domestic use ... may open or have opened, both day and night, vehicles used professionally for the transportation of animals ... may have opened, in the presence of a member of the police or a law enforcement officer, any vehicle parked in direct sunlight ..."

They exercise their supervisory powers either through regular inspections, following a programme established at *département* level, or through targeted investigations, at the request of the central authorities, pursuing specific objectives: checking the conditions in which animals are transported, checks on pet shops or any other activity connected to pets, checks on the conditions in which animals are taken for slaughter and slaughtered, inspections of establishments providing animals for experimentation purposes, checks on the conditions of rearing pigs, calves, laying hens, etc. They are also responsible for checks on conformity in connection with authorisations (animal experimentation establishments, livestock transporters, etc.) or certification for activities involving domestic pets.

Veterinary services may "order the removal of animals suffering ill-treatment and entrust them to an animal protection association or foundation until the case is judged".[1] The veterinary services' ability to decide to remove animals greatly assists their efforts in the animal protection sphere, where swift intervention is necessary to ensure that animals are kept in proper conditions. Whatever the case, any removal of animals must be accompanied by conventional judicial proceedings. But if animals are seriously ill or in very poor physiological state, it is also possible to use an administrative procedure which sadly often concludes with the animal being put down.

There is a very wide range of animal protection associations in France, from those with a general vocation (National council for animal protection, Animal protection society, French Animal Rights League, Animal Assistance) to more specialised bodies (abattoir beasts assistance charity, French horse protection league). With their obviously front line involvement they are systematically consulted when any new text is drawn up on animal protection within the Advisory committee on animal health and protection. They are also able to bring criminal proceedings for ill-treatment of or acts of cruelty against animals as well for the deliberate killing of animals. Dialogue between the authorities and associations is often excellent, and initiatives to improve conditions for animals are sometimes undertaken in close collaboration between the two.

As for the *département* committees on animal health and protection, the prefect may choose to set up specialised training in animal protection within them; the committees bring together local representatives of authorities that may be involved in animal protection issues (emergency services, gendarmerie), representatives of the agricultural sector and professionals working in an animal-related capacity in the *département*, the veterinary profession, representatives of animal and nature protection associations, etc. The committees' role is to

1.
Article L.214-23 of the Rural Code.

co-ordinate initiatives in the area of animal protection and cater for the concerns of society in this respect. They are a means of:

- facilitating implementation of a true animal welfare policy in the *département*;

- improving the response to ill-treatment;

- co-ordinating the inter-commune management of stray animals;

- facilitating the handling of problems involving dangerous animals;

- providing opinions on initiatives concerning domestic pets or animal experiments.

Finally, texts relating to stray or dangerous animals are also prepared by the Animal protection bureau, with mayors bearing responsibility for their management.

General principles of legislation on animal protection

Initially, the Grammont law of 1850 prohibited the ill-treatment of animals in public. At the time it was a matter of protecting the image of humankind through a ban on degrading acts committed in public. In the 20th century, from the 1960s onwards, the law shifted in favour of animals, extending this prohibition to all ill-treatment, whether committed in public or not. The emphasis was no longer on the image of people but on the welfare of the animals themselves. In French law, animal protection as enshrined in current legislation is based on the law of 10 July 1976, which was the real starting point for the legal texts. It must be realised that the Council of Europe played a decisive role in the early development of regulations protecting animals and promotion of awareness of the needs of animals kept by humans. Community directives and regulations in turn marked major milestones in the development of texts and due consideration of animal welfare.

The legislative provisions are grouped in Chapter IV of section I, book II of the Rural Code, under the title "animal protection".

Article L.214-1 of the Rural Code stipulates that:

> "Any animal, as a sensitive creature, must be provided with conditions by its owner that are compatible with the biological imperatives of its species."

A person who owns or keeps animals is therefore placed under obligation by the law to provide the conditions of upkeep best suited to the animal.

The second fundamental article of the Rural Code, L.214-3 (1976) states that:

> "[...] it is prohibited to ill-treat domestic or tamed or captive wild animals. Decrees of the Council of State shall determine the measures to be taken to ensure that animals are protected against ill-treatment or abuse and avoid their suffering during handling inherent to various techniques of livestock breeding, penning, transportation and slaughtering."

This article is the foundation stone of all regulations on animal protection, regardless of species, situations or uses of the animal (livestock farming, keeping, transportation, slaughtering, circus performances). The implementing decrees vary in terms of the uses or categories of the animals concerned, individually defining the "abuses" considered as ill-treatment.

The criminal penalties punishing the perpetrators of ill-treatment or acts of cruelty relate to one of the following.

1. A misdemeanour (the perpetrator must go before a criminal court). In this case, they are specified in law:

> "An act, committed needlessly in public or in private, of serious ill-treatment or cruelty towards a domestic or tamed or captive wild animal shall be punishable by two years' imprisonment and a fine of €30000."[2]

The same penalties apply to the abandonment of an animal. These are acts committed with a manifest desire, to be assessed by the judge, to harm the animal. In such cases the judge may pass a further penalty prohibiting the individual from keeping animals, either definitively or temporarily.

2. A petty offence, applied to failure to comply with regulatory texts and scaled to reflect the seriousness and nature of the infringements.

2.
Article 521-1 of the Criminal Code.

In all cases, the reports drawn up by veterinary service officers are forwarded to the Prosecutor's office, which chooses to prosecute or file the case without further action.

Finally, it is fairly significant that the status of animals, classified as moveable assets in the Civil Code, changed in 1999 to distinguish them from inanimate objects. Thoughts are now being turned to granting animals reinforced protection status within that code, indicating a clear desire to take account of changes in mentality and society where animals are concerned.

Different spheres of animal protection

The spheres described below illustrate how these general principles are incorporated into French regulations and the procedures for applying checks.

Protection of livestock

Since 1980 a founding decree on animal protection has laid down the general obligation to feed and water animals and provide them with care and appropriate shelter. The text applies to all situations in which animals are kept or farmed and reiterates the provisions of the European Convention for the Protection of Animals kept for Farming Purposes. The texts adopted to implement this decree, which also incorporate the provisions of Directive 98/58 on the Protection of Animals kept for Farming Purposes, are geared to laying down in detail the minimum welfare conditions for keeping or raising animals kept for farming purposes, horses and pet animals.

By way of example, the community provisions on the farming of pigs, calves and laying hens are transposed on the basis of the decree. To ensure that methods of checking are harmonised in France and that the results gathered and then forwarded to the European Commission under directives applying to those species are uniform throughout France's *départements*, checklists and model annual reports are provided as references.

Pet animals

The keeping of domestic pets in France has now become a phenomenon of society. One household in two has at least one dog or cat, and for that reason French legislation and regulations have developed since 1999 in order to provide protection for these animals in keeping with the substantial role played by these creatures of companionship and also to cater for concerns linked to cohabitation, particularly in urban areas (problems of dangerous dogs).

The animal protection provisions applying to pet animals hinge on:

- mandatory reporting to the prefect of any activity concerning pet animals: keeping, transit, breeding, sale, impounding, sanctuaries, training and public showing;
- obligation of qualifications for individuals engaged in such activities;
- exacting standards for facilities, in terms of both hygiene and criteria for the respect of animals' general and specific biological needs;
- very exacting requirements governing the showing and sale of animals (authorised places, prohibition from fairs and markets, documents of sale, minimum ages for animals, classified advertising for the sale of dogs and cats);
- the setting up of pounds and sanctuaries, for better management of the problem of stray animals and, consequently, easier conditions for the rehoming of animals.

At a time when more and more people find themselves unable to cope with a domestic pet bought for the wrong reasons and when problems of trafficking in dogs and cats are becoming a concern of the public and the public authorities – particularly on health grounds – and of animal protection associations, making the breeding and sale of animals subject to regulations will improve animal welfare, ensure greater transparency in the trade in pet animals and enhance breeding in France.

In 2004 the European Convention for the Protection of Pet Animals (ETS No. 125) was eventually ratified. It is a useful complement to the very strict rules governing activities involving domestic pets by:

- prohibiting the sale of a pet to a minor under 16 years of age without the express consent of the parents;
- prohibiting surgical operations for the purpose of modifying the appearance of a pet animal or for other non-curative purposes;
- developing the selection of animals in a manner that avoids the passing on of genetic flaws that might alter their well-being or health.

Animals used for scientific purposes

The regulations on animal experimentation are derived from European Community and Council of Europe provisions. The aim is to cut down the number of animals used, to guarantee a match between the numbers of animals used and the protocols envisaged and to diminish any suffering that protocols might cause. The Criminal Code stipulates that the carrying out of experiments or research of a scientific or experimental nature on animals without complying with a decree is punishable by the penalties applicable to acts of cruelty or serious ill-treatment, that is, for a misdemeanour. Consequently, the regulatory text defines:

- which experiments are considered as legal;
- which animals may be used, their origin and identification;
- the procedures for authorising researchers;
- the procedures for approving establishments;
- the training to be undergone by technicians or animal keepers involved in experiments or animal upkeep.

It is a good example of implementing specific regulations generated by debate at international and community level, leading to improvements in the conditions in which animals live and are used, a cut in the number of animals used and greater responsibility on the part of the people involved. There are also texts providing for animals' housing conditions. All these texts are adjusted in line with developments at Community or Council of Europe level.

A national committee on ethical considerations in animal experimentation was recently set up, bringing together animal experimentation professionals in the public and private sectors, eminent specialists from the fields of law, philosophy and sociology, animal protection associations, representatives of the veterinary sphere and authorities responsible for research and agriculture. This committee will have the task of drawing up a national charter of ethics in respect of animal protection and issuing any useful recommendations on methods likely to improve animal welfare.

Transportation of animals

Public opinion regularly conveyed by the media is particularly sensitive to the conditions of livestock transportation, particularly on long journeys. The regulations, initially drawn up at the Council of Europe, are based on Community law. Transport is indeed a phase putting animals placed in strange and apparently hostile surroundings under substantial stress. France clearly has strong interests in animal transportation, owing both to its geographical location linking the north and south of Europe for road transport and to the importance of livestock farming in French agriculture. That is why inspections of animal transportation conditions are among the priorities pursued from year to year by the Ministry of Agriculture. In this area, France has elected to develop training validated at national level for animal transporters, which is undeniably a factor in engaging the responsibility of all those involved in the relevant sectors and therefore in improving conditions for animals in all types of transport.

Slaughtering and killing of animals

Obviously, it is vital that animal protection be implemented at this ultimate stage, when the animal is to be killed, particularly where animals kept for farming purposes are concerned. The stunning of animals in abattoirs was made compulsory as early as in 1964. The French regulators also quickly set about laying down requirements for the use of abattoir equipment, making stunning equipment subject to mandatory approval. A 1993 community directive broadened the scope of these provisions to all the operations carried out on a live animal in an abattoir, from unloading to bleeding as well as to all methods of killing animals outside abattoirs (farmed game, animals reared for fur). These particularly delicate phases call for constant vigilance on the part of the veterinary services through regular ante mortem checks on animals and inspection guideline material for use by abattoir professionals. Special considerations regarding ritual slaughter are covered in the regulations in this area.

These few examples of regulation in the area of animal protection are obviously far from exhaustive, but they do form the base architecture around which the other more specific texts are constructed. As a result, it is these main texts, very much under constant scrutiny by the champions of animal protection, that come in for review, amendment and in some cases criticism. In this respect, in-depth analysis of their origin and development provides a perfect reflection of man's perception of animals in line with his own sociological evolution.

Trends and outlook

Amendments and adaptations to texts are based on trends in the scientific process and new findings in ethology in particular, but they are primarily conditioned by a social demand. In each of the aforementioned sectors, there are national, community or international working groups considering the ongoing adjustment of texts as science progresses. Indeed, community directives are quite clear on this point, providing for regular review of some of their provisions.

Research in this field

It is important to realise the necessity of developing research programmes on animal welfare. Negotiations at community level can only be improved as a result, and all the more so since the countries most active in this field are also the countries where voluntary movements are most vigilant. France decided several years ago to take account of this vital factor and developed research on the conditions of transportation of cattle and pigs, the conditions of rearing calves, turkeys, chickens, laying hens, animal experimentation (animals' housing conditions, etc.), the breeding of pet animals and other areas. Fundamental research work on animals' sensitivity to pain or stress is very important in this connection. These programmes are developed in technical institutes, the national institute of agronomic research, the French agency for food safety, and veterinary colleges.

Development of the notion of qualifications

It is obvious that the better an individual's qualifications and knowledge of the physiological and behavioural needs of animals and the greater their ability to recognise signs of suffering or distress, the more the aims of animal protection can be fulfilled. It must not be forgotten, either, that animal-related qualifications and know-how reduce the risk of work accidents.

The notion of training or qualifications for those in contact with animals is now applied across the board. It is incorporated in European Community texts and in the Council of Europe instruments regarding livestock. For pet animals, it exists in the Council of Europe convention and was made obligatory by the law of 6 January 1999, which introduced certification. It has long been mandatory in the animal experimentation sector, where training is demanded and approved for researchers, technicians and animal keepers. Finally, in the transport sector it is a decisive requirement for the approval of carriers, and the training in this area must be validated. Overall, we will doubtless be seeing a future reshaping of relations between man and the animals used by man.

Supervision and public awareness

Alongside the development of regulations and growing public interest, the veterinary services are having to develop their supervisory function in the animal protection field. This is resulting in farm or transport inspection programmes as previously mentioned but also in more checks on domestic pets in the last few years, through surveys of pet shops, shelters and kennels in the summer season.

But checks alone are not enough. Each person involved in the process and every animal owner must be able to take on board the information necessary to the animal's welfare. To this end, the state has run campaigns to raise awareness among the owners or future owners of pets (a booklet setting out responsibilities) and developed specific training modules on animal welfare in numerous sectors. The voluntary sector and local councils have launched numerous initiatives with the same aim of making animal protection everyone's business and not just for specialists.

Economic aspects

Catering for animal welfare criteria has undeniable economic repercussions for all the professionals involved: conversion of buildings, purchase of new equipment, training of staff, changes in livestock farming and feeding methods, all have a cost that must be evaluated. A further example is the application since 1998 of community rules which adjust refunds granted for the export of live cattle to third countries according to their conditions of transport.

It is also clear that debate on animal welfare can have a very substantial impact on certain sectors: fattened waterfowl, beef calves, etc. It remains to be seen what impact it will have on prices for consumers and how far consumer demands can go in this respect. In the agricultural sector, the risks of price distortions with third countries must be considered and a future broadening of debate at international level is likely. Finally, the introduction of animal welfare standards on which aid to farmers will be conditional from 1 January 2007 (reform of the Common Agricultural Policy) is bound to influence perceptions in the farming world.

In conclusion, while animal welfare appears as a constraint arising from the various regulations in this area, it lays down a new definition of relations between us and animals that are more considerate of animals' needs and certainly in closer harmony with nature. Discussion in major research institutes and also within federations of professionals show that the requirements of animal protection are no longer perceived as mere idyllic fancies of people not conscious of the realities. On the contrary, scientific approaches are now moving towards a proper grasp of the concept of animal welfare, suggesting that another conception of agriculture is certainly on the way. If we are so attached to our domestic pets, as the number of pets in French households suggests, it is vital that we devise and apply ethical principles for the entire animal kingdom living alongside us, which will only enhance the image of ourselves that we leave reflected in nature.

The Council of Europe and animal welfare

by Egbert Ausems

As has been the case in many other areas, such as nature conservation, architectural heritage, urban renewal and bioethics, the Council of Europe was the first intergovernmental organisation to express concern about the fate of animals used by man.

In this way, over 40 years ago in September 1961, the Parliamentary Assembly addressed a formal recommendation[1] to the Committee of Ministers. In this text, the Assembly stated that "the humane treatment of animals is one of the hallmarks of western civilisation, but (...) even in member states of the Council of Europe, the necessary standards are not always observed", and accordingly requested the drafting of a convention to regulate the international transit of animals.

Why animal welfare?

From the beginning, the Assembly – and it has been followed in this by the Committee of Ministers – has based its activities for the welfare of animals on two considerations:

- among the ideals and principles which are the common heritage of all member states, respect for animals is undoubtedly one of the obligations underpinning the whole dignity of the European citizen;

- the general public in all Council of Europe member states is genuinely concerned about unnecessary suffering on the part of animals, and pressure is being brought to bear on governments to remedy this situation.

Over the last few years, other arguments have been put forward in support of animal welfare. It has long been recognised that education must play a major role in the protection of the natural environment. But how can younger generations be persuaded to safeguard nature and wildlife if they do not first learn to respect the animals around them? Furthermore, it has

1.
Recommendation 287 (1961) on the international transit of animals.

been established that where modern stockbreeding systems do not take account of all the elementary requirements of the animals kept, this can have adverse effects on public health and exacerbate environmental pollution.[2]

There has been a growing awareness since the early 1960s that animal welfare is not just an hysterical obsession on the part of a few eccentrics, or a mere hobby indulged in by a few well-to-do pensioners; this issue has become a legitimate concern for an ever-growing section of society which is endeavouring to apply basic ethical and moral principles in everyday life. Most political parties have come to take this concern seriously, and the Council of Europe's Parliamentary Assembly was the first international parliament to become active in this field.

Possible approaches to animal welfare

In each of its recommendations on animal welfare the Assembly has insisted that animals must be respected. This respect is based on the realisation that human beings are entitled to use animals to meet their needs in terms of food, clothing, companionship or in their quest for knowledge, health and safety. This is why the Assembly, in its concern for the economic and social progress of European citizens, has never advocated a blanket ban on the transport of animals, intensive breeding, the slaughter of animals, hunting or animal experimentation. Nor has it ever tried to put unreasonable limits on the right to keep animals as pets.

However, in its overall approach to the issue the Assembly has been careful about two aspects. Firstly, it has endeavoured to transpose into international law the ethically and morally acceptable norms and standards for allowing animals to be transported, bred, kept, slaughtered, hunted or used in experiments. Secondly, it has striven to ensure that animals which have to be subjected to any of these activities are treated in a way that does not inflict on them any avoidable pain, suffering, distress or lasting harm. The Assembly's recommendations therefore urge the prohibition of such practices as the transport of animals under inappropriate conditions, non-religious slaughter without prior stunning, hunting non-selectively,

2.
Two recent examples have been bovine spongiform encephalopathy (BSE) and avian flu.

keeping animals in an unsatisfactory environment and superfluous experiments on animals.

This realistic approach has proved successful. Not only has the
Committee of Ministers followed each of the Assembly's recommendations and drawn up five different conventions to
improve the welfare of five categories of animals, but these
conventions have been largely signed and ratified by the member states: the current totals of 109 ratifications and 122 signatures indicate that the Council of Europe's message has been
received.

These conventions have also proved useful to the European
Union, which, in its pursuit of a common market, has to harmonise the national legislations of its member states on animal
welfare. As we shall see below, the European Community is
party to the Council of Europe's conventions on farm animals
and laboratory animals and is considering acceding to the convention on animal transport. This transposes the provisions
formulated by the Council of Europe directly into Community
law, thus avoiding imposing parallel or even different rules on
Community member states.[3] For all its legal complications, this
unique co-operation in the field of animal welfare between the
Council of Europe and the EU has functioned in an exemplary
manner.

The various conventions

European Convention for the Protection of Animals during International Transport[4]

This convention was the first international legal instrument in
which sovereign states declared in the Preamble that they
were "animated by the desire to safeguard, as far as possible,
animals in transport from suffering" and that progress in this
respect might be achieved "through the adoption of common
provisions".

The preparation of this convention follows the recommendation of the Parliamentary Assembly of 1961. The Committee of
Ministers agreed only in October 1963 to mandate a commit-

3.
Which are also mem-
ber states of the
Council of Europe in
any case.

4.
European Treaty
Series (ETS) No. 65.

tee of experts to draft the said convention; the expert committee was established in 1965 and held six meetings between 1965 and 1967. Observers from the World Federation for the Protection of Animals,[5] the International Air Transport Association, the Central Office for International Railway Transport, the International Union of Railways, the International Road Transport Union, the International Office of Epizootic Diseases and the European Cattle Trade Union participated. The Customs Co-operation Council and the United Nations Economic Commission for Europe were consulted, as were the International Chamber of Shipping and the International Union for the Conservation of Nature and Natural Resources.

The Committee of Ministers adopted the draft convention in 1968 and finally, on 13 December of that year, the European Convention for the Protection of Animals during International Transport was opened for signature. This delay of over seven years after the Assembly's recommendation bears witness, on the one hand, to the complexity of the subject and, on the other, to the seriousness of the drafting.

The convention entered into force on 20 February 1971, following the deposit of the requisite four instruments of ratification. This further delay in implementing the measures advocated by the Assembly almost ten years earlier is attributable to the time taken by the individual states which had signed up in 1968 to bring their national legislations into line with the provisions of the convention, because although these provisions seem far from revolutionary if we compare them with current norms and standards, in 1968 they were new and in most legislations not as clearly defined as in the convention.

The convention lays down general but elementary requirements such as fitness on the part of the animals, veterinary inspection of livestock before loading, suitable equipment for loading, unloading and transporting the animals, adequate space for each animal and expeditious completion of transit formalities. The convention sets no limit on the distance over which animals may be transported or on the duration of such transport, merely requiring that animals are not left for more than 24 hours without food and water – unless the destination

5.
Which later merged with the World Society for the Protection of Animals.

can be reached within a reasonable time thereafter. The convention goes on to lay down special provisions for transport of animals by rail, by road, by water and by air.

However, another aspect excluded from the convention was a legal basis for the parties to meet and adopt further common provisions on the transport of animals. This situation was remedied when – without amending the convention – the Committee of Ministers in 1987 authorised the Secretary General to convene so-called multilateral consultations of parties to monitor the implementation of this convention and also of the European Convention for the Protection of Animals for Slaughter.[6]

From 1987 onwards, these consultations, again with the assistance of observers from the leading animal transport organisations and animal welfare associations, devised highly detailed codes of conduct on the transport of horses, pigs, cattle, sheep and goats, and poultry, respectively. These codes have no other relation with the convention than a reference to it; yet they were formally adopted by the Committee of Ministers as Council of Europe recommendations and addressed to all member states, whether parties to the convention or not.[7]

Since 1968, harmonisation of legislation on the transport of animals had become a major issue for the European Economic Community (EEC), which had adopted Community legislation on this subject, thereby, according to its internal rules, acquiring so-called "concurrent competence" in matters of international transport of animals. The Community therefore asked the Council of Europe to open up its animal transport convention to enable the EEC to become a full party to the instrument. This was achieved in May 1979, when an additional protocol to the European convention was opened for signature. It was ten years before all parties had signed and ratified (mainly because EEC competence in this particular area was contested in some EEC member states), but in November 1989 the additional protocol came into force.

On 19 March 1996, at the first meeting of the working party for the preparation of their third multilateral consultation, the parties to the convention acknowledged, in the wake of a new Par-

6.
ETS No. 102.

7.
Committee of Ministers recommendations by definition "recommend" a course of action to governments which they may or may not subsequently choose to follow; the legal duty to act on a so-called "recommendation ex Article 15 of the Council of Europe's Statute" goes no further than to consider in good faith whether or not it should be implemented.

liamentary Assembly recommendation on animal welfare and livestock transport, that its provisions should possibly be revised in the light of scientific progress and experience accumulated since the adoption of the convention.

The long process of revision led to the formulation of a revised convention, which built on the lessons learnt from the previous 30 years of experience and scientific breakthroughs. It takes the form of a framework convention laying down essential principles applicable to all species. It also provides for technical protocols on allocation of space and rest intervals, which can be amended in accordance with a simplified procedure, thus facilitating their updating. The revised convention still applies mainly to international transport, although it urges all parties to endeavour to apply the relevant provisions to national transport.

The convention was opened for signature in Chișinău (Moldova) on 6 November 2003. 15 member states have signed it so far, as has the European Community, and three of them have ratified it. When ratifying the revised convention states must concurrently denounce their ratification of the original 1968 text.

Four new codes of conduct are also currently being prepared on the rail, road, water and air transport of animals. These new texts will replace the existing codes of conduct for the transport of different species adopted in 1987, 1988 and 1990.

European Convention for the Protection of Animals kept for Farming Purposes[8]

As was the case with the transport convention, the initiative to draw up a convention on the protection of industrial stock-breeding was taken by the Assembly in its Recommendations 620 and 641 (1971). Again, governments were invited to appoint an official to sit on the so-called Committee of Experts on the Protection of Animals, and professional organisations and animal welfare associations were allowed to send observers.

This time, an active role was played in the committee by the observers from the Commission of the European Communi-

8.
ETS No. 87.

ties. Since the Communities were at the time deeply involved in their Common Agricultural Policy, harmonisation of national legislations on intensive breeding in their member states was of the utmost interest to the European Commission. Right from the outset, therefore, it had clearly voiced the European Economic Community's interest in becoming an actual contracting party to the future convention. This request for a community of states to become one party to a legal instrument of another organisation of partly the same states presented a number of interesting legal questions, but it did nonetheless come to fruition in 1988.[9]

In only four meetings between May 1972 and January 1974, the Committee of Experts had revised the Assembly's text and presented a draft convention to the Committee of Ministers. After thorough examination (not least of the provisions on the possible accession of the European Economic Community), the Committee of Ministers adopted the convention and decided to open it for signature in March 1976.

In the early 1970s many farmers considered intensive stock-breeding as a way of ensuring the survival of agriculture, which was in decline, and were therefore reluctant to make any concessions in husbandry methods which might endanger the competitiveness of the livestock industry. Both sides, the animal breeders and the animal welfarists, agreed that in order to breed healthy animals a number of basic conditions had to be met in fields such as food supply, adequate space provision, exercise, care and attention. But there was no agreement on the composition and exact amount of the food supplied, or on how much space, exercise and care were necessary to guarantee the bare minimum in terms of animal welfare. For every demand from the animal welfare side in terms of improving breeding conditions for the various categories, be it more space for animals in crates or cages, greater possibilities for exercise or easier access to natural food, the breeders would ask for scientific evidence as to the absolute need for such changes, which they felt would only lead to increased costs. To complicate matters even further, the member states themselves were divided into those which had flexible animal welfare legislation or wanted to protect their domestic

9.
In the meantime, the European Community has become a Party to other Council of Europe conventions, including the Bern Convention on the Conservation of European Wildlife and Natural Habitats (ETS No. 104), the Convention on the Elaboration of a European Pharmacopoeia (ETS No. 50) and the European Convention for the Protection of Vertebrate Animals used for Experimental and other Scientific Purposes (ETS No. 123).

stockbreeding industry, and those which had already enacted strict laws on animal protection. It was clear from the outset that identifying detailed criteria for the minimum welfare of each category of farm animal acceptable to both sides would be a lengthy and intensive process which would not be suited to direct codification in conventional provisions.

For that reason, the drafters of the convention opted for a so-called framework convention, namely a text which would lay down the fundamental principles of good husbandry and provide a machinery for the joint elaboration of more precise criteria governing each category of farm animal. The convention thus begins by listing the basic requirements for safeguarding the welfare of animals kept for farming purposes: appropriate housing and feeding, freedom of movement and regular inspections, all of which must comply with their physiological and ethological needs in accordance with established experience and scientific knowledge. The convention then provides for the setting up of a standing committee of parties to the convention and entrusts it with the detailed formulation of these basic requirements so as to ensure an acceptable minimum level of protection for each animal. In this way the convention lays down a basic code for animal husbandry but postpones the real codification of detailed instructions, which would also become binding, to a later juncture.

Council of Europe convention-making practice[10] has shown that member states are reluctant to embark on international legal instruments which go much further than their own current legislation. By splitting the convention into one part which would be fairly easy for most member states to accept because it would not significantly alter their stockfarming practices, and a second part which would allow them to work out for themselves the more detailed instructions for the implementation of the fundamental principles, the drafters aimed at circumventing this reluctance on the part of member states which had less strict laws on farm animal welfare. However, in so doing they imposed a heavy workload on the future standing committee.

10.
Some 200 conventions have been concluded by the Council of Europe to date.

In order to enable the Standing Committee to carry out its mandate, the convention provides for a working method whereby parties have time to examine the scientific evidence, take cognisance of acquired experience, draft the relevant provisions, settle any disagreements emerging and agree on compromises – all this without any other obligation for the parties than to consider them at home, consult their own breeders and welfare organisations, and after six months or more inform the Committee whether they accept the conclusions thus drafted. If two or more parties object, the conclusions are withdrawn and the Standing Committee has to start all over again. If the conclusions are accepted they become binding on all parties; they acquire the same conventional force as the provisions in the convention, and the parties have to implement them.

Because the conclusions of the Standing Committee are not initially binding, the convention refers to them as "recommendations of the Standing Committee". While it is true that by definition recommendations have no other force than having to be considered in good faith, the "recommendations" adopted by the Standing Committee lose this flexibility once they have been accepted by the parties and become "directives", that is, they take on mandatory force. It has also been pointed out that the Statute of the Council of Europe defines recommendations as one of the tools for intergovernmental co-operation[11] and that there is a risk of confusion between such recommendations, which are addressed by the Committee of Ministers to the governments of all member states, and the "recommendations" adopted by the Standing Committee and aimed exclusively at the parties to the farm animals convention. Be this as it may, the system has been successfully operating since 1986.

The European Convention for the Protection of Animals kept for Farming Purposes was opened for signature in March 1976, and in September 1978 it became effective after its fourth ratification. In 1982 the Standing Committee, assisted by observers from leading stockbreeders' organisations and animal welfare associations[12] who provided much of the scientific evidence and practical experience, started its work on the elaboration of "recommendations". The committee adopted recommendations on pigs and poultry (1986), cattle (1988), fur animals (1990), sheep and goats (1992), ratites (1997), domes-

11.
See footnote 7 above.

12.
European Confederation of Agriculture, Federation of Veterinarians of the EEC, International Society for Applied Ethology, World Society for the Protection of Animals and Eurogroup for Animal Welfare.

tic ducks, domestic geese, Muscovy ducks and hybrids (1999) and turkeys (2001). It is currently finalising a new recommendation on fish farming, and working on a similar new instrument on rabbits.

While the first task of the Standing Committee seems to be carried out in accordance with the convention, its second mandate, explicitly outlined in the Explanatory Report on the convention, is to examine periodically each of its "recommendations" and complete and amend them in the light of new scientific evidence. This work will ensure that the rules on the keeping of animals for farming purposes in Europe remains in line with the most recent knowledge on their welfare. The Standing Committee has in the meantime revised its recommendations on domestic fowl (1995), fur animals (1999) and pigs (2004). It is currently revising its recommendation on cattle.

Over the years, a second institution has become active in overseeing the implementation of the provisions of the convention and the "recommendations" of the Standing Committee: the European Commission. Since April 1989 the European Community is a party to the convention, which involves the EU giving effect to the principles of animal welfare laid down in the convention and implementing the "recommendations" of the Standing Committee. This is done by means of directives which transpose these principles and "recommendations" into Community law, the implementation of which directives is monitored by the European Commission. As mentioned above, this unique form of co-operation between the Council of Europe and the EU has led to some interesting legal questions, which fall outside the scope of this chapter.[13]

Biotechnology

Since the conclusion of the convention in 1976, science has progressed, and biotechnology in particular has reached levels of application to intensive breeding which had not been taken into account when the convention was drafted. In May 1991, the Standing Committee concluded that progress in biotechnology presented both positive and negative aspects for animal welfare and that in the absence of a specific international agreement it was highly desirable to define certain principles

13. For instance, in a Communication from the Commission of the European Communities to the Council and the European Parliament, on the protection of animals (document COM (93) 384 final, dated 22 July 1993) reference is made to a judgment of 23 February 1988 of the European Court of Justice (Cases 68/86 and 131/86): the protection of animals, being part of the Common Agricultural Policy, is a matter of exclusive Community competence. However, the Communication goes on to say that in the animal welfare field case law does not go so far as to impose the direct applicability of the Council of Europe rules to which the Community adheres; the Community must adopt its own legal framework in order to provide uniform application in the member states.

to be respected for the welfare of animals subjected to or resulting from biotechnological procedures. However, since the convention contained no explicit reference to problems of animal welfare connected with biotechnology and identified by the committee in the course of its work, it drew up a protocol of amendment to the convention which would empower the committee to deal in its "recommendations" also with biotechnological aspects of intensive breeding.

The Protocol of Amendment to the European Convention for the Protection of Animals kept for Farming Purposes[14] was opened for signature in February 1992. Pending ratification by all 30 parties – including the European Community – the protocol has not yet become effective. In practice, however, the Standing Committee continues to comply with its terms of reference and to base its work on all available scientific knowledge, biotechnological or other. Furthermore, national and EU legislation has taken most of its provisions on board.

European Convention for the Protection of Animals for Slaughter[15]

It was only logical for the Assembly, in its endeavours to improve the fate of farm animals during the stages of breeding and transport, finally to come to the terminal stage, namely the slaughter of the animal. In July 1973, the Assembly presented the Committee of Ministers with its Recommendation 709 inviting the governments to conclude a convention on the humanisation and harmonisation of slaughtering methods.

In 1973, national legislations on the slaughter of animals differed from one member state to the next. Some countries did not have enough slaughterhouses, and animals were still slaughtered on farms and at fairs or markets. Smaller slaughterhouses in remote areas were not always equipped to comply with elementary welfare rules. Closing down such slaughterhouses would entail longer transport for the animals for slaughter. In other states, the rules on hygiene and public health were strictly applied, and the EEC member states in particular were committed to implementing specific directives in these fields. This disparity in the norms and standards implemented within the borders of the Council of Europe was not

14.
ETS No. 145.

15.
ETS No. 102.

only confusing but also partly jeopardised the measures taken to improve animal welfare in industrial breeding and during transport.

As had been the case with the previous conventions on transport and on farm animals, the Committee of Ministers mandated the Committee of Experts on the Protection of Animals to prepare a draft text. The Committee of Experts started its work in June 1975, with the assistance of observers from the European Confederation of Agriculture, the International Committee on Laboratory Animals, the World Federation for the Protection of Animals and, of course, the Commission of the European Communities. This time, observers from the United States were also admitted, presumably because of US interest in the possible consequences for the world meat trade of a European convention on slaughter. The Committee of Experts presented its draft in June 1977; the convention was opened for signature in May 1979 and entered into force in June 1982.

The convention lays down two general principles: in all forms of slaughter animals must be spared any avoidable pain and suffering and, secondly, slaughterhouses must be designed in such a way as to enable all the applicable conditions in the convention to be met. Chapter II of the convention regulates the delivery of animals at the slaughterhouse and their lairaging, the moving of animals within the slaughterhouse and care to be given in general. Finally, the rules on the slaughter itself, inside or outside the slaughterhouse, appear in Chapter III.

The convention requires animals to be restrained when necessary before slaughtering, and also to be stunned. This requirement gives rise to a particular problem in the field of humane slaughter: the precept in some religions that the animal to be slaughtered must be drained of its blood before death, sometimes without prior stunning. At the time of drafting of the convention, religious slaughter without stunning was permitted in most member states; it was, however, forbidden in Iceland, Norway, Sweden, Switzerland and some Austrian *Länder*. The convention therefore allows parties to authorise derogations from the obligation to stun the animal before slaughter.

Like the convention on transport, the convention on slaughter does not provide for regular meetings of the parties to monitor implementation of the provisions, to improve them or to elaborate new rules. In 1987, as advocated by the parties themselves, the Committee of Ministers authorised the Secretary General to convene multilateral consultations of parties to the slaughter convention. The first consultation resulted in a code of conduct for the slaughter of animals, based on the convention but much more detailed and enriched with new scientific knowledge and acquired experience. This code of conduct was also formally adopted by the Committee of Ministers and addressed to all Council of Europe member states as Recommendation (91) 7.

European Convention for the Protection of Vertebrate Animals used for Experimental and other Scientific Purposes[16]

Experimentation on animals is probably one of the most sensitive subjects in the field of animal welfare. Every government encourages and stimulates scientific research as a key to economic development and improved living conditions. At the same time, governments must ensure that no new product is released on to the market before thoroughly testing as to possible side-effects, and legislation accordingly provides for experimentation, usually on animals. This applies particularly to medical research, where newly developed medication might save human lives but might also cause undesirable harm. The most logical way to ascertain any harmful effects is to test the new drug on animals.

As early as 1971, the then Consultative Assembly recognised that to protect animals against abusive and unnecessary experimentation, certain norms should be established at international level enabling states to harmonise the regulations on such experiments in their domestic law.[17] The Assembly had opened yet another Pandora's box: while animal welfare organisations applauded the initiative, researchers, and in particular the pharmaceutical and cosmetic industries, protested that any such international regulation might impede the development of science. Both sides started lobbying the governments, and

16.
ETS No. 123.

17.
Recommendation 621 (1971) on the problems arising out of the use of live animals for experimental purposes.

only in 1973 did the Committee of Ministers reach agreement on the elaboration of a draft convention.

Again, the Committee of Experts on the Protection of Animals was entrusted with the task of drawing up a text. However, the Committee preferred first of all to finalise the slaughter convention, and the real work on animal experimentation did not start until January 1978. Five years later, in April 1983, a draft was presented to the Committee of Ministers for adoption. But even within the Committee of Ministers, the political body, the avalanche of amendments submitted by the various governments was such that the technical Committee of Experts had to be reconvened in order to sort them out and suggest compromise solutions.[18] Finally, in May 1985, the convention was adopted and opened for signature on 10 March 1986. On 1 January 1991, the European Convention for the Protection of Vertebrate Animals used for Experimental and other Scientific Purposes entered into force, but by virtue of Article 3, parties had five years to give effect to the provisions.

The very preamble to the convention constitutes progress in the actual concept of animal welfare: for the first time in an animal welfare convention the member states recognised explicitly "that man has a moral obligation to respect all animals and to have due consideration for their capacity for suffering and memory".[19] The explanatory report on the convention – which admittedly has no legal force, but the publication of which must be explicitly approved by the Committee of Ministers – points out that "the states signatories to the convention, while accepting the need to use animals for experimental and other scientific purposes, recognise that everything possible should be done to limit such use with the ultimate aim of replacing such experiments, in particular by alternative methods".

The convention itself pursues three objectives: reducing the number of experiments with animals, reducing the number of animals used in such experiments and ensuring that these animals suffer as little as possible.

To reduce the number of experiments, the convention limits the purposes for which experiments on animals may be carried

18.
Although confidential at that stage, the text of the draft had leaked out and the lawn in front of the Council of Europe building was flooded with animal welfarists demonstrating for a stricter convention.

19.
Cf the Preamble to the Convention on the Conservation of European Wildlife and Natural Habitats (Bern 1979, ETS No. 104): "Recognising that wild fauna and flora constitute a natural heritage of aesthetic, scientific, cultural, recreational, economic and **intrinsic** value that needs to be preserved and handed on to future generations".

out: prevention and treatment of diseases in man, animals and plants (including testing of products); research on physiological conditions in man, animals and plants; environmental protection; scientific research; forensic enquiries; education and training. Moreover, the convention prohibits experiments with animals where other scientific methods are available.[20] Finally, in order to help avoid the unnecessary repetition of experiments, the convention requires parties to recognise, under certain conditions, the results of each other's procedures.

The number of animals used in experiments is also reduced by the convention: the species to be used must be carefully selected, and where there is a choice of procedures, precedence must be given to the type of experiment which requires the smallest number of animals. Furthermore, an animal may be used again if it is healthy and well and will not suffer seriously from the next experiment.

Thirdly, the convention seeks to improve the care given to the animals. Before or during the experiment the animals must be given such accommodation, environment, some freedom of movement, food, water and care as are appropriate to its health and well-being. During the drafting of this provision, it became clear that it would be impossible to lay down in the convention specific, detailed rules on accommodation and care to be given to each category of laboratory animal. The drafters agreed on a compromise: they appended to the convention an appendix containing detailed guidelines on the physical facilities, the environment and the care to be provided to the animals. Even though this appendix is an integral part of the convention, it is a mere recommendation without mandatory force: the only obligation on the parties is to consider in good faith the extent to which they can apply the guidelines in Appendix A.

One of the main emphases of the convention is the animal's suffering during experimentation; this must obviously be reduced to the minimum; anaesthesia must be used unless this would jeopardise the objective of the experiment, but in that case the need for such an experiment must be double-checked. The convention goes even further for experiments in which the animal will experience enduring severe pain: in such cases

20.
One of the draft articles illustrates the extreme prudence with which governmental experts formulate future obligations for their governments: "Each Party should (1) seek to (2) take steps (3) as it deems appropriate (4) to encourage (5) if possible (6) scientific research into the development of methods which could provide the same information as that obtained in procedures". In its wisdom, the Committee of Ministers deleted precautions 2, 3, 4 and 6.

the competent national authority must be informed or its authorisation obtained. Proposals to introduce a straightforward system of permits here was rejected.

The convention requires the animal to be killed after the experiment if it cannot be restored to normal health and well-being. If the animal is kept alive it must be cared for; if healthy and well it may be used again in a painless experiment; or if necessary for the experiment it may be set free.

For the rest, the convention regulates such conditions as the qualifications of people involved in experiments and those in charge of breeding and supplying the animals, the registration of establishments that breed or supply laboratory animals and those which carry out experiments, and the registration of laboratory animals. The convention attaches great importance to the collection and dissemination of statistical information on animal experimentation as one of the tools for monitoring the use of animals for these purposes. To ensure harmonised information, Appendix B to the convention, which is mandatory, presents a set of standard tables.

The convention is open for signature by the European Communities, which signed in February 1987 and approved the convention in April 1998. Before doing so, in November 1986, the Council of the European Communities adopted a Directive on the approximation of laws, regulations and administrative provisions of the member states regarding the protection of animals used for experimental and other scientific purposes (86/609/EEC). This directive is largely based on the Council of Europe convention, but it is not identical owing to pressure from the European Parliament which found the convention too lax.[21] Notwithstanding these differences, no serious problems have arisen yet in respect of states which are bound by both, that is, Community member states which are party to the convention, principally thanks to the close co-operation between the Council of Europe and the Commission of the European Communities.

Unlike the transport and the slaughter conventions, the animal experimentation convention does provide for multilateral consultations of parties. The first consultation, in November 1992,

21.
The differences between the convention and the directive have been analysed in a study by Amelia Tarzi, trainee at the Council of Europe's Directorate of Legal Affairs.

assessed information from the representatives of the parties and identified a number of problem areas in the implementation of the convention, arising mainly from divergent interpretations by different parties of selected provisions. The consultation meeting therefore adopted a resolution fleshing out the scope of the convention in respect of transgenic animals and remodelling certain statistical tables.

The second multilateral consultation took place in November 1993, adopting a resolution on the education and training of persons working with laboratory animals. The third consultation, held in May 1997, led to the adoption of two new resolutions on the acquisition and transport and on the accommodation and care of laboratory animals, respectively.

From the strict animal welfare angle, the laboratory animals convention has not added much to the national legislation that was already in force in 1986 in some member states. Nevertheless, the adoption of the convention by the Committee of Ministers was an important step forward in that all other member states explicitly acknowledged that experiments with animals could give rise to welfare problems, that these problems could be partly solved and that this should be done at international level. Secondly, eight years of research and negotiations have led to a Europe-wide codification of norms, standards and principles accepted by governmental experts, delegates from animal welfare organisations, scientific researchers and representatives of the industries in question. This codification was subsequently used as the basis for further improvement by the parties and, at the specific Community level, for EU legislation.

European Convention for the Protection of Pet Animals[22]

In May 1979 the Parliamentary Assembly recommended the Committee of Ministers to draw up a convention to regulate the trade in animals and to control animal populations.[23] In January 1981 the Committee of Ministers instructed the Committee of Experts on the Protection of Animals – which was at that time busily drafting the laboratory animals convention – "to examine the legal aspects of animal protection with a view to preparing appropriate instruments". The Committee of

22.
ETS No. 125.

23.
Recommendation 860 (1979) on the dangers of overpopulation of domestic animals for the health and hygiene of man, and on humane methods of limiting such dangers.

Experts started work on domestic animals in November 1983 and presented a draft convention in June 1986. The Committee of Ministers adopted the convention in May 1987, and in November 1987 the European Convention for the Protection of Pet Animals was opened for signature.

The origins of the pet animal convention are slightly different from those of the previous conventions. First of all, the Parliamentary Assembly's basic recommendation was inspired by public health concerns rather than animal welfare. Secondly, the Committee of Ministers was not immediately convinced of the need for a convention to protect pets. When the Assembly's recommendation was referred to it, it first of all sought the opinion of the Committee of Experts on whether a convention was really needed in this matter. After the Committee of Experts had recommended studying the problem at the European level, the Committee of Ministers instructed it to do precisely that "with a view to preparing appropriate instruments", implying that it was still not convinced of the need for a convention. It is to the credit of the Committee of Experts, assisted as usual by observers from the World Society for the Protection of Animals and the Eurogroup for Animal Welfare, representatives of the pet animal trade organisations and of hunting and falconry associations, that the convention on pet animals nevertheless saw the light of the day.[24]

To meet the concerns expressed by the Assembly and to convince the Committee of Ministers, the Committee of Experts adopted a broad approach. The final outcome was a draft convention which would ensure international legal protection to pet animals, based on safeguarding their health and welfare. The scope of the convention is therefore limited to "animals sharing man's companionship and in particular living in his household". However, the convention also takes into consideration the conservation of threatened wild animal species, the inconveniences caused by stray animals, the danger that certain animals may present to human health and safety and disease control. This broad approach is already apparent in the preamble, where parties explicitly consider the risks inherent in pet overpopulation to human hygiene, health and safety, the range of animal species which can be kept as pet animals, the

24.
Although doubt subsisted until the final adoption of the convention by the Committee of Ministers, when, before the vote, one of the Permanent Representatives wondered whether the Council of Europe had no better things to do than to look after cats and dogs ...

lack of knowledge and awareness in this field, as well as the need to discourage people from keeping wild fauna as pets. In conclusion, the convention does not encourage the keeping of pet animals, but advocates responsible ownership.

This concept of responsible ownership underlies the basic principles laid down in the opening provisions of the convention: nobody shall cause a pet animal unnecessary pain, suffering or distress, nobody shall abandon a pet, and any person who keeps a pet animal (or has agreed to look after it) shall be responsible for its health and welfare. The latter provision includes the obligation to take all reasonable measures to prevent its escape. The convention also prohibits inbreeding for commercial purposes, the breeding of abnormally aggressive animals or animals with hereditary defects or other physical characteristics required by certain pedigree standards. Training animals in a way that is detrimental to the animal's health and welfare is prohibited, as is the unrestricted use of pet animals in advertising, entertainment, competition and similar events unless certain conditions have been met.

The convention also prohibits surgical interventions on pet animals for non-curative purposes, such as tail docking, ear cropping, devocalisation and declawing, unless a veterinarian considers the intervention necessary for veterinary medical reasons. Opposition came from breeders and hunters, particularly in respect of the docking of tails of certain hunting dog species, but these objections were rejected by the majority of experts. Furthermore, the convention lays down that except in emergencies, pet animals may only be killed by a veterinarian or other competent person and, in principle, not by means of drowning, suffocation, poisoning not preceded by anaesthesia and electrocution without prior loss of consciousness. A special chapter in the convention is devoted to stray animals. When their numbers present a problem, parties may capture them with a minimum of physical and mental suffering and keep or kill them, though still in accordance with the convention.

Because in the preamble the signatory states expressed concern about lack of knowledge and awareness of pet animals, the convention particularly emphasises information and education programmes, which parties undertake to encourage. In this way, it is prohibited to give children pet animals without their parents' agreement, or to offer pets as prizes, awards or bonuses. Parties must also discourage unplanned breeding of pet animals, which was considered as one of the main causes of the proliferation of stray animals. The convention entered into force in May 1992, four and a half years after its opening for signature. To date, 21 states have signed, 18 of which have also ratified the instrument. The convention provides for multilateral consultations to be convened every five years from its entry into force, geared to examining the implementation of the provisions and the need for revision or extension. Such a consultation was held in 1995, during which the parties adopted three resolutions on surgical operations on pet animals, the breeding of pet animals and the keeping of wild animals as pet animals respectively.

The European Convention for the Protection of Pet Animals remains the only international legal instrument codifying the fundamental rules on the keeping of animals as pets.

The room for animal welfare activities has been drastically reduced in the Council of Europe's current work programmes, with no budgetary lines and no specialised staff. The Committee of Experts on the Protection of Animals, which had so successfully prepared all texts required by the Parliamentary Assembly, was abolished in 1987, just as it was about to start examining the welfare of animals in exhibition situations (zoological gardens, safari parks, circuses, bullfights, etc.).

In 1993, the Parliamentary Assembly asked[25] for a convention to be drawn up "covering bioethical aspects of biotechnology applied to the agricultural and food sector". In its reply, the Committee of Ministers promised to convene a conference. In 1999 in Oviedo (Spain), at the Council of Europe's International Conference on ethical issues arising from the application of biotechnology, a whole session was given over to animal welfare. However, the Committee of Ministers rejected the recommendation based on the conclusion of the conference to

25.
Recommendation 1213 (1993) on the development of biotechnology and the consequences for agriculture.

continue developing activities in this field. This decision may be regretted considering the international pioneering role played by the Council of Europe in this field.

The Council of Europe's work on the welfare of animals is impressive both in volume and quality. With the exception of animals in exhibition situations, it has covered virtually all the areas in which animals are directly used by humankind. All its work, embracing conventions, recommendations and codes of conduct, has been based on extensive scientific research and accumulated experience, also taking account of the opinions of the professionals concerned and of the whole range of animal welfare organisations. It has therefore laid the vital foundations upon which further rules can be grafted in order to guarantee proper animal welfare.

But the work has not yet been finished. Firstly, the Council should continue to update its conventions, recommendations and codes of conduct by pursuing its scientific work on animal welfare. The influence it continues to have on EU legislation testifies to the importance of that work. Secondly, it should not only ensure that its instruments are implemented by its older member states, but should also assist the new member states to adapt their legislation and administrative practice to the animal welfare norms and standards which it has established. It must continue be a driving force in this field, enabling its work to retain its status as an international level reference point.

Conclusion – Animal welfare and the ideal of Europe

by Colin Tudge

Britain's former Prime Minister Harold Wilson said of the Labour Party, that it "is a crusade or it is nothing". The same, surely, can be said of the European construction. If it is just a marketing cartel, or just another power base, then so what? The world has surely seen enough of them. If ordinary Europeans like me are to take Europe seriously, treat it as more than a pest with nit-picking rules or as a holiday resort, a place to drink good coffee, then it has to stand for something. It must emerge as a serious version of civilisation – not the only version there is but an excellent one nonetheless: one that truly contributes to the world as a whole. Europe in reality has been all kinds of things in its time (and still is) but traditionally, and ideally, we think of it in Renaissance terms, as summarised in the panels on the ceiling of the Uffizi Gallery: the arts, the sciences, theology, all manners of philosophy, and economics (the Medicis were bankers first and foremost) all flourishing, all in balance, for the greater benefit of all humankind and for the enhancement of the world; hearts and minds in harmony.

Yet our claim to civilisation should be judged not by occasional magnificence – not by the wonders of Renaissance Florence – but in moral terms. The greatest test lies in our treatment of those who are vulnerable, and cannot fight back if we treat them badly: vulnerable people, and all non-human species. In short, whether the lofty ideals of the Renaissance and all that has followed are worth a hill of beans can very properly be judged by our treatment of chickens and cows, cage birds and laboratory mice, foxes and songbirds, zoo lions and circus elephants. This present Council of Europe report is even more relevant than it seems, in short. To a significant extent it measures the worth of the European ideal.

Optimists, of the kind who in Britain are known as "Whiggish", like to think that the world is getting better; that the process of civilisation itself inexorably shifts us, click by ratchet click, from barbarism to sweetness and light. Others, observing the mayhem of the 20th century and the unabated disasters that have followed us into the 21st, are doubtful. The treatment of animals in Europe this past few thousand years and even in the past few decades provides powerful support both for Whigs and for the most extreme pessimists.

We can be cheered, first of all, that animal welfare is at last on the agenda. Twenty years ago, in most countries and in most situations, it was not. The idea that governments, or the putative supergovernment of Europe should bother with such stuff, would in many circles have been considered ludicrous. But as outlined in several of the excellent essays in this report, minds are changing. Deep and elusive notions such as "animal rights" are now discussed in public and sometimes translated into law, while rigorous science is applied to find out what animals actually need and want, as opposed to what we, anthropomorphically, might guess should make them happy. The very fact that the Council of Europe has produced this report is a step forward – although, of course, it is much easier to produce reports with statistics and fine prose than it is to make a real difference.

Assuming, though, that we really do take the welfare of animals seriously, what in practice should we do?

Actually, this innocent question raises issues of seemingly endless depths that we – humanity as a whole – have hardly even begun to explore. To begin with, why do we suppose that animal welfare is even an issue? It is not an issue unless animals are capable of suffering. We do not discuss the happiness of chairs or the well-being of wardrobes, so why of animals? If they do suffer, how do we know what measures will improve their lot? The great 20th-century zoologist Sir Peter Medawar tells how as a boy he tucked up a frog in a nice warm bed – only to find it dry as a crisp in the morning. Might not we make the lives of animals worse in our attempts to improve them? George Bernard Shaw's adage is surely relevant – that the road to Hell is paved with good intentions.

Many other societies have taken it for granted that other animals can and do suffer because, quite simply, they drew no sharp distinction between "them" and "us". It is as least widely reported (and presumably is true) that many peoples of North

America apologised to the various animals that they were obliged to kill for food, and to the gods of those animals, who were also their own gods. The Hindu tradition, with its Buddhist derivative, as outlined here by Daniel Chevassut, sees all life as a series of reincarnations: all of us were animals in past lives, and present-day cows and hamsters may be humanity's future princes. Europeans perhaps come closest to the spirit of such attitudes in St Francis who, in the early 13th century, acknowledged other animals as his brothers and sisters. Francis is often perceived as the most Christ-like of the Christian saints – although it is not obvious that other Christians have necessarily followed his lead.

But post-Renaissance Europeans in general have been made of sterner stuff. Above all, our tradition is analytical. René Descartes in the 17th century suggested that although non-human animals may often seem to be like us – sometimes thoughtful, sometimes sad, sometimes joyous – we should not be deceived. After all, he said, the clockwork mannequins that were popular in his time imitated human manners wonderfully – but no one would suggest that they have truly human qualities. The key seemed to lie with verbal language. Humans seem to think in words. Animals clearly do not have words – or at least they do not string the noises they make together to fashion brand new thoughts. But if thought requires verbal language, then it follows that animals cannot think. If they do not think, they cannot be conscious. If they are not conscious – well, they may scream when assaulted but this signifies nothing. A corpse may twitch, after all. Voltaire was among the Enlightenment philosophers who thought this altogether too glib. Animals (at least vertebrate animals) have the same kinds of nerves and brains that we do, and the same organs in general, so why suppose that they are more like clockwork toys than they are like us? If they are like us, then how can they not be capable of suffering?

This kind of discussion could have gone either way but in practice, in the early 20th century, the coin flipped towards Cartesian rationalism. The logical positivists based in Vienna in effect declared that nothing that could not be directly measured and analysed was worth taking seriously at all. This for a time virtually became the orthodox agenda of science (and in some circles still is): everything that is not readily definable and pin-downable, is fit only for dreamers. A powerful school of psychologists, anxious to turn their subject into a true science, seized on this line of thinking. From before the First World War until well into the 1970s, behaviourism dominated: psychology based entirely on the study of what animals *do* – how they observably and measurably behave. All the traditional trappings – ideas of mind, and emotion, and suffering – were stripped away, confined to the wastebin along with metaphysics in general. To imagine that animals may suffer as we do is to fall into the trap of anthropomorphism: attributing human qualities to non-human entities. When I first studied biology formally in the 1950s and 1960s, anthropomorphism was seen as the cardinal sin, the apotheosis of muddle-headedness.

This brings us into a paradox. In much of the world, it seems, people routinely treat animals with indifference, and often with what looks like extreme cruelty. It is common to see animals in traditional markets in Europe or Asia or Africa tightly tied by the neck or the feet in the noonday sun. Chickens are peremptorily slaughtered as often as not with a blunt penknife. Yet the same, traditional societies who administer such assaults – lacking the rationalist, Cartesian tradition – take it for granted that animals can suffer. But then, in traditional societies, life is hard. We all suffer. If animals suffer now and again – well, that's life.

Europeans, with our primarily Christian background, tend to take it to be self-evident that it is bad to inflict pain on others. But our Cartesian rationalism, reinforced by logical positivism and the (highly successful) agenda of behaviourism, has apparently convinced us (or at least, many of us) that animals do not *really* suffer so it still does not matter what we do to them. Animal welfarists have often been assured from on high that their concerns are "merely" sentimental; that there is no "scientific evidence" that animals know or care much what is happening to them, despite appearances, so there is no problem. So the rationalism of which we are rightly so proud has also often prevented us from behaving with what to many people seems simply to be common sense and common humanity.

Of course in large part the ultra-rationalists are right. There is no "scientific evidence" that animals suffer. If they squeal – well, Descartes' point applies. Mannequins can be made to squeal, too (even those of Descartes' day). We do not *know* that animals really feel anything, or register their own feelings. This, however, is simply the first of a series of deep philosophical traps. To begin with, the adage applies – that "absence of evidence is not evidence of absence". To be sure, the only way to know that an animal suffers is to get inside its head and become the animal: to experience the world through its own brain and senses. But we cannot do that. So there is no evidence. More profoundly, though, we have to question the whole logical positivist agenda. Is it really true that what cannot be directly measured is not worth taking seriously? Here there are two points. First, mind and consciousness cannot directly be observed and measured – but does it make any sense to say that they therefore do not exist? We *know* that we ourselves are mindful (indeed as Descartes himself pointed out, it is the only thing we can be certain of). Yet we do not *know* that other human beings are mindful for precisely the same reason that we do not know that animals are. We cannot get inside other people's heads any more than we can project ourselves into cows and chickens. But is it sensible to deny that other people are mindful? If not, why not? Because everything that other people do suggests that they do know what is going on around them. Yet to a significant extent this is true of animals, so why doubt that they are mindful too? We are back to Voltaire's point.

In truth, the behaviourist agenda that dominated so much of the 20th century was a success. It did help to put psychology on to a sound scientific footing. But it has led too many people into nonsense nonetheless. Thus, the behaviourists were perfectly right to leave mind and consciousness out of account precisely because they are metaphysical concepts that were and are too difficult to study by experiment. To quote Medawar again (who was misquoting Bismarck): "Science is the art of the soluble". This means, however, that the behaviourists left "mind" out of account simply as a matter of convenience, to tidy up their scientific protocol. But it is a deep and obvious nonsense to suggest that ideas that we leave out for convenience thereby cease to exist, or to be important. That, nonetheless, is the nonsense that many Europeans in influential places have allowed themselves to fall into this past century or so, and have subjected the rest of us to. Science, they have all too often seemed to think, has somehow demonstrated that animals cannot suffer to any significant extent. Therefore they can reasonably be treated simply as possessions: not bashed about too much, but only because this lowers their value.

But even if (still a "biggish" if) we agree that animals can suffer and as sentient beings should be treated well, what in practice does this imply? As a general question, can we improve on common sense?

Actually we can. To be sure, we abandon common sense at our peril (and at everything else's). But it is the general task of science to improve on common sense and in this sphere it certainly can. Medawar's frog story applies. Even though we may acknowledge that it makes sense to compare other animals to ourselves in general terms it is a huge mistake to suppose that they resemble us in detail. If in all the practicalities we simply observe the ancient intuitive rule (albeit formalised by Immanuel Kant) of "do as you would be done by", we might end up by torturing them. This is where science, and hard-nosed philosophy of a practical kind, have a very positive role to play: finding out, as far as we can, what the different species do actually like, and what they dislike, so that we can truly cater to their predilections. Though no one can truly see the world from the animal's point of view, scientists can and do gain objective insights by various routes, for example by measuring the animals' output of various hormones associated with stress, or measuring the discomforts they will put themselves through in order to achieve desired ends. Hens, for example, will overcome serious obstacles to find their way to nests to lay their eggs. To start this report, Professor Donald Broom spells out the principles and progress so far: absolutely vital if we truly seek to improve the lot of animals, and not simply to salve our own consciences; and absolutely within the European tradition of philosophical analysis and objective scientific inquiry.

But in this as in all else Europe has a less acceptable face as well. Increasingly in Europe as in the world as whole, human affairs are driven by commerce. If there is money to be made, then ordinary sensibilities are all too easily sidelined. Thus we may discover that hens like to scratch and make nests (as pigs do), and that cows feel at home in herds of a dozen or so. But commerce has driven us to keep dairy cows in herds of a 100 or more (a thousand or more is already common in the US) and to keep pigs in factories of a million-plus – already unexceptional in the US, and now coming to the newly-expanded Europe. We can pass laws to improve practice ad hoc, but when the system as a whole drives farmers and beasts towards ever greater productivity such reforms, which require so much effort to bring about, begin to seem rather forlorn. Britain's police, commendably self-critical, recently accused themselves of "institutionalised racism". Perhaps in the ultra-commercial, industrialised farming of Europe and America, we have institutionalised cruelty. Yet the commerce that drives the industrialised system is perceived to be extremely "rational". It is, after all, geared to "efficiency", which is often equated with rationalism. Here too we see the ambivalence of science. Good science is essential if we are truly to find out what animals want and what makes them unhappy, without which welfare measures are hit-and-miss. But science in another guise makes industrialisation possible – for example to supply the antibiotics and other anti-infective measures that are required in extremely intensive husbandry. On the other hand – can we really be sure that hens in cages are better off than hens in free-range flocks? Apparently, the mortality rate in cages is lower. So what is actually preferable? Common sense can take us a very long way and is abandoned at our peril but we need more, good, objective, science-based studies as well.

Science and commerce too lie behind the modern pharmaceutical industry which uses, worldwide, many millions of animals for experiments and for testing drugs. In most countries, apparently, including most European countries, this raises few qualms. Most people seem to take it for granted that animals can reasonably be sacrificed and even endure some suffering, to save human lives. As a broad generalisation we may accept this. If it is reasonable to kill pigs for bacon it is surely reasonable to sacrifice mice to develop drugs to save the lives of children. In some countries at least (including Britain) laws to protect laboratory animals from unnecessary pain are stringent, and stringently applied; and laboratory animals, cared for by professional technicians, are often far better off than pets (who raise another huge raft of problems). But many people nonetheless are uneasy. Some feel as I do, that although we may grant ourselves the privilege of sacrificing animals for our own benefit, we cannot give ourselves carte blanche. Speaking personally, perhaps I am not too many years away from Alzheimer's. I have seen how horrible it can be. I do not relish it. But I disagree nonetheless with those doctors and scientists who argue that because Alzheimer's is vile, then we can do whatever it takes to rabbits or monkeys in order to put a stop to it. I feel personally (and such feelings are personal) that to a significant extent, humans just have to put up with whatever life throws at them, and that ends do not always justify means. Concern for laboratory animals seems far more powerful in Britain than in most of Europe. I know of no formal studies on this, on why it should be so. We may guess – and perhaps one guess is as good as another, that Britain lacks the peasant tradition that is still so powerful in most of Europe. Our bona fide peasants disappeared as a class with the rise of the industrial revolution, which for us was well over 200 years ago. Now, in Britain, only one per cent of the workforce works full-time on the land. Perhaps because we are so urbanised, we allow ourselves to be more "sentimental" about animals than other Europeans do, or Asians or Africans. Whether this "sentiment" is a good thing or merely effete, is still up for discussion. Does "urbanised" really imply more "civilised"? Both words literally mean "citified" – one Greek, one Latin – but their connotations are clearly very different.

In general, in order to do good, we have to know what is the case: in this case, what do animals really want, and what truly is helpful to them. But as philosophers have pointed out at least since David Hume (Scotland's greatest player in European Enlightenment) what is the case, is not necessarily what ought to be. Science can tell us what is, but not what is good. For this we need moral philosophy. In general, worldwide, this past few thousand years, morality has taken three forms. The Utilitarians argued that what is right can be judged purely by outcome: as England's Jeremy Bentham put the matter, "the greatest happiness of the greatest number". Others have sought moral absolutes. Religions traditionally do this: in general (to put the matter crudely) what is good is what God says is good. But some moral philosophers have sought "secular" absolutes – notably Immanuel Kant, who identified his "categorical imperatives" which, he said, even God should not ignore. Finally, many have stressed the overriding need for attitude: the tradition of "virtue ethics". Hume, who in so many other ways inspired Kant, seems to be on the side of virtue ethics. He concluded that in the end, moral principles are based on "passion". We know good when we see it because we *feel* it to be good.

Although religions are associated with moral absolutes – the Ten Commandments; the Torah; the will of Allah – in truth they focus at least as much on attitudes. Their roots are in virtue ethics. As reflected in this report, the various traditions of Christianity speak above all, as Christ did, of love and mercy. In Jewish law, as Albert Guigui tells us, "It is forbidden, as a Torah precept, to cause pain to animals". The Talmud has an eye for rustic detail: "Thou shalt not plough with an ox and an ass harnessed together" (because the two beasts move at different speeds); "Thou shalt not muzzle the ox when he treadeth the grain" (because this would frustrate him). Raoutsi Hadj Eddine Sari Ali quotes the Koran: "No creature is there crawling on the earth, no bird flying with its wings, but they are nations like unto yourselves". The Buddha spoke, above all, of "compassion", for all sentient beings.

Religious detractors – and the more zealous within each of the religions – tend to emphasise the differences between religions. Then they argue: "They all claim to know the truth, but they can't all be right". But far more striking is the deep similarity of religious approaches – not at the level of manners, customs, and traditions, but in their underlying attitudes to life: the qualities they claim as virtues. Indeed, the 19th century Hindu mystic Ramakrishna said that when all the pronouncements of all the great prophets of all the great religions are boiled down, then just three prime virtues – not rules! – emerge, from which all else derives: personal humility; respect for other, sentient creatures; and a sense of reverence for God – or for those of more secular mien, reverence for the universe as a whole. To me, Ramakrisha's summary indeed seems unimprovable. Apply these virtues ("passions") to any moral situation, and all starts to become clear. Immediately, for example, we start to ask whether we truly have a *right* to treat animals as we will, purely for our own convenience – or to meet some entirely arbitrary economic goal. Where is the humility in this, or the respect? If we don't ask such questions, and continue to ask them, then we can have no moral agenda at all.

Europeans have often taken it for granted that we are a good thing: that we are in the end the prime begetters of civilisation, setting the standards for the whole world. Thus over the centuries we have justified our empires: that we have a right to tell others what to do because we are better, and for their own good. The horror of this attitude has now been abundantly exposed. But even if there is no excuse at all for empire, or for European conceit, we do have a great deal to offer. Europe above all, at its best, combines the traditions of what Thomas Aquinas identified as faith and reason; or might more broadly be seen as romanticism and classicism, of Dionysius and Apollo; or might most simply be presented as heart and mind. Christianity and Judaism have been with us from the beginning. Islam has been a huge presence, first in Moorish Spain and now again in modern times. Buddhism and other eastern religions are modern incumbents, again with a growing presence. All these religions have a huge role to play not as creators of sects but in defining and reinforcing the underlying attitudes on which all moral behaviour rests. But science too is vital for pragmatic reasons: to establish what is the case – in this case what animals want and need – and to show what can be done truly to improve their lives.

But I am left with a feeling that it is all to do. The idea that animals should be treated well is not universal. Basic knowledge, of what animals really need or want, is lacking – and although there is excellent research here and there it is not frontline. Legislation is slow. Such new laws as there are generally delayed, for practical reasons, for several years, but if a practice is cruel in five years' time then it is cruel now.

This report, then, excellent though it is, can be seen only as an interim. The moral principles still need spelling out. The science, or most of it, still has to be done. Above all, perhaps, we need to integrate different ways of looking at any one problem. In the ceiling of Uffizi the various agenda of the renascent Europe are presented in separate panels. The Renaissance was wonderful because it established the necessary specialisms so clearly – fine art, astronomy, theology, economics, and so on. But for the same reason it was also deeply pernicious, destroying the mode of thought that was taken for granted in the Middle Ages, which was all-embracing; embedding the study of what is actually the case, within a moral framework. If 21st-century Europe is really to be worthwhile, we need to get that pre-Renaissance habit back: learn to feel the different threads of thought – science, economics, philosophy, theology – all as one. Otherwise we will get nothing right. The world needs an approach to life that is both humane and sensible, and Europe is at least as well placed as any to show what this entails. The way we treat animals can be taken as a measure of our success in general; of whether ordinary Joes, like me, should take "Europe" seriously at all.

Appendices

Appendix I – Some key concepts

Animal welfare

There are many different definitions of animal welfare but the general theme is the concern for the well-being of individual animals so they do not suffer unnecessarily. The Farm Animal Welfare Council (FAWC) states that the welfare of an animal includes "its physical and mental state and [...] that good animal welfare implies both fitness and a sense of well-being". The FAWC considers an animal's welfare in terms of "five freedoms":

1. **Freedom from hunger and thirst** – by ready access to fresh water and a diet to maintain full health and vigour.

2. **Freedom from discomfort** – by providing an appropriate environment including shelter and a comfortable resting area.

3. **Freedom from pain, injury or disease** – by prevention or rapid diagnosis and treatment.

4. **Freedom to express normal behaviour** – by providing sufficient space, proper facilities and company of the animal's own kind.

5. **Freedom from fear and distress** – by ensuring conditions and treatment which avoid mental suffering.[1]

Animal rights

Animal rights as a concept is different from animal welfare in that it is the movement to protect animals from being used or regarded as property by human beings. It aims not merely to attain more humane treatment for animals, but also to include species other than human beings within the moral community and to treat them as subjects of law rather than object of law. See the article by Elisabeth de Fontenay p. 29.

1.
www.fawc.org.uk/
default.htm

Appendix II – A selection of useful websites

Some international/European sites

www.coe.int
See: Legal affairs/Legal co-operation/Biological safety, use of animals.
Site of the Directorate of Legal Affairs of the Council of Europe dedicated to biological safety and use of animals by humans.

europa.eu.int/comm/food/animal/index_en.htm
The European Union Animal Health and Welfare site (available in several of the official languages) provides information about animal health strategies, the latest news about animal diseases and details about European legislation.

www.eurogroupanimalwelfare.org/
The Eurogroup for Animal Welfare represents the leading European animal welfare organisations. The site has dossiers available about various animal welfare issues as well as information about animal welfare legislation and links to their member organisations' websites.

www.ebra.org/aboutebra/index.html
The European Biomedical Research Association (EBRA) promotes laws, regulations and controls on animal research and provides statistics for Europe and details about the animal research regulations in European Union member states.

www.ifaw.org/ifaw/general/default.aspx
Available in several languages. Site of the International Fund for Animal Welfare.

www.oie.int
The site of the World Organisation for Animal Health, (available in English, French and Spanish) has information about animal health throughout the world and animal health standards.

worldanimal.net
World Animal Net is a website for those interested in campaigning for animal welfare. It has links to organisations (there

are also links to French organisations) and resources for those wanting to know more about animal welfare.

www.wspa.org.uk/
Site of the World Society for the Protection of Animals.

www.wwf.org/ and
www.panda.org/
Site of the global environmental conservation organisation WWF. Available in several languages.

Some European countries' sites

www.minlnv.nl
Site of the Dutch Ministry of Agriculture, Nature and Food Quality. Select "International Homepage" for the English translation. See, in particular "Livestock" and then select "Animal Welfare".

www.dyrenes-beskyttelse.dk/
Site of a Danish animal welfare association.

www.tours.inra.fr/BienEtre/accueil.htm
Website (in French) of the Institut National de la Recherche Agronomique (INRA) which deals with animal welfare research throughout France.

www.rspca.org.uk
The Royal Society for the Protection of Animals (RSPCA) works to prevent cruelty to animals. The website has general advice about caring for animals and information aimed at the general public about animal welfare campaigns and education and more specific information intended for scientists and researchers.

www.bmelv.de
Site of the German Federal Ministry of Food, Agriculture and Consumer Protection. Available in German and English. Select "Animal Welfare and Protection".

www.min-agricultura.pt
Site of the Portuguese Ministry of Agriculture, Rural Development and Fisheries (site in Portuguese only).

www.djurskyddsmyndigheten.se/
Site of the Swedish Animal Welfare Agency.

www.mmm.fi
Site of the Finnish Ministry of Agriculture and Forestry. Select "Veterinary Services" and then "Animal Welfare". Site also available in English.

www.politicheagricole.it/
Site of the Italian Ministry of Agricultural Policy (site in Italian only).

www.mapa.es/
Site of the Spanish Ministry of Agriculture, Fisheries and Food. Available in several languages. Click on "Livestock" and select "Animal welfare".

www.protection-des-animaux.org/
Site (in French) of an association for animal protection. See "Législations" for a list of European and French laws on animal protection and welfare.

Appendix III – Council of Europe treaties dealing with animals

European Convention for the Protection of Animals during International Transport
ETS No. 65

European Convention for the Protection of Animals kept for Farming Purposes
ETS No. 87

European Convention for the Protection of Animals for Slaughter
ETS No.102

Additional Protocol to the European Convention for the Protection of Animals during International Transport
ETS No. 103

Convention on the Conservation of European Wildlife and Natural Habitats
ETS No. 104

European Convention for the Protection of Vertebrate Animals used for Experimental and other Scientific Purposes
ETS No. 123

European Convention for the Protection of Pet Animals
ETS No. 125

Protocol of Amendment to the European Convention for the Protection of Animals kept for Farming Purposes
ETS No. 145

Protocol of Amendment to the European Convention for the Protection of Vertebrate Animals used for Experimental and other Scientific Purposes
ETS No. 170
Treaty open for signature by the Signatories to Treaty ETS No. 123

European Convention for the Protection of Animals during International Transport (Revised)
ETS No.193
Treaty open for signature by the member states and by the European Community and for accession by non-member states

Sales agents for publications of the Council of Europe
Agents de vente des publications du Conseil de l'Europe

BELGIUM/BELGIQUE
La Librairie Européenne -
The European Bookshop
Rue de l'Orme, 1
B-1040 BRUXELLES
Tel.: +32 (0)2 231 04 35
Fax: +32 (0)2 735 08 60
E-mail: order@libeurop.be
http://www.libeurop.be

Jean De Lannoy
Avenue du Roi 202 Koningslaan
B-1190 BRUXELLES
Tel.: +32 (0)2 538 43 08
Fax: +32 (0)2 538 08 41
E-mail: jean.de.lannoy@dl-servi.com
http://www.jean-de-lannoy.be

CANADA and UNITED STATES/
CANADA et ÉTATS-UNIS
Renouf Publishing Co. Ltd.
1-5369 Canotek Road
OTTAWA, Ontario K1J 9J3, Canada
Tel.: +1 613 745 2665
Fax: +1 613 745 7660
Toll-Free Tel.: (866) 767-6766
E-mail: orders@renoufbooks.com
http://www.renoufbooks.com

CZECH REPUBLIC/
RÉPUBLIQUE TCHÈQUE
Suweco CZ, s.r.o.
Klecakova 347
CZ-180 21 PRAHA 9
Tel.: +420 2 424 59 204
Fax: +420 2 848 21 646
E-mail: import@suweco.cz
http://www.suweco.cz

DENMARK/DANEMARK
GAD
Vimmelskaftet 32
DK-1161 KØBENHAVN K
Tel.: +45 77 66 60 00
Fax: +45 77 66 60 01
E-mail: gad@gad.dk
http://www.gad.dk

FINLAND/FINLANDE
Akateeminen Kirjakauppa
PO Box 128
Keskuskatu 1
FIN-00100 HELSINKI
Tel.: +358 (0)9 121 4430
Fax: +358 (0)9 121 4242
E-mail: akatilaus@akateeminen.com
http://www.akateeminen.com

FRANCE
La Documentation française
(diffusion/distribution France entière)
124, rue Henri Barbusse
F-93308 AUBERVILLIERS CEDEX
Tél.: +33 (0)1 40 15 70 00
Fax: +33 (0)1 40 15 68 00
E-mail: prof@ladocumentationfrancaise.fr
http://www.ladocumentationfrancaise.fr

Librairie Kléber
1 rue des Francs Bourgeois
F-67000 STRASBOURG
Tel.: +33 (0)3 88 15 78 88
Fax: +33 (0)3 88 15 78 80
E-mail: francois.wolfermann@librairie-kleber.fr
http://www.librairie-kleber.com

GERMANY/ALLEMAGNE
AUSTRIA/AUTRICHE
UNO Verlag GmbH
August-Bebel-Allee 6
D-53175 BONN
Tel.: +49 (0)228 94 90 20
Fax: +49 (0)228 94 90 222
E-mail: bestellung@uno-verlag.de
http://www.uno-verlag.de

GREECE/GRÈCE
Librairie Kauffmann s.a.
Stadiou 28
GR-105 64 ATHINAI
Tel.: +30 210 32 55 321
Fax.: +30 210 32 30 320
E-mail: ord@otenet.gr
http://www.kauffmann.gr

HUNGARY/HONGRIE
Euro Info Service kft.
1137 Bp. Szent István krt. 12.
H-1137 BUDAPEST
Tel.: +36 (06)1 329 2170
Fax: +36 (06)1 349 2053
E-mail: euroinfo@euroinfo.hu
http://www.euroinfo.hu

ITALY/ITALIE
Licosa SpA
Via Duca di Calabria, 1/1
I-50125 FIRENZE
Tel.: +39 0556 483215
Fax: +39 0556 41257
E-mail: licosa@licosa.com
http://www.licosa.com

MEXICO/MEXIQUE
Mundi-Prensa México, S.A. De C.V.
Río Pánuco, 141 Delegacíon Cuauhtémoc
06500 MÉXICO, D.F.
Tel.: +52 (01)55 55 33 56 58
Fax: +52 (01)55 55 14 67 99
E-mail: mundiprensa@mundiprensa.com.mx
http://www.mundiprensa.com.mx

NETHERLANDS/PAYS-BAS
De Lindeboom Internationale Publicaties b.v.
M.A. de Ruyterstraat 20 A
NL-7482 BZ HAAKSBERGEN
Tel.: +31 (0)53 5740004
Fax: +31 (0)53 5729296
E-mail: books@delindeboom.com
http://www.delindeboom.com

NORWAY/NORVÈGE
Akademika
Postboks 84 Blindern
N-0314 OSLO
Tel.: +47 2 218 8100
Fax: +47 2 218 8103
E-mail: support@akademika.no
http://akademika.no

POLAND/POLOGNE
Ars Polona JSC
25 Obroncow Street
PL-03-933 WARSZAWA
Tel.: +48 (0)22 509 86 00
Fax: +48 (0)22 509 86 10
E-mail: arspolona@arspolona.com.pl
http://www.arspolona.com.pl

PORTUGAL
Livraria Portugal
(Dias & Andrade, Lda.)
Rua do Carmo, 70
P-1200-094 LISBOA
Tel.: +351 21 347 42 82 / 85
Fax: +351 21 347 02 64
E-mail: info@livrariaportugal.pt
http://www.livrariaportugal.pt

RUSSIAN FEDERATION/
FÉDÉRATION DE RUSSIE
Ves Mir
9a, Kolpacnhyi per.
RU-101000 MOSCOW
Tel.: +7 (8)495 623 6839
Fax: +7 (8)495 625 4269
E-mail: zimarin@vesmirbooks.ru
http://www.vesmirbooks.ru

SPAIN/ESPAGNE
Mundi-Prensa Libros, s.a.
Castelló, 37
E-28001 MADRID
Tel.: +34 914 36 37 00
Fax: +34 915 75 39 98
E-mail: liberia@mundiprensa.es
http://www.mundiprensa.com

SWITZERLAND/SUISSE
Van Diermen Editions – ADECO
Chemin du Lacuez 41
CH-1807 BLONAY
Tel.: +41 (0)21 943 26 73
Fax: +41 (0)21 943 36 05
E-mail: info@adeco.org
http://www.adeco.org

UNITED KINGDOM/ROYAUME-UNI
The Stationery Office Ltd
PO Box 29
GB-NORWICH NR3 1GN
Tel.: +44 (0)870 600 5522
Fax: +44 (0)870 600 5533
E-mail: book.enquiries@tso.co.uk
http://www.tsoshop.co.uk

UNITED STATES and CANADA/
ÉTATS-UNIS et CANADA
Manhattan Publishing Company
468 Albany Post Road
CROTTON-ON-HUDSON, NY 10520, USA
Tel.: +1 914 271 5194
Fax: +1 914 271 5856
E-mail: Info@manhattanpublishing.com
http://www.manhattanpublishing.com

Council of Europe Publishing/Editions du Conseil de l'Europe
F-67075 Strasbourg Cedex
Tel.: +33 (0)3 88 41 25 81 – Fax: +33 (0)3 88 41 39 10 – E-mail: publishing@coe.int – Website: http://book.coe.int